D0221945

CULTURE IN THE
COMMUNICATION AGE

What does it mean to live in the Communication Age? What is the nature of culture today? How have cultural identities changed in globalization?

Culture in the Communication Age brings together some of the world's leading thinkers from a range of academic disciplines to discuss what 'culture' means in the modern era. They describe key features of life in the 'Communication Age', and consider the cultural implications of the rise of global connectivity, mass media, information technology, and popular culture. Individual chapters consider:

- Culture of the Mind
- Rethinking the Foundations of Culture
- Culture in the Global Ecumene
- From 'Ways of Life' to 'Lifestyle'
- Cultural Gender
- Cultural Fronts
- Superculture
- Popular Culture and Media Spectacles
- Visual Culture
- Star Culture
- Computers, the Internet, and Virtual Cultures.

Contributors: David C. Chaney, Jorge A. González, Ulf Hannerz, Stephen Hinerman, Steve Jones, Stephanie Kucker, Mirja Liikkanen, James Lull, Paul Messaris, Eduardo Neiva, Michael Real, Edward C. Stewart.

James Lull is Professor of Communication Studies at San José State University, California. He is author or editor of ten books, including *Media, Communication, Culture: A Global Approach* (Polity 2000), *Media Scandals* (Polity 1997), *Popular Music and Communication* (Sage 1992), *China Turned On* (Routledge 1991) and *World Families Watch Television* (Sage 1988).

COMEDIA
Series editor: David Morley

Other *Comedia* titles from Routledge:

CULTURE IN THE COMMUNICATION AGE

Edited by James Lull

London and New York

First published 2001
by Routledge
11 New Fetter Lane, London EC4P 4EE

Simultaneously published in the USA and Canada
by Routledge
29 West 35th Street, New York, NY 10001

Routledge is an imprint of the Taylor & Francis Group

Typeset in Bembo by RefineCatch Limited, Bungay, Suffolk
Printed and bound in Great Britain by
TJ International Ltd, Padstow, Cornwall

British Library Cataloguing in Publication Data
A catalogue record for this book is available from the British Library

Library of Congress Cataloging in Publication Data
A catalog record for this book has been requested

ISBN 0–415–22116–1 (hbk)
ISBN 0–415–22117–X (pbk)

CONTENTS

v

CONTENTS

NOTES ON CONTRIBUTORS

David C. Chaney is Professor of Sociology at the University of Durham, England. His academic specialty is the sociology of contemporary cultural history. He has published extensively, combining studies on institutions such as the shopping center and public festivals with more theoretical concerns regarding the discourses of culture. His latest books include *The Cultural Turn* and *Lifestyles*. He is currently working on a book on cultural change and everyday life for Macmillan.

Jorge A. González is Director of the Culture Program, University of Colima, Mexico. He is editor of the journal *Estudios Sobre las Culturas Contemporaneas* (*Studies of Contemporary Cultures*), and is a member of Mexico's Complex Communication Network. He is also a member of the Executive Committee of the International Sociological Association. His most recent book is *La cofradia de las emociones (in)terminables* (*The Brotherhood of Unending Emotions*). His research interests are cognition, technology, and culture, and the further development of a network of communication researchers across Mexico and Latin America.

Ulf Hannerz is Professor of Social Anthropology, Stockholm University, Sweden. He has taught at several American, European, and Australian universities. He is a member of the Royal Swedish Academy of Sciences and the American Academy of Arts and Sciences, and is former Chair of the European Association of Social Anthropologists. His research has been especially in urban anthropology, media anthropology, and transnational cultural processes. Most recently, he has been engaged in a study of the work of news media foreign correspondents, including field research in four continents. Among his books are *Soulside*, *Exploring the City*, *Cultural Complexity*, and *Transnational Connections*. He is also Anthropology editor for the new *International Encyclopedia of the Social and Behavioral Sciences*.

Stephen Hinerman is Lecturer in Communication Studies at San José State University, California. He has written extensively on cultural studies and rhetoric for many academic and popular publications, and writes regularly on popular music for several newspapers. He is co-editor (with James Lull) of *Media Scandals: Morality and Desire in the Popular Culture Marketplace.*

Steve Jones is Professor and Head of the Department of Communication at the University of Illinois-Chicago. He is author or editor of several books, including *Doing Internet Research, CyberSociety, Virtual Culture,* and *The Internet for Educators and Homeschoolers.* Additional information can be found at *http://info.comm.uic.edu/jones*

Stephanie Kucker received a master's degree in Communication from the University of Illinois-Chicago in 1999, where she studied computer-mediated communication and Internet technologies. She has co-authored several articles on the role of computer-mediated communication in scientific work and consulted for the Pew Charitable Trust on the role of the Internet in education and everyday life. She currently works in Chicago as marketing and communications coordinator for VRCO, Inc., a hi-tech industry firm, and as Adjunct Instructor of Communication at the University of Illinois-Chicago.

Mirja Liikkanen is a Senior Researcher in the Unit for Culture and Media Statistics, Helsinki, Finland. Her licentiate's degree is in Sociology from the University of Helsinki. She has published several articles and chapters on culture, leisure, cultural consumption, media use, and gender. She is especially interested in the role of cultural hierarchies, processes of exclusion and inclusion, and national cultures. Recently she has been consulting the European Union and UNESCO on improving transnational information on culture.

James Lull is Professor of Communication Studies at San José State University, California. He also teaches regularly at several universities in Latin America. He is author or editor of many books, including *Media, Communication, Culture: A Global Approach, Media Scandals, Popular Music and Communication, China Turned On, Inside Family Viewing,* and *World Families Watch Television.* He holds an honorary doctorate in Social Sciences from the University of Helsinki, Finland. Home page: *http://members.aol.com/JamesLull*

Paul Messaris is Professor at the Annenberg School for Communication, University of Pennsylvania. He teaches and does research in the area of visual communication. His research has dealt with the way in which people make sense of visual representations in still and moving images; with the persuasive uses of visual media; and with the cultural implications of narrative conventions in movies and other forms of visual storytelling. He is author of *Visual Literacy: Image, Mind, and Reality* (winner of the National Communication Association's Diamond Anniversary Award) and *Visual Persuasion: The Role of Images in Advertising.*

Eduardo Neiva is Professor of Communication Studies and Director of the Center for Communication Research at the University of Alabama-Birmingham. He has also taught in his native Brazil at the Catholic University of Rio de Janeiro, the Federal University at Fluminense, and the State University of Rio de Janeiro. He is a former Fulbright scholar at Indiana University. A specialist in semiotics, he has published *Mythologies of Vision: Image, Culture, and Visuality* and numerous books in Portuguese.

Michael Real is Professor and Director of the Scripps School of Journalism at Ohio University. He is the former Director of the School of Communication at San Diego State University. His writings on media events, sports, popular culture, and communication theory have appeared in dozens of scholarly and general publications. His books include *Exploring Media Culture*, *Super Media*, and *Mass-mediated Culture*.

Edward C. Stewart is a cultural psychologist living in Silver Springs, Maryland. He has taught at Lehigh University and George Washington University, as well as universities in Japan and Scotland. He is co-author (with Milton J. Bennett) of *American Cultural Patterns*, and has published widely in many journals and in many languages. Lately he has concentrated on cultural memories of war, and is conducting research on the meaning of pain and the role of emotion in cultural identity and aggression.

INTRODUCTION
Why the Communication Age?

James Lull

To describe the spectacular nature of what's happening today as the 'Information Age', the 'Digital Age', or the 'Internet Age' takes most of the life out of this exciting era and puts the analytical emphasis in the wrong place. No doubt we live with much more information now than ever before; lots of that information comes to us in digital form; and the Internet has certainly become an indispensable resource. But for what?

Symbolic exchanges facilitated by high technology and the new networks of 'complex connectivity' in place today (Tomlinson 1999) are contemporary elaborations of what is really a very basic activity – human communication. Although information technologies have greatly accelerated and altered some of the ways human beings communicate with each other, motivations behind the signifying practices that people create in order to construct their social and cultural worlds remain fundamentally unchanged. High-technology jargon unfortunately often detracts from the vital and complex processes that motivate and manifest communication, as it dehumanizes one of life's most fundamental undertakings. Compounding the problem, the technocratic language of the current period generally privileges the rational side of communicative interaction. We might easily get the impression nowadays that imperfect, real human contact has somehow transmogrified into seamless robotic conversations with databanks located somewhere in cyberspace.

The expression 'Communication Age' serves as an umbrella term that can be used to broaden, humanize, and make more accurate a description and interpretation of the exciting new era. The Communication Age refers not only to the efficient transmission of digitized bits and bytes from here to there, but also to the significance that communication processes hold for real people as they engage the entire range of material and symbolic resources at their disposal. Those resources include not only the tele-mediated and computer-mediated symbolic forms that get so much attention these days, but the whole stock of traditional less-mediated cultural influences that make up the most taken-for-granted aspects of everyday life.

Unlike previous eras when values and ways of life were tied mainly to local contexts and influences, cultural forms today circulate far more widely and are used in ever more innovative ways. The resulting struggles over culture and identity on a global scale have become core issues for scholars across a wide range of disciplines in the social sciences and humanities. This book adds to the ongoing debates and does so with an open mind. The diverse perspectives presented in the following chapters have been brought together here in order to give advanced students an opportunity to discuss and debate the very terms of the future.

Communication and cultural globalization

Communications technology has become decisive in sociocultural transformations taking place worldwide. This book attempts to take full account of technological developments in contemporary cultural activity, including the nuances and subtleties of computer-mediated communication, but it considers the more directly experienced and 'non-rational' sides of life too. Human emotions and routine everyday experience – factors which are often left out of theoretical discussions about culture and society in the Communication Age – occupy a central place in this volume. The emphasis given to communication is key. By focusing on *processes* of human interaction and on their constitutive *signifying practices* rather than simply on the *hardware* or *content* of information transmission and exchange, we keep the human considerations in the forefront of the analysis where they belong.

That is an especially consequential priority in an age when technocratic thinking and language – which operate interdependently with the same dispassionate mentality that drives most global economic activity – have assumed such tremendous visibility and allure. The technological and information revolution that created the Communication Age in the late twentieth century took place during a 'period of the global restructuring of capitalism' (Castells 1996: 13). Clearly, the economic incentives and rewards of global capitalism continue to be supported and advanced by the institutional use of state-of-the-art information and communications technology. Patterns of economic domination that have long been in place are now being extended even more by the rush of high technology and global connectivity.

When we turn our attention to the cultural dimensions of globalization, however, we see that 'informational capitalism' has also created 'historically new forms of social interaction' (Castells 1996: 18) that embody and provoke a multitude of contradictory tendencies which often shake up traditional power relations. We must be careful therefore not to oversimplify things by blaming technology and globalization for all the world's ills, as Zygmunt Bauman (1998) and others have tended to do. The hub of the Communication Age, the

Internet, for example, is widely used in extremely creative, even revolutionary ways that defy supervision and control, and has even begun to democratize 'routine' global communication in some respects. The Internet has evolved to become less a *technological form* and more a *communications medium*, which opens up limitless cultural possibilities. Rather than just reinforcing traditional structures of political-economic-cultural authority, information technology, the Internet, and mass media make those structures all the more porous (Lull 2000).

The profound diversification of symbolic forms and the attendant growing number and variety of occasions for asserting *symbolic power* (Thompson 1995; Lull 2000) in cultural contexts are inevitable consequences of mediated communication and globalization, a development that in many ways disturbs the hegemony of political, economic, and cultural influence that dominant institutions and ideologies hold over individual persons. The global availability of ever more diverse and mobile symbolic forms emanating from the culture and information industries, when combined with increased access by individuals to micro-communication technologies, uniquely empowers many people. To conceptualize power in symbolic and cultural terms harmonizes theoretically with the indeterminate character of human communication processes overall.

The digital divide

The other side of the rosy optimism often expressed about life in the Communication Age is the undeniable fact that the tangible benefits brought about by present-day technology and connectivity accrue very unevenly across social categories inside individual nations and between nations in the global context. Just as the Communication Age is a global phenomenon, so too is the digital divide. Large areas of the world including North American inner cities, African shanty towns, Brazilian *favelas*, and the deprived rural areas of China or India are almost completely 'switched off' from information technology and the global 'network society' (Castells 1996: 33–4).

By now home computers with an Internet hookup have become more a necessity than a luxury in many parts of the relatively developed world. Still, in the United States – where more than half the homes were hooked up to the Internet by 2000 – extreme differences between economic and racial groups continue to divide the society into computer/Internet 'haves' and 'have nots'. In Europe, Internet hookups in 2000 were far less pervasive overall than in the USA – some 12 per cent of total homes. Internal social and technological differences in the European nations are least severe in the Scandinavian countries and the rest of the northern part of the continent. By comparison southern European nations are far less connected overall and reveal the widest internal gaps. While social and technological gaps in Japan are not as extreme as they are in many other nations, the internal digital divide is growing there too as the collective nature of Japanese society also edges toward the global trends of consumerism and individualism.

The chapters

This book features stage-setting essays written by several of the world's best thinkers about communication and culture representing a range of academic disciplines – communication studies, sociology, cultural studies, anthropology, psychology, semiotics, and media studies. The book is divided into three sections.

In the first section, 'The foundations of culture', we encounter a lively spectrum of theoretical approaches to culture in the Communication Age ranging from analysis of the perceptions of individual persons to the most expansive, multimediated processes of global cultural flows and interactions. Beginning with psychologist Edward C. Stewart's provocative essay on the 'Culture of the mind', and the Brazilian-American semiotician Eduardo Neiva's equally arousing 'Rethinking the foundations of culture', we find that the origins of cultural organization must account for emotion, fear, and the close relationship between nature and culture, particularly as it manifests in the 'predation paradigm' and in struggles for human survival. These contemporary Darwinian-influenced essays resonate with current theoretical trends in molecular biology and genetics, and reflect the important 'recent surge of interest in the connections between biology and semiotics' (Laubichler 1997: 248), particularly as it applies to cultural analysis. In a far less deterministic argument that radically opposes the first two essays, the Swedish social anthropologist Ulf Hannerz argues for a cosmopolitan understanding of culture that is constructed through the analytical framework of the dynamic, multicultural 'global ecumene'.

Section II explores various crucial ways for 'Making sense of culture'. The British sociologist David Chaney continues to develop his work on 'lifestyle' in the first essay by contrasting current cultural modalities and styles with more traditional and stable 'ways of life'. Writing from her home in Helsinki, Finland, where in 2000 a single mother had been elected the country's first female president, the cultural sociologist Mirja Liikkanen evaluates the tremendously important role of gender in culture and cultural analysis. The third chapter in this section marks the first comprehensive discussion published in English about an especially intriguing theoretical idea, 'cultural fronts', by the Mexican cultural theorist and sociologist Jorge González. Finally, I take an opportunity in this section to offer my own perspective on cultural ecology in the Communication Age by outlining the key features of a broad concept I term the 'superculture'.

The last section of the book is labeled 'Contemporary cultural forms'. It features incisive perspectives on four analytical domains that have become especially prominent in the Communication Age. Media studies theorist

Michael Real begins the section with an introductory essay on how popular culture and media spectacles have influenced the development of contemporary cultural theory. Annenberg School communication theorist Paul Messaris argues for the central place of visual forms in cultural analysis. Communication studies scholar Stephen Hinerman puts forward an argument for what he considers to be the positive role of global media stars in cultural life. Finally, emphasizing the extraordinary influence of computer-mediated communication in contemporary cultural construction, communication researchers Steve Jones and Stephanie Kucker discuss 'virtual cultures' and how the skills of 'Internetworking' influence social and cultural reality in the Communication Age.

It should be clear from this brief overview of the book's chapters that no single perspective on culture emerges from these pages. I hope to have steadfastly avoided editing a volume that could easily be said to represent a 'postmodernist' or 'essentialist' or 'social scientific' or 'cultural studies' position. The range of voices and views expressed in the book reflects the diverse and dynamic state of culture in the Communication Age, and they are brought together here to help provoke the discussions that these matters clearly merit.

References

Bauman, Z. (1998). *Globalization: The Human Consequences.* Cambridge: Polity Press; New York: Columbia University Press.

Castells, M. (1996). *The Rise of the Network Society.* Oxford: Blackwell.

Laubichler, M. (1997). 'Introduction'. *S: European Journal for Semiotic Studies*, 9: 248–50.

Lull, J. (2000). *Media, Communication, Culture: A Global Approach* (revised ed.). Cambridge: Polity Press; New York: Columbia University Press.

Thompson, J. B. (1995). *The Media and Modernity.* Cambridge: Polity Press.

Tomlinson, J. (1999). *Globalization and Culture.* Cambridge: Polity Press.

Section One

THE FOUNDATIONS
OF CULTURE

1

CULTURE OF THE MIND

On the origins of meaning and emotion

Edward C. Stewart

The theory pursued here begins with the assertion that the origins of modern human nature and the foundations of culture were constructed during the last Ice Age. Living in the hostile environment of the glacial period, and in a fierce struggle to survive, Paleolithic humans confronted large wild animals each day and faced a deadly fight to secure flesh for food and pelts for clothing. During the glacial period men and women competed with, and were the frequent prey of, carnivores. By bonding in small groups, early humans increased their chances of surviving the attacks of ferocious predatory animals. The need for protection against predators, and for security from counter-attacks of the prey hunted, gave early men and women powerful incentives to develop vital inter-personal networks or 'cultures' of belonging and identity. The human nature which was formed was defensive and aimed to compensate for human vulnerability. Even so, social strategies developed by prehistoric humans for preserving life allowed the species to survive only by a razor-thin margin, according to some scientists.

What early humans learned about survival by the end of the Ice Age has endured in human relations. Studies conducted by anthropologists in Asia, Africa, and Australia in the 1800s and more recently show that when living under the threat of attack by large predators, such as tigers, people live clustered together in small communities, while people who are not threatened by such predators tend to live spread out over the land, singly or in small groups. Modern social scientists continue to find the same social tendencies in each 'unique' culture.

In this chapter I will describe the formation of human nature and culture, and argue that key foundational paths of personal and social development are common to all cultures. The discussion will highlight the tension between 'predator' and 'prey' in human survival. I will demonstrate briefly how such a dangerous condition endures today in various forms of aggression, especially war. I will then link biological processes of cultural evolution to symbolic

9

interaction by defining culture as 'meaning'. Finally, I will make a brief sketch of what I call the 'Cultural Trilogy', a framework for understanding and theorizing culture that embraces individual, social, and primordial elements. Underlying the entire chapter is a distinct emphasis on the importance of emotion in culture and cultural theory.

Emergence of modern humans

Two subspecies of modern humans lived in Europe during the last Ice Age, beginning about 110,000 years ago. The Neanderthals (*Homo sapiens neanderthalensis*) lived in Europe and the Middle East from around 120,000 years ago. The second subspecies of fully modern humans (*Homo sapiens sapiens*) left fossil remains in Africa which date to slightly more than 100,000 years ago. Very soon afterward, modern humans appeared in Israel, where they were in contact with the Neanderthal. Between 35,000 and 45,000 years ago fully modern humans spread throughout Europe and also came in contact with the Neanderthals. As the Ice Age entered its coldest phase, *Homo sapiens sapiens*, in a swift and decisive transition, completely replaced the Neanderthals. Reasons for Neanderthal extinction remain unclear (Scarre 1993: 43, 49).

During the Ice Age wild game animals were plentiful. Steppe bison, wild goats, and wild ox among other herd animals existed in great numbers and were effectively hunted. Groups of drivers composed of men, women, and children drove animals over cliffs to their deaths and then stripped the carcasses to the bones. In other cases, the animals were ambushed or driven into enclosed places where they were slaughtered. Around 15,000 BC, the world gradually began to warm, changing the environment and bringing the last Ice Age to a close around 8000 BC. Earth's terrain was no longer habitable for some species of animals. Other animal groups were destroyed by over-hunting as human populations began to grow in warmer climates throughout the world.

By 12,000 BC, at the end of the Paleolithic and beginning of the Mesolithic epoch, the supply of large game animals had declined in many parts of the world. It became less possible for men and women to drive a herd of animals over a cliff or to surround and drive them into a cul-de-sac. Hunters had to track individual animals and kill them one by one (Ehrenreich 1997: 110). Consequently, the cunning and efficiency of individual hunters in stalking the prey became very important. During the same period of time, wars and warlike raids took place. Finally, between 12,000 and 8000 BC, a third change developed. The first 'arms revolution' consisted of the production of the bow and arrow, the sling and dagger, and the newly invented spear and knife. First used for hunting animals, these weapons were later converted into arms for war (Ehrenreich 1997: 117–25).

The predator–prey paradigm

The predator–prey paradigm is the origin of human sacrifices, of warfare, and of conflict as a way of life. The paradigm also establishes certain forms of social relations between predator and prey, among predators, and among prey. When human–predator relations first evolved in the Ice Age, humans were much weaker than the powerful elephants, lions, and leopards. But what humans lacked in strength, swiftness, claws and teeth, they made up for with intelligence, manual skills, and language. Their specialties allowed them to develop technologies of weapons and tools, and to create social relations among members of the band that were intended to equalize, and then to give the edge in encounters with the beast.[1]

Around 10,000 BC human communities turned to agriculture. As hunting animals gave way to war as a way of life, people from other tribes replaced animals as prey, and human beings took the place of animals in sacrifices. In some cultures, the Aztec for example, war and human sacrifice were practiced institutionally right up until the civilization ended. In the cultures of Europe and Asia Minor, humans switched from preying on wild animals to preying on domesticated herds. Hunting became a sophisticated sport for kings and other royalty. The killing of animals perpetuated cultural blood rites. In all these cases of killing and sacrifice, in hunting and in war, of humans and of animals, the blood rites reassured humans that they were no longer the prey, but the predators. Man's life-driving force during the glacial period thus found behavioral expression in the aggressive pursuit of becoming a predator and attempting to escape the vulnerability of being a prey. The shift from prey to predator involved adopting both the behavior and the relations of a predator.

Cognitive archaeologists have reconstructed the primal scenes of Paleolithic people's procedures for obtaining food during the last Ice Age, beginning around 125,000 BC. Not only did early humans drive herds of animals over cliffs or into ambuscades, they also scavenged for the meat of animals killed by the large carnivores. For self-protection against the more powerful predators, early humans banded together in small hunting parties to launch scavenging expeditions. Because a carnivore typically leaves behind some of the prey's flesh, the carnivore could be forced to abandon the carcass, thereby allowing human scavengers to feast on choice pieces of meat. Small bands of prehistoric men apparently approached carnivorous hunters – such as a tiger devouring a stag – and would try to frighten the predator away with noise, fire, or rocks.

In a world dominated by large predators on the prowl, the great carnivores and man selectively became both predator and prey, both with and against each other. The fear that humans were the prey and would be killed and eaten became implanted in circuits of the brain. The human nature that was activated by the circuits was the anguished struggle of humans convincing themselves that they had conquered the predator monster, and had escaped from the fate of being a prey by themselves becoming the predator. This neurological process demonstrates Ovid's idea of *metamorphosis* – that a strong emotion changes the 'form' of the person – and is central to the notion of human nature (Hughes 1997: 18). The nightmare of remaining a prey none the less persists and continues to haunt the human spirit. To neutralize the prey's feeling of dread, humans turn fear into anger, revealing the strange bond that exists between prey and predator.

In all Western societies and probably in others as well, anger is like a moving object that assumes the form of a wild beast out of control ('He was so angry, he roared like a lion!' or 'Be careful, she's a tigress when offended!'). The beast is uncontrollable, so the angry person cannot be held responsible for his rampages. It is the 'other', the person who precipitated the anger, who is deemed responsible for the damage. The irrationality of such a profound feeling is something like the mysterious realm of pain.[2]

Children with no direct experience of large predatory animals naturally seem fearful at first exposure. Charles Darwin himself noticed this fear when visiting the zoo with his young son. Darwin wondered where the fear came from (Ehrenreich 1997: 87). Does the brain contain an innate residue of the truly fearful experience of predation? How does such a reaction link up with aggression in human nature? Many theorists since Darwin's day have tried to understand the social consequences of fear and aggression. If aggression is indeed an instinct, then it is necessary for society to suppress aggression in every conceivable form and to prevent its automatic discharge. On the other hand, if aggression occupies an intermediate status in the repertoire of instincts and voluntary behavior, then the challenge for society is to canalize this energy in ways that are least destructive to others, and most productive for the individual (Storr 1968: 31).

The physical human being is equipped with a fear–fight–flight reaction and with anxiety, which is a close relative to the fear of imminent attack. Panic disorders, phobias, and chronic anxieties all represent evolutionary adaptations to dangerous environments. Furthermore, the innate perception of the 'stranger' and the 'other' assumes the presence of a 'predator beast'. But how? Barbara Ehrenreich argues:

> What we seem to inherit, then, is not a fear of specific predators, but a capacity to acquire that fear – for example, by observing the reaction of adults to various potential threats – with efficiency and tenacity. Hence, perhaps, the surprising frequency of predator animals in dreams . . .
>
> So we can say . . . that human beings inherit certain patterned responses to threats and that the threat which originally selected for these responses was probably that of predation. It seems likely, then, that the primordial experience of predation at least *colors* our emotional

responses to situations other than predation itself – the sight of violence or bloodshed occasioned by our fellow humans, for example.

(Ehrenreich 1997: 90–1)

Grief, depression, and helplessness are all experiences of the prey. To escape these dismal states, folkloric narratives describe how the weak rise up against the strong, how lions are defeated by foxes and, in general, how small and weak animals and birds, deemed to be wiser than big animals and birds, are ultimately victorious in their tasks and struggles (Ehrenreich 1997: 83, 139). Because fear and anxiety continue to reside in humans today, our thoughts and feelings are drawn back to the perpetually unfinished revolt of the prey against the predator.

In the fearful struggle to avoid the suffering and death of being prey to animals or other predators such as bands of people from other cultural groups, the cerebral cortex of *homo sapiens* has developed the enduring potential to construct representations of the 'other' – the one who is different from me/us, and who does not qualify for my/our own identity. 'Other' is a representation originating in dread and pain, nurtured in suffering, and activated by the innately sensed predator–prey paradigm. The image of the one who is different is held in the mind as a feeling of terror, a symbolic wild beast.

In the poetry of William Blake (1982), for example, we can experience this beast in its full terror and beauty, and in its uneasy relation to humankind and to the deity:

> Tiger! Tiger! burning bright
> In the forests of the night
> What immortal hand or eye
> Dare frame thy fearful symmetry?
> . . .
>
> When the stars threw down their spears,
> And watered heaven with their tears,
> Did he smile his work to see?
> Did he who made the Lamb make thee?

Fear and anger

Emotional expression appears in sight, sound, smell, and touch early in the life of a child. When only a few days old, an infant sees the smile of the mother, and by the age of two to four months responds in kind. The exchange of smiles between mother and child reflects the evolutionary origins of emotions as control mechanisms in human relations (Johnson-Laird 1988: 91). Emotion saturates and guides interpersonal interaction. To communicate with others successfully, an individual must have a refined perception of how those others feel.

But what is the nature of the potentiality of nuclear emotion in the new-born that through the course of development will construct the infant's view of the world? The answer is predominantly *fear*. Evidence collected by developmental psychologists suggests that the newborn infant responds to a loud noise with a startle reflex, followed by fear. The sudden loud noise probably triggers a response of pain, forming a connection between the startle reflex and sound-pain-fear. Other sources of stimulation such as hard knocks on the infant's body, rashes, and gastrointestinal disturbances, for example, certainly reinforce connections among pain-fear-anger through Pavlovian conditioning, and establish the primacy of the fear response. Then, when the infant begins to move about on its own, towards the end of the first year of life, it develops fear of strangers and, in counterpart and at the same time, has a strong attachment to its mother or other primary caretaker (Brown 1991: 135, 179).

When fear is great and the frightened one freezes, the body closes in upon itself. The color of the skin changes, the limbs and torso turn clammy and cold. The body shivers. The feeling of fear is that of defeat, impelling the individual to look outside for help, but at the same time the external world appears to have gathered against the individual. In the experience of panic, distortions of symbolic space may precipitate the fears of claustrophobia or the reverse, agoraphobia. There seems to be no rational escape from the causes of fear, real or imaginary. The powerlessness that is rendered by fear makes the individual vulnerable to *anger*.

In the Western world anger is perceived as a 'mass', an 'object under pressure', hot 'fluid' coursing through the body. The emotion of anger noticeably increases body heat, blood pressure, and muscular activity, and interferes with perception ('I was so mad, I couldn't see straight!'). Anger is understood to be inside the body, which is viewed as a container ('She was brimming with rage' or 'She couldn't contain herself'), that increases physical agitation ('She was shaking with anger'). The angry person runs the risk that the container will boil over or explode. Cultural control imposes a shared belief that the explosion may be prevented by application of sufficient force and energy to contain the energy inside, but when the anger increases beyond a certain limit, the pressure does in fact explode and the person loses control ('He blew his stack!').

When anger threatens others in Western cultures, the beasts appear:

> There is a part of each person that is a wild animal. Civilized people are supposed to keep that part of them private, that is, they are supposed to keep the animal inside them. In the metaphor, loss of control is equivalent to the animal loose. And the behavior of a person who has lost control is various passions – desire, anger, etc. In the case of anger, the beast presents a danger to other people.
>
> (Lakoff 1987: 492)

The folk mind imagines that the animal is sleeping and is dangerous to awaken ('He has a monstrous temper'). The dangerous animal's aggressiveness is angry behavior ('He unleashed his anger' or 'His anger is insatiable') (Lakoff 1987: 392–4).

The fearful person may become panic-struck in an open space, or pressed completely out of reason if surrounded by a thicket of things, events, or people. Fear drives the individual into his or her own solitude, close to the province of pain. The only routes of escape other than pain are paths that cross the frontier into anger or flight into the refuge of reason mediated by language.

The demon of war

Throughout the ages men and women have debated the causes of war. An early explanation was given by Thucydides, who believed that people go to war out of fear, interest, and honor (Kagan 1995: 8). War attained a privileged position in human affairs by developing a means for resolving differences between human groups. War has roots in cultural elements that are much more fundamental than the derivative political aspects (Keegan 1993: 12–24). In her analysis of war, for instance, Ehrenreich asserts that the causes of war are not necessarily the same as its origins. She advances the disturbing idea that a chief cause of war is an earlier war. Warfare demonstrates *functional autonomy*, with one war leading naturally to the next war. The autonomy of war thus looms as an important issue that needs to be confronted. The nature of war rules out any single issue that can serve as an explanation, however, because war depends on a broad and complex ecology: political leadership, the economy, the social order, patterns of interpersonal behavior, and so on. Still, the best model for understanding war is to treat it as a self-reproducing cultural entity comparable to a living organism, and like a contagious disease that spreads. War fever reached epidemic proportions in the last century and, up to now at least, no vaccine or effective treatment has been found.

The demon of war is encountered in the predation paradigm which human beings have inherited from their ancestors. The human dynamic of pain-fear-anger installs the charge. Its potential power exceeds the integrity of the body and mind of the individual, and the cohesion of the social community. War destroys personal and social ethics, replacing them with the ethic of heroic sacrifice. But war also offers the pleasure and excitement of a predator at work – hence, the appeal of violent action and the 'romance' of battle. The dynamic is based on biology; it is hereditary and imperious. The drive of predation constitutes the state of nature in human beings.

Pain and fear are major sources of sociocultural control, but if reason is cunning, then the demon is insurgent. Cultural control refers to the development of discipline and moral behavior according to societal norms, and allows organized violence only under the authority and control of the society itself. Control mechanisms in societies thus blend with designs for daily life. Cultural control mechanisms consist of manners, accepted modes of expression, shared values, and virtually all ways of thinking about the self in relation to others in daily life. The ultimate dimension of culture equips individuals with supreme beings, beliefs, rituals, codes, and feelings that compose spiritual and religious systems that transcend the here and now to address the very design and meaning of life.

Symbolic evidence for the formation of human nature

Prehistoric drawings, paintings, carvings, engravings, and sculptures discovered in caves used by Paleolithic man provide many insights into human nature formed during the glacial age. Rowland has summarized the meaning of pictorial expression found in Paleolithic art between 40,000 and 5000 BC:

> This first dawn of pictorial expression . . . was the art of the hunters who depended for food and clothing on the great herds of beasts that roamed Europe . . . This is an art magical, rather than esthetic, in purpose, intended to give the tribe power over, and possession of, the animals drawn by artists dedicated to this cult of hunting magic. The art of the men of the Paleolithic period is located in the depths of grottoes that were used not so much for habitation as for the ritual insuring the success of the hunt. These drawings were not made for public exhibitions, nor for the playful joy of the artist in recording aspects of his world . . . Their purpose was strictly a utilitarian magical one, a matter of life and death. The effectiveness of the ritual probably depended upon the naturalness of the drawing as a veritable counter-feit of the animal to be conquered. The painted darts and spears are like the pins the witch sticks in the wax effigy of an intended victim in an entirely similar exercise of sympathetic magic. Once the ceremony of 'killing' the game in the painted effigy was over and the hunters sallied forth in quest of the real quarry, the drawing lost all further effectiveness.
>
> (Rowland 1965: 15–16)

The main preoccupation of prehistoric humans was to secure food and shelter and to protect their vulnerability. When these vital needs were satisfied, the will to survive was nourished. This will to live was the main theme of pre-historic art. The earliest images were linear, formed by delineating contours and outlines that convincingly isolated a single impression from the confusion of reality (Rowland 1965: 16). Even very early paintings and engravings of animals are so realistic that archeologists can identify the species of animals depicted. Later, sophisticated methods of shading and polychromy were used to improve the images' lifelike qualities. Apparently the effect sought was to enhance the potency of the animal depicted. Human figures that inhabit the walls were usually armed and in pursuit of animals, fighting one another, or dancing.

The images' vivid quality reveals the sacred nature and magical power of the great predators. Emotion and danger permeate the symbolic atmosphere represented in the caves. The images seem to portray the animals from the inside – displaying their primal power – rather than from the outside, as the predator or prey would appear in real life. In contrast to the vivid and realistic depiction of animals, human forms often take a simpler form. They appear as stick figures such as hunters, warriors, and shamans.

The universal rites of blood letting and the killing of animals as sacrifices were part of the rituals of magic that were invented to gain power over animals. Complex religious beliefs aimed at pain, fear, anger, and the need for power clearly underlie the content and distribution of cave art.

Cave art offers evidence of warfare in the Paleolithic period too. From a cave in Spain, for example, archers fight archers with each one depicted as a kinetic stick figure. The stick limbs of all archers are lengthened, because in the act of running they feel long. The stylization works; the figures are dynamic. From the right side, three archers on the run close in on a single archer who is dashing towards them from the left side. A second archer runs behind from the left to support the forward archer threatened by encirclement. At a greater distance, three other supporting archers run toward the central fracas from the left side.

The politics of cultural relativism

Edward O. Wilson attributes the low explanatory power of the social sciences to the fact that social scientists spurn the idea of the hierarchical ordering of knowledge that unites and drives the natural sciences. He insists that a science can be valid only with 'consilience', the interlocking of causal explanations across disciplines. Physiological psychology founded on biology, for example, has taken huge strides in its knowledge base primarily because it has begun to interlock causal explanations at the molecular, cellular, and organic levels of the organism. The natural sciences have constructed a network of causal explanation that begins with quantum physics and extends to the brain sciences. They have also examined deep origins which, in the case of physiological psychology, are isolated in evolutionary biology (Wilson 1998: 125).

The explanatory network now reaches the edge of culture, where it enters and engenders a state of confusion. The anthropologist Franz Boas, aided by his famous students Ruth Benedict and Margaret Mead, led a crusade against the threat of eugenics and racism many people believe to be implicit in Social Darwinism. 'With caution swept aside by moral zeal', they created the new ideology of cultural relativism, believing that all cultures are equal but in different ways. This position supports the politics of multiculturalism in the

United States, for instance, where the effect of political ideology on culture has been especially intense, and in other Western societies (Wilson 1998: 184–5). But outside the American academic world and other 'contained areas', cultural relativity is difficult to defend with respect to human nature. Wilson observes:

> Where cultural relativism had been initiated to negate belief in heredi-
> tary behavioral differences among ethnic groups – it was then turned
> against the idea of a unified human nature grounded in heredity.
> A great conundrum of the human condition was created: If neither
> culture nor a hereditary human nature, what unites humanity? The
> question cannot be left hanging, for if ethical standards are molded
> by culture, and cultures are endlessly diverse and equivalent, what
> disqualified theocracy, for example, or colonialism? Or child labor,
> torture, and slavery?
>
> (Wilson 1998: 185)

The social sciences are thus unable to make valid and powerful explanations because they lack consilience and generally ignore deep origins. The 'Standard Social Science Model' has endured primarily by authority of its moral appeal, not for its truth.

Evolutionary psychologists take a contrary position to direct mental or cultural descriptions, and argue for consilience. For them, the mind is biology, and its state of nature for human beings is genetic inheritance as it has developed throughout the millennia of human existence. Tracing its history in the biological process of evolution and reconstructing its nature through the science of cognitive archaeology establishes the configuration of abstract human nature. The original contemporary inheritance probably was in place some 100,000 years ago. The differences that anthropologists describe between groups of modern people today are matters of constructed culture, as well as biology. Moreover, those differences were certainly not self-evident, valid social values present in the cultural life of early humans; in fact, quite the opposite is true.

The actualization of inherited cultural potential is what I call *nuclear culture*, to be discussed later. In the world today an urgent need exists for a paradigm of cultural analysis that places culture at the center of the social sciences, not at the periphery. The solution for accomplishing such an ambitious and important project rests in large measure in operations of the mind, processes of meaning construction, and human communication generally.

Culture as meaning

Culture defined as a 'reserve of meaning' is now gaining favor among anthropologists, communication theorists, sociologists, and other social scientists. Ulf Hannerz (1992) is among those who theorize culture as meaning. All the major elements of culture are mentioned or implied in the following passage authored by Hannerz, a narrative which emphasizes five basic principles that are also present in culture as it was imagined years ago by the famous Russian psychologist, L. S. Vygotsky. Hannerz observes:

> in the recent period, culture has been taken to be above all a matter of meaning. To study culture is to study ideas, experiences, feelings, as well as the external forms that such internalities take as they are made public, available to the senses, and thus truly social. For culture, in the anthropological view, is the meanings which people create, and which create people, as members of societies. Culture is in some way collective.
>
> (Hannerz 1992: 3)

This narrative of culture as a 'matter of meaning' begins inside the mind where it takes the form of perceived 'ideas, experiences, feelings'. When such a description is made more explicit, it includes language and attention, and the word 'consciousness' is sometimes used. Cross-cultural psychologists have referred to these 'internalities' as 'subjective culture' (Triandis 1972), a phrase we can profitably use to refer to the psychological side of culture.

The central process in the mind is perception. Meaning, when psychologists talk about it, refers to processes people use to organize information impinging on their sensory organs about experiences with objects and events in the external world. Psychologists also commonly emphasize that perception is not a passive process that dutifully receives a 'hard copy' of the external world and replicates it, but an active operation that transforms neural information of the external world picked up by the sensory organs into mental reconstructions in the mind. Psychologists variously call these 'products of the mind', 'impressions', 'feelings', 'emotions', 'images', 'concepts', and the like.

Ideas, experiences, and feelings are transformed into language not only in the audible sounds of speech, but in the signs that make up all forms of communication – expressions seen on the face, the love felt in an embrace, the pain endured from blows delivered. Central to the thought of Vygotsky are the communicative mechanisms which are used to transform ghostly forms residing inside the mind into observable actions. He called such mechanisms 'tools', but other writers have used the word 'artifact'.

The basic premise about tools or artifacts is that cultural evolution is the medium in which the tool or artifact as 'Human psychological processes emerged simultaneously with a new form of behavior in which humans modified material objects as a means of regulating their interactions with the world and one another' (Cole 1996: 108). All artifacts possess a 'dual material-conceptual nature' (Cole 1996: 117). The *material* side is hard and clear in examples of a pitcher, a loom, or a bow and arrow. Each of these 'tools' is available to the senses. Simultaneous with the material side, the *ideal* (conceptual) side regulates how the artifacts function in everyday human activities.

With their hands, early human beings constructed pitchers for storing water, looms for weaving cloth, and bows and arrows for killing game. The production and use of these three artifacts, as well as an infinite number of other artifacts endowed with hard material surfaces, left indelible marks on daily life.

But Vygotsky considered language to be by far the supreme artifact operating in human interaction. The material side of language – the sounds of speech – is software compared with, for instance, the hardware structure of a pitcher for storing water. But the *ideal, conceptual* side of language is incomparable to the ideal aspect of any other cultural artifact. Vygotsky believed that *word meaning* is the unit of verbal thought, and that the primary function of the sounds of words in speech is to construct culture and to communicate with others in social interaction (Vygotsky 1962: vi–vii, 4–6).

Mediated action

When language is the specific tool that transforms internalities into speech, the process can be labeled 'language-mediated action'. Such actions aimed at others induce reactions, leading Vygotsky to believe that all communications tools are ultimately based on assumptions and procedures of interpersonal exchange, and are heavily contextualized. The individual's repertoire of socially enacted, tool-mediated actions constitutes his or her culture.

The action mediated by the tool of language is implied in the Hannerz quotation, 'the external forms that internalities take as they are made public' (Hannerz 1992: 3). In Vygotsky's view, language is an integral part of cultural mediation. As an artifact, language mediates behavior in two courses of action: direct and instrumental. The consequence of the duality of application for the basic structure of behavior is that 'instead of applying directly its natural function to the solution of a particular task', an instrumental means intervenes between the function and the task, by the medium of which an individual is led to perform the task (Cole 1996: 108).

We are talking about the cultural turn in psychology. Jerome Bruner calls the new psychology 'culturalism' (Bruner 1996: 3). Bruner's culturalism emphasizes language-mediated actions. Its development is linked to a way of life where 'reality' exists in the form of symbolism – primarily language – shared by members of a cultural community who organize and construe a technical-social way of life according to their symbolic expressions:

> This symbolic mode is not only shared by a community, but conserved, elaborated, and passed on to succeeding generations who, by virtue of this transmission, continue to maintain the culture's identity and way of life. Culture in this sense is *superorganic*. But it shapes the minds of individuals as well. Its individual expression inheres in *meaning making*, assigning meanings to things in different settings on particular

20

occasions. Meaning making involves situating encounters with the world in their appropriate cultural contexts in order to know 'what they are about.' Although meanings are 'in the mind,' they have their significance in the culture in which they are created. It is this cultural situatedness of meanings that assures their negotiability and, ultimately, their communicability.

(Bruner 1996: 3)

A second point of interest is that artifacts function in cultural mediation in

a mode of developmental change in which the activities of prior generations are cumulated present as the specifically human part of the environment. This form of development, in turn, implies the special importance of the social world in human development, since only other human beings can create the special conditions needed for that development to occur.

(Cole 1996: 145)

The division of mind/brain, mind/body, or individual/society has been a thorn in the side of Western scientists and philosophers, dimming their vision of the reality of the mind. Social scientists have failed to understand or explain culture well because they have thought about human behavior as if only single-coded, pure cognition mattered. The dual nature of artifacts eliminates the dichotomy of individual/society, and restores double coding to culture. Both the individual and the group are simultaneously incorporated in artifacts that mediate interpersonal interaction and the evolution of culture. Finally, the individual mind emerges as a social product in the ongoing process of cultural evolution. Like a tide that emerges from the deep ocean, flows in to cover the shore, then ebbs out to reveal marks left behind on the sand, the mind is a tide and an ocean at the same time. The tide's ebb and flow are subject to the general laws of gravity, and to the action of the sun and the moon, but the nature of the local tide can be known only from how the wind, ocean floor, and shoreline govern the ebb and flow on each meeting of water with land. Tide and ocean are the same, but double-coded like human consciousness in sensations of the body and perceptions of the world.

Returning briefly to the Hannerz passage cited on p. 19, his claim that 'culture is in some way collective' stresses what Vygotsky called the social origin of human thought processes and the social essence of all tools (Cole 1996: 110). But Hannerz's definition of culture then ends with the quixotic statement, 'For culture is the meanings which people create, and which create people'. The implications of such an assertion are truly profound. Culture is the *medium* through which we think and feel and, simultaneously, it is an *object* of thought.

It should be clear that culture as meaning defies ordinary scientific thought and all the theoretical and methodological assumptions of any social science that pretends to be 'objective'. Because the mind emerges from and develops in joint, mediated human activities, cause–effect and stimulus–response theories simply fail to explain how culture works. Advances in neurophysiology, however, provide theoretical openings for grounding developmental theories of human nature in biology based on a genetic template that transcends not only the shortcomings of comparative methods in cross-cultural psychology but also the banalities of simple-minded assertions such as, 'it's in the genes' or 'you're born with it!'

Mapping nuclear culture: the Cultural Trilogy

In recent years many explicit and implicit meanings of 'culture' have been deployed in the social sciences and circulated in the mass media. The concept has come to be seen as important, even romantic, but scientifically soft. Hence it is necessary to define rigorously what I mean by *nuclear culture*, beginning with the idea that 'nuclear' brings together the many concepts minted, and observations made, that position culture as the foundational discipline of the social sciences.

Culture's elusiveness can be reduced by projecting on to the map's cognitive space the social, life, and physical sciences, the humanities, and the arts. Each discipline is seen as a continent that is connected to, or separated from, other continents, but ultimately integrated as a world. When we cross a regional frontier and explore the mental activities of the human minds existing in the region, we have entered a particular state of culture that is different from, yet shares a general identity with, all other states on the continent. The qualities of culture that are universal throughout the continents compose the nuclear culture.

'Nuclear', therefore, refers to the interlinked relation of culture and biology in which biology determines the culture of the individual through a process of experiential development and, in turn, culture determines the biology of the species through the evolutionary process of natural selection. In the long run, no theory of the individual is satisfactory until it has explained development, and no theory of the species is satisfactory until it has explained human evolution.

Nuclear also refers to cultural differences, but only in the sense that universal principles found in all cultures, such as language and perception, serve to identify the similarities between cultures and are also used to measure differences in cultural practices. Functioning both as foundational discipline and agent in evolution, nuclear refers to theoretical trajectories that link to all the sciences, arts, and humanities. Such a system of nuclear culture is represented in the Cultural Trilogy (Appendix 1.1), which is based on four assumptions:

(1) *Double coding of experience.* The double-coding assumption asserts that

meaning has two sides, individual and social. On the psychological side, meaning is to 'make sense' of the ideas, experiences, feelings, and images that pervade our lives. On the social side, meaning is to be 'sensible' about the external
forms we use to make our internal creations public, available to the senses, and
therefore truly social. The idea of 'making sense' therefore suggests the 'sensibility' of the solitary individual, while the 'common sense' of the social side
implies community. Meaning, from the viewpoint of culture, thus refers to the
individualistic and collective coding of experience (Hannerz 1992: 269).

(2) *Identity and belonging in human relations.* The second assumption involves
a complex double coding of meaning centered on consciousness, a process of
the internal world of the mind. True consciousness 'makes sense' only when its
cognitive and emotional elements are verified in the perceptual reality of the
external world. Specific people and concrete objects and places out there are
linked to consciousness in the internal world of the mind. When the internal
experience of consciousness activates the connection to the people and objects
of the outside world by a glimpse, a sound, by touch or pain, by an utterance or
a question, and so on, the internal–external relationship is verified. Reality –
the external object – is linked to internal consciousness. *The connection creates
meaning.* Such connections are patterned and organized socially. Cultural
meanings are based on human relations and emotionally laced sentiments of
belonging. Belonging then develops in the formation and maintenance of
cultural identities.

(3) *Cultural control.* An important idea in social science is that culture functions as a *control mechanism* which governs behavior, and can be compared to
plans, recipes, rules, instructions, and computer programs (Geertz 1973: 44).
Because culture as meaning imposes form and direction on behavior, it can
logically be considered 'cultural control'.

(4) *Cultural survival.* The fourth assumption asserts that of all the species
of life, human beings are the most helpless in surviving the harshness of the
natural environment. The biological resources of reflexes, instincts, and genetic
circuits of the brain on their own are simply inadequate to generate the knowledge and repertoires of skills needed for survival. The genetic resources of the
cerebral cortex in the brain function more like a generator than a director. An
enormous information gap thus exists between biological endowment, on one
side, and the systems of knowledge and repertoires of skills that are required for
survival, on the other. Basic survival and, to a much greater extent, civilization
require the accumulated knowledge and skills of many generations to fill in the
information gap. Without the advantages of cultural belonging and control, and
without cultural procedures passed on from generation to generation, both the
cultural individual and the cultural community are destined for rapid extinction.
Culture is a strategy for survival, and the human being is the creature which
most desperately depends on 'such extra genetic, outside-the-skin control
mechanisms' of culture for ordering his behavior (Geertz 1973: 44). This idea
I call cultural survival.

Elements of the Cultural Trilogy

Individuals acquire subjective culture through interactions with other human beings and with their environments. In this process of development, what makes (common) sense and becomes reality for each individual is selected and internalized from physical and social experience. Consciousness is constructed through repeated contact with others who have already acquired patterned cognition and behavior from those experiences. Language, traditions, customs, ethnicity, region, religion, and race all contribute to the construction of cultural identity through social bonding in a process of enculturation. A synthesis of the social and psychological processes of enculturation continually changes and develops to create consciousness and the psychic content of the individual's personal culture. Although the locus of personal culture is the individual, the nature and quality of individual cultural meanings are socially constructed through communicative interaction.

I shall use a paradigm with three parts, called triads, to explain the development and functioning of nuclear culture. The first triad provides a theory of perception (the individual level), the second triad a theory of situations (the social level), and the third triad a theory of emotions and identification (the primordial level). (See Appendix 1.1.)

The first triad deals with internal psychological processes in the body and brain centered on *perception*. The origin of all that we learn and all that we know is found in the sensory processes of perceiving. Perception has been compared to the Roman deity Janus, with two faces looking in opposite directions: one to the past, the other to the future. Janus served as the god of gates and doors and received the prayers of Romans at the beginning and at the end of courses of action, especially wars. The Janus-like duality in perception qualifies as the central process in psychology. One face looking outward is riveted to sensory stimuli that impinge upon and enter the organs for vision, hearing, smell, touch, and the other sensory modalities. The other face looks inward where all information about the external world and even about the body arrives in the brain through the gates of perception (see Triad I).

The second principle introduces the social side. For a cognitive form such as 'the value of equality' to qualify as culture, it must exist simultaneously as a psychological value of the individual and a social value of the society. The value becomes an element in a national culture, for instance, only when it is incorporated into the social norms and institutions of the society and concretely influences the patterns of daily life. The social side of culture is *time-factored*, meaning that culture is a dynamic process, constantly evolving according to the collective experiences of the cultural community. The cultural flow is neither uniform nor homogeneous. It is composed of at least three currents of human activities: interpersonal, economic-technical, and political-social. Each 'movement' of the current is contextualized in specific places and is time-factored in real time so that specific 'moves' – for example, making a decision –

can be described in context as 'timely', 'too early', or 'too late'. The time factor in each current of activity also correlates with each dominant motive in the stream of activities: interpersonal culture is present-oriented for the belonging; economic-technical culture is future-oriented for the motive of achievement; and political–social culture is past-oriented for the motive of power (Triad II).

Third, the union between the individual and the cultural community is formed on the emotional charge of what has been called *primordial sentiments* toward language, territory (region), traditions (customs), religion, ethnicity, and race. The six primordial sentiments refer to emotions in interpersonal life that help create the social organization of culture. The social side of a primordial sentiment points to the functions of sentiments in society. Principles and issues integrated in the primordial sentiments invigorate emotions of belonging, of ethics, and of loyalty surrounding the communal group. Emotions associated with primordial sentiments thus provide the vital affective bonds for the social organization of culture (Triad III).

The trilogy's three dimensions offer a broad and strong definition of culture in which the content of civilization, the ideals and values of humanism, and the norms of human nature are theorized to derive from culture, not the reverse, and not in any other causal configuration. A paradigm of culture must include parameters that account for the psychology, sociology, politics, economics, and history of human beings. The trilogy constitutes just such a foundation. It is designed to replace folk ideas about human nature in order to establish a base for constraints on culture as meaning. The cultural trilogy is founded on a neurophysiological template of the brain.[3]

The importance of basic emotions

Beginning with the discussion of the emergence of modern man in the opening paragraphs of this chapter, I have been concerned to express the importance of emotion in human nature and culture. Development of the modern view of emotions can be said to begin with the publication of Charles Darwin's *The Expression of the Emotions in Man and Animals* (1872/1998). Darwin described how fundamental emotions find expression in the overt behavior of human and lower animals in simple forms such as fear and anger. But Darwin's materialistic ideas were too controversial for psychologists and philosophers intent on describing human nature as rational, constructive, benevolent, even sublime. William James turned conventional wisdom upside down in 1884, however, when he published the celebrated paper, 'What is an emotion?'. James's answer to the question insisted that facial expressions and visceral reactions, previously thought to be the *result* of an emotional experience, were instead the emotion itself in the form of perceptual responses to changes in the physical body. The physiological nature of emotion was argued to include processes such as faster heartbeat and breathing, and excitement from adrenaline released into the bloodstream. The body, it was reasoned, takes the lead, perhaps playing the *only* role in the experience of emotion (James 1952: 738–66).

Today it is accepted that bodily reactions play an important part in creating and sustaining emotions. Models of the brain now show how the brain influences emotion. Scientists have demonstrated that the limbic system and the right hemisphere of the brain are involved in mediating emotional feelings and behavior. Even so, human feelings are too complicated to be reduced to hormonal and neural activity. In addition to the autonomic arousal in emotion, 'attention and scanning mechanisms are directed towards important aspects of the environment' and alerting and marking mechanisms identify events that are important (Mandler 1987: 220). Cognitive evaluations of both the exciting event and of the bodily reactions are crucial elements in mediating emotional feelings.

In the field of cross-cultural psychology, emotions captured the attention of the experimental psychologist Charles Osgood and his colleagues (1975), who pioneered a massive classic study of the universals of affective meaning based on single words – the *Cross-Cultural Universals of Affective Meaning*. Subjects from many cultures rated a list of words used to measure their affective meanings. In this way, Osgood collected information on cultural feelings towards particular words. The hypothesis driving the study was that regardless of language or culture, human beings throughout the world use the same qualifying emotional framework to allocate affective meaning to concepts (Osgood *et al.* 1975: 6). The study is a monumental effort to construct a universal culture of the type I call 'nuclear culture'.

Following in the tradition of the universal culture of emotion, the psychologist Paul Ekman identified six basic universal emotions: happiness, sadness, anger, fear, disgust, and surprise (Ekman, Friesen and Ellsworth 1972). Each of the six emotions has a distinctive physiological pattern among all peoples in body temperature, blood pressure, muscle tone, body agitation, and perceptual accuracy. The receptor organs for warmth, pressure, movement, and all the other sensory impressions convert sensory stimulation into electric impulses which stream to the brain, where neuronal firing is organized into a single pattern, such as anger.

None the less, more recently Anna Wierzbicka in *Emotion and Culture* (1994) confronts what she calls the 'shallow universalism' of the idea that a 'finite set of discrete and universal basic human emotions can be identified by English words'. Continuing the thought:

> Cross-cultural lexical research undertaken by linguists and anthropologists demonstrates that concepts such as happy or angry are not universal, but constitute cultural artifacts of Anglo culture reflected in, and continually reinforced by, the English language . . . Another conclusion emerging from this research is that the set of emotion terms

available in any given language is unique and reflects a culture's unique perspective on people's ways of feeling. It also reflects the links between feelings, cognition, moral norms, and social interaction.

(Wierzbicka 1994: 134–5)

The universal culture of emotion in the work of Osgood's and Ekman's universalisms stands for one extreme on a continuum of nuclear culture, while Wierzbicka's 'culture's unique perspective' stands for surface culture at the opposite end, where each perception is unique, garbed as it is in the myriad of circumstances and accidents of occurrence.[4]

In my Cultural Trilogy, universalism goes into *deep culture*. Concrete uniqueness is categorized in *surface culture* as perception. States of emotional expression that fall between deep and surface culture belong to *procedural culture* – the 'how' of culture. In the province of procedures, surface and deep culture combine in the individual and in the community by merging contexts and goals into experiences.

Procedural culture mediates operations of the human mind and is comparable to the operation system that drives a computer. Procedural culture combines deep thoughts, values, and logic with surface percepts in the form of recipes shared among members of a cultural group. In the process, deep culture provides the human engineering required by the system while surface culture designs the architecture of feedback from experience for learning and producing adaptations rooted in biology. As with the computer program, it is important to note that procedural culture functions as an artifact for building adaptations to situations according to the norms of the cultural community. Procedural culture uses the thoughts, values, and logic of deep culture as tools adapted to the architecture of surface culture. The constraints of the neurophysiology of perception guide human behavior along the paths our cultural ancestors have blazed.

Conclusion

In the late twentieth century, dissatisfaction with the objectivist paradigm in psychology and other social sciences was met by advances in understanding the neurophysiology of the brain, a regeneration of Darwin's theory of natural selection, and communication-based theoretical approaches to culture such as the language mediations of Vygotsky. In a new view of the mind, human nature becomes a cognitive interpretation of innate circuitry in the brain. The brain is a system of mental modules, and its modularity can be analyzed more concretely as an assembly of artifacts used to attain practical consequences. From this perspective culture is composed of tool-mediated actions collaborating with symbolic resources.

In the view of evolutionary psychologists, the present architecture of the brain was established in the prehistory of the species about 100,000 years ago.

Since then changes in human nature have formed through cultural evolution. The mind emerges as an organ adapted to avoid threats and to exploit opportunities our ancestors faced hunting and foraging in the hostile environment of the glacial period. The harsh circumstances of survival created in the human's perceptual systems the potential to perceive animals and people with fear, and to defend the self and allies with an algorithm of aggression based on anger and on predator–prey relationships. In responding to external events, human perception developed a doubled–coded process of sensation and emotion that forms in perception and cognition. All of this makes 'reality' an intuitive, implicit feeling beyond the reach of reason, a process that is coded in language and the senses. In order to decode the complex processes of the mind, it is necessary to map the structures and operations of culture. The Cultural Trilogy presented here is one such approach to mapping nuclear culture as innate human nature.

Appendix 1.1: The twelve parameters of the Cultural Trilogy

Triad I: Individual analysis of behavior

1 Surface culture: Content is observable behavior (speech, facial expressions, gestures, actions, etc.), artifacts (foods, dress, architecture, farmland, etc.); psychology is external perception, contextualized in time, place, and conditions of experience.
2 Deep culture: Content is cognition, emotions (thinking, values, systems of knowledge); psychology is internal perception in the absolute and universal time and space of the body.
3 Procedural culture: Content is performance and communication; agent in interaction is in pursuit of goals in context (pattern of managing self–others, decision-making, counseling, conflict resolution, modes of production, etc.); psychology is synthesis of surface and deep culture.

Triad II: Time-factored activities in social environments

4 Interpersonal culture: Activities of interior life pursued with family and others known face-to-face to satisfy physiological, security, and belonging needs; time-factored in cyclic present.
5 Economic-technical culture: Activities of work life pursued with others as experts to satisfy achievement need; time-factored in near future in linear form of time.
6 Political-social culture: Activities of public life pursued to satisfy power need; competition between civil and cultural time-factored identity formed in time-factored episodic past.

Triad III: Primordial sentiments in social organization of culture

7 Language: Cultural belonging and identity through interpersonal and mass communication.
8 Traditions and customs: Traditions develop belonging in social side of procedural culture; customs as social manners.
9 Ethnicity: Extended family-community.
10 Region (Territory): Attachment to style of life and locus of homeland.
11 Religion: Ideal form of human relations and governing moral sentiment.
12 Race: Attachment and identity based on physical differences.

Notes

1 Throughout this chapter, and specifically in this section, I rely on Barbara Ehrenreich's *Blood Rights* (1997) as the chief source for the predator–prey paradigm, and on Steven Mithen's *The Prehistory of the Mind* (1996) for the evolution of human culture.
2 George Lakoff's *Women, Fire, and Dangerous Things* (1987) is the original source for the analysis of anger in American and other Western societies.
3 The first publication of the cultural trilogy was an intercultural application of the paradigm to the Persian Gulf crisis (Stewart 1991). A second critical application was made to the cultural change in American society beginning in the 1960s (Stewart 1998). A third application of the trilogy is towards peace-building, using Germany as a case study (Emminghaus, Kimmel, and Stewart 1998).
4 Since his original publications on basic emotions, Paul Ekman has modified his position that each basic emotion, such as anger, stands for a discrete affective state. Ekman has replaced affective singularity with a family of related states. Moreover, Ekman has identified more than one universal expression for each basic emotion (Wierzbicka 1994: 143).

References

Blake, W. (1982). *The Complete Prose and Poetry of William Blake*. New York: Anchor Books: 'The Tiger'.

Brown, D. E. (1991). *Human Universals*. New York: McGraw-Hill.

Bruner, J. (1996). *The Culture of Education*. Cambridge, MA: Harvard University Press.

Cole, M. (1996). *Cultural Psychology*. Cambridge, MA: Belknap/Harvard University Press.

Darwin, C. (1872/1998). *The Expression of Emotion in Man and Animals*. Oxford: Oxford University Press.

Ehrenreich, B. (1997). *Blood Rites*. New York: Henry Holt.

Ekman, P., Friesen, W., and Ellsworth, P. (1972). *Emotion in the Human Face*. New York: Pergamon Press.

Emminghaus, P., Kimmel, R., and Stewart, E. C. (1998). 'Primal violence: Illuminating culture's dark side'. In E. Weiner (ed.), *The Handbook of Interethnic Coexistence*. New York: Continuum.

Geertz, C. (1973). *The Interpretation of Cultures*. London: Hutchinson. New York: Basic Books.

Hannerz, U. (1992). *Cultural Complexity: Studies in the Social Organization of Meaning*. New York: Columbia University Press.

Hughes, T. (1997). 'On Ovid's metamorphosis.' *New York Review of Books*, 17 July: 52–6.

James, W. (1952). *The Principles of Psychology*. Chicago: University of Chicago Press.

Johnson-Laird, P. N. (1988). *The Computer and the Mind*. Cambridge, MA: Harvard University Press.

Kagan, D. (1995). *On the Origins of War*. New York: Doubleday.

Keegan, J. (1993). *A History of Warfare*. New York: Alfred A. Knopf.

Lakoff, G. (1987). *Women, Fire, and Dangerous Things*. Chicago: University of Chicago Press.

Mandler, G. (1987). 'Emotion'. In. R. L. Gregory (ed.), *The Oxford Companion to the Mind*. Oxford: Oxford University Press.

Mithen, S. (1996). *The Prehistory of the Mind*. London: Thames and Hudson.

Osgood, C. E., May, W., and Miron, M. S. (1975). *Cross-Cultural Universals of Affective Meaning*. Urbana, IL: University of Illinois Press.

Rowland, B. Jr (1965). *Drawings of the Masters: Cave to Renaissance*. New York: Shorewood Publishers.

Scarre, C. (1993). *Smithsonian Timelines of the Ancient World*. London: Dorling Kindersley.

Stewart, E. C. (1991). 'An intercultural interpretation of the Persian Gulf crisis'. *Intercultural Communication Studies* 4: 1–47.

—— (1998). 'The feeling edge of culture in the American sensitivity shift'. In R. A. Javier and W. G. Herron (eds), *Personality Development and Psychotherapy in Our Diverse Society*. Northvale, NJ: Jason Aronson.

Storr, A. (1968). *Human Aggression*. London: Penguin Books.

Tocqueville, A. de (1945). *Democracy in America*. New York: Vintage Books.

Triandis, H. C. (1972). *The Analysis of Subjective Culture*. New York: Wiley-Interscience.

Vygotsky, L. S. (1962). *Thought and Language*. Cambridge, MA: MIT Press.

Wierzbicka, A. (1994). 'Emotion, language, and cultural scripts'. In S. Kitayama and H. R. Markus (eds), *Emotion and Culture*. Washington, DC: American Psychological Association.

Wilson, E. W. (1998). *Consilience*. New York: Alfred A. Knopf.

2

RETHINKING THE FOUNDATIONS OF CULTURE

Eduardo Neiva

Despite being currently considered the solid ground of communication studies, or better because of it, culture needs radical reformulation. The antiquated perspective on culture defined it as an idealized abstraction, as a means of distinguishing human beings and the variety of their social groups, as well as an edge severing humanity from the natural world. In that sense, culture is conceived as a set of immanent rules of social integration, whose purpose is to separate what is *ours* in opposition to what is *other*. The distinctions are neat: social groups are different because they have different cultures, and culture draws a line disengaging human beings from both animal and natural life.

These assumptions are untenable. The separation of cultures in the world of global communication simply cannot hold any more. Nowadays, no culture can aspire to isolation. Cultural identification is more than ever under the global pressure of information exchange. And why should we accept uncritically the opposition between what is natural and what is cultural, between what is given by genetic inheritance and what is acquired through human interaction? The separation of nature and culture stems from an inaccurate assumption that the natural world and the human mind belong to universes without bridges. It implies that the natural world is a realm ruled by blind necessity, resulting from the mechanical properties of matter and determined by unchanging links of cause and effect, inasmuch as human life and social interaction are basically free. This assumption is based on the premise that matter and mind are isolated dualities. But the dualism of nature and culture, or of matter and mind, merely reflects an archaic metaphysical polarity: the one between body and soul.

A critique of the anthropological illusion

How can we continue to believe that human cultures are radically autonomous from each other, when even anthropologists embracing this conception of culture inevitably return from their field research saying that the studied group is a meaningful whole, and that it can be understood? Anthropological interpretations may be right or wrong, but anthropologists consistently offer an interpretation of social gatherings.

Yet, paradoxically, anthropology disseminated the idea of culture as conventional and that singular patterns of thought form an invisible but potent barrier that grants collective and excluding identity to social actors. Culture then becomes a set of rules antedating social actors – the cause of relative social determination, a stable grid resisting change. But why did it seem reasonable to understand culture as a fixed frame acting over social life making it resistant to change?

At the foundation of anthropology in British universities, anthropologists were incapable of dealing with a pressing social problem that was very near to them: the destruction of the urban working class by the Industrial Revolution. And, without inclination or desire to idealize the English peasantry, they transferred their expectations of domesticity and social equilibrium – so inbred in the upper crust from where anthropologists were recruited – to primitive social groups subjugated to British colonial rule. It is an anthropologist (Leach 1984: 4) who recognizes that his discipline suffered, since its beginnings, from this kind of arcadian illusion. In any case, anthropological thought is mixed with a superior attitude that, in a condescending manner, identifies what is its *other*.

Even for authors (Gass 1989: 189) writing from the fringes of contemporary social thought, culture is seen as a term that cannot be easily stripped from prejudice and bad consciousness. How can we forget that the apparently neutral anthropological approach to societies branches out into two trends superficially contradictory that are – deep inside – complementary?[1]

On one hand, in classrooms, anthropology claimed to be the defender of the legitimate humanity of the people it studied. But, on the other hand, it furnished the necessary knowledge for the transformation of natives of colonized societies into servants that would be bought with beads. Anthropology, whose birth is a consequence of the colonialist legacy, presented a bad deal for the natives. In exchange for their symbolic validation as humans, the colonized would receive a religion that was foreign to their traditions; at the same time the integrity of their society was almost always destroyed. Colonized societies would never be the same; they became part of the general plan of humankind, to which they contributed unconsciously and at their own expense.

The idea of cultural singularity was marginal in early cultural theory. The set of values prevalent in a particular social group was seen as part of a unique whole organizing the apparent diversity of humanity. The lines separating human groups were less important than the recognition of a legacy underlining the multiplicity of cultures. Edward B. Tylor's (1871) influential project of a cultural and anthropological theory was a typical nineteenth-century pseudo-evolutionary scheme[2] that had its foundations in the Enlightenment conception of a progressive development of humankind. This would change. But, at the beginning of anthropological research, universals mattered much more than particulars.

During the nineteenth century, the encounters of cultural theorists with actual and singular cultures were indirect. As I am about to explain, cultures different from one's own were not known from lived experience. This is not to say that early cultural theory held a sloppy or careless approach to particular cultures. Encountering a culture was a means of collecting data, never an end in itself. Collecting data served a higher purpose.

Anthropology started under the sign of a clear-cut division of labor. Government officials, missionaries, travelers, explorers, and other tentacles of colonialism would experience intercultural contact, leaving the processing and the reflection of data to armchair theorists with deficient second-hand knowledge of actual cultures. Tylor, for instance, thought that his role was to deal with the conjectural aspect of anthropological imagination, fitting singularities into an overall design. Meanwhile, the actual contact with specific groups was left to missionaries already in the field, like Lorimer Fison and Robert Henry Codington, or to explorers such as Everard Im Thrun (Stocking 1983: 78). It is therefore no surprise that culture, the key notion of such an odd undertaking, could be regarded as suspicious, however careful the British Association on Anthropology may have been, requesting rigorous information, and demanding data to follow a meticulous prescription. Informers were ordered not to ask uncalled-for questions and, above all, to be precise (Stocking 1983: 72–3). Informers should follow step by step the script of *Notes and Queries on Anthropology*, blessed by the British Association on Anthropology.

The great transformation in cultural anthropology came when this division of labor was unraveled, at the onset of the First World War, after Malinowski's involuntary but deep immersion in the native life of the Trobriand Islands. Malinowski's experience would reveal the importance of living in the social group to be interpreted. The interpreter of a culture should learn to be a native; the anthropologist must be able to comprehend the native culture from the inside.

With the lived experience of dwelling among the members of a society, a whole new insight on culture emerged. To separate a fragment of a culture from the conditions of its use was deemed a hopeless distortion. Nothing could repair it, not even the high purpose of inserting the segment in the evolutionary metamorphosis of humankind.

Cultural function and singularity

In Malinowski's terms, the basic rule to understand society was to dispense with establishing the sequence of historical and comparative links between social groups. The main objective now was to provide 'a functional analysis of culture' (Malinowski 1931: 624). Looking towards the past was replaced by consummate immersion in the present. The functionalist conception of culture maintained that social experience was an integral whole offering collective cohesion to social interaction. The task of anthropological analysis was to identify the cultural values and regulations in actual and occasional behavior (Stocking 1989: 98). Every incident in a group loomed from culture.

After Malinowski, cultural interpretation ought to be anchored in contexts.[3] The major condition for cultural analysis was the observation and the actual interaction of the ethnographer with the interpreted society. Any other contention outside of the present context matured into a fuzzy supposition. Linguistic exchange, and by extension all exchange in a culture, was 'only intelligible when placed within its *context of situation*' (Malinowski 1923: 306). The trace perfusing all cultural events and whatever communicative act occurred in a social group was singularity.

The impact of Malinowski's recommendation was deeply felt throughout anthropology. More than anyone else, he 'emphasized that the effect of a spoken word is entirely dependent upon the context in which it is uttered' (Leach 1957: 131). Linguistic meaning could not be grasped by philological and historical concepts. Malinowski's idea of a situational context as a criterion of meaning led the interpreter to link one lived stimulus to another, expanding the conditions for his understanding to encompass more than actual utterances. Language in context implied culture, and correct interpretation of meaning needed 'a detailed account of the culture of its users' (Malinowski 1923: 309).

Literal translation of an utterance, word by word, from one language to another, would never be sufficient to cope with the intricate question of meaning. If speech is 'one of the principal modes of human action' (Malinowski 1923: 333), how could we do away with the cultural frame in which the action occurred, and which itself allowed this action to be performed? In *Argonauts of the Western Pacific*, Malinowski (1922: 459) declared that 'no linguistic analysis can disclose the full meaning of a text without knowledge of the sociology, of the customs, of the beliefs current in a given society'.

Malinowski's pragmatic conception of language may have been innovative, but it was marred by his unwarranted conclusion that in utterances everything amounted to a mere reiteration of the very culture into which they occur. Linguistic exchange was then reduced to *phatic communion*. Language grew into the fulfillment of a social function.[4]

For Malinowski, cultural acts were the transformation of biological impulses. Culture had a tendentious practical nature. Kinship was the cultural answer to reproduction; health was obtained by cultural notions of hygiene (Piddington 1957: 35). To the functionalist interpretation, culture was a form of practical reason whose restricted goal was survival.

If that was the case, did biological needs generate culture; or did culture create organic needs? The circularity of answers to easily interchangeable questions indicated that this was a false problem, a tautological merry-go-round, haunting Malinowski's understanding of culture. But it is valuable to recognize in Malinowski's definition of culture the traces of a resilient idea of culture as a rupture with an original natural state severing humans from the natural world.

On the other hand, it is quite true that Malinowski's functionalist theories were criticized by anthropologists themselves. The most harrowing critique can be found in Claude Lévi-Strauss's *Totemisme, aujourd'hui* (1962a) and *La pensée sauvage* (1962b). Lévi-Strauss argued against the disqualification of thought in archaic societies. The 'savage' was quite capable of sophisticated and legitimate thinking. For Lévi-Strauss, all human languages can express the intricacies of abstractions; primitive classificatory systems are as sophisticated as the theoretical enterprise of modern science; their dissimilarity should be accounted as a result of a diverse interest and intention, without being considered a symptom or a judgment of greater or lesser intellectual achievement.

The logic of the modern engineer had to be distinct from primitive thinking's *bricolage*. The achievements of primitive thought and science vary as a result of how each culture approaches nature. The primitive mind pursues a strategy leveled at perception and imagination; science aims at reaching nature through the grasping of its structure, moving away from what is given to the senses. The *bricoleur* manipulates nature, handles what is at his or her disposal. The outcome of scientific inquiry is different. Nature is not a limit, nor a hedge, but an object to be treated in an altogether distinct light. As a product of scientific thought, the engineer is immersed in a world of concepts; his or her goal is to transcend natural events, trying to capture them conceptually, thus providing a discernment of their structure.

In Lévi-Strauss's terms, culture had a positive stand in itself, not to be reduced to a mere transformation of biological drives or needs. Culture could never be 'an immense metaphor for reproduction and digestion' (Lévi-Strauss 1988: 28), as Malinowski hastily suggested.

Social life followed models that were different from organic and biological interpretations. Nature and culture belonged to dissimilar realms. The way to interpret culture should be in strictly cultural terms. Thus, the appropriate interpretation of culture should be inspired, although cautiously, by linguistics. Lévi-Strauss's claims endorsed a sociocentric, and therefore a strictly conventionalist, discernment of culture and social life.

However, Lévi-Strauss's idea of culture kept much of what Malinowski defined as the traits of cultural experience. Culture was distinctively local and singular. It was an autonomous whole, prior to any behavior in a social group. Culture was a departure from our biological order. The duality of orders – one natural, the other cultural – in a state of mutual exclusion was clearly visible in both Malinowski's and Lévi-Strauss's notion of culture.

Nature, culture

The roots of the anthropological dogma separating nature and culture may be found in the intellectual legacy of Jean-Jacques Rousseau (1712–78). Indeed, anthropologists with methodological concerns have already acknowledged

Rousseau's influence over anthropology. When Marshall Sahlins (1977: 9) said that Rousseau was the true ancestor of anthropology, he was just reinforcing what Lévi-Strauss (1976: 33–43) had previously stated. For Lévi-Strauss, Rousseau was the originator of an attitude without which anthropology would be unthinkable.

Lévi-Strauss asserted that Rousseau did more than just adopt a dichotomy excluding nature and culture. In itself, that would never be an original contribution, because the segregation of mind and matter, reason and emotion, soul and body has been an old and recurrent theme in the Western philosophical tradition.

The whole point of Rousseau was to affirm a synthesis that transcended the rift between human order and the natural world. He contended that understanding occurs only after the subject is free from his (or her) original position, and begins to think of his (or her) self as an *other*. Then, the subject goes beyond his (or her) intimate preconceptions. It is a cognitive attitude similar to the aims of anthropological understanding; prejudices should be abandoned in favor of a relativistic stance. The result is a sense of profound identity between me and the other, my society and others, nature and culture, the sensible and the intelligible, humanity and life (Lévi-Strauss 1976: 43).

Forceful as Lévi-Strauss's assessment of Rousseau may be, it is also clear that he sentimentalized the philosopher's vision of the natural world. For Rousseau, the distinction between nature and culture remained untouched. Animals were radically alien to the basic principles of human social life; they could never have enlightenment and freedom. According to Rousseau, only civil societies, where human beings aggregated, could experience the sentiment of compassion. Compassion would not be within the reach of animals. As with many thinkers who secluded nature from culture, Rousseau moved in circles; he talked of compassion as a condition of sociability, but it is in the midst of social interaction that compassion is possible. Human societies are a radical break from the natural world. In Rousseau, anything that is part of the natural world was completely left aside. The natural world ignores any kind of social contracts.

Civil society would have started from an act of territorial demarcation, yet fundamentally different from the disputes in animal conflicts. Someone may have declared 'this is mine', but society subsequently envisaged property as a legitimate possession. What was an individual and solitary act became, from then on, part of a socially shared convention. And convention will lead to the acceptance of mutual rights for all members of the group. Nothing like that could be accessible to animals. They would never grasp the notion of property, nor of any other aspect of society. Animals do not possess the necessary light to apprehend the proper laws of human groups. Likewise, Rousseau (1973), in *Du contrat social*, disqualified natural force as the ground of judicial order. Political power demanded another kind of authority, stemming from shared conventions. Only conventions could legitimize authority. Sooner or later even the most blatant despotism requires more than the exercise of force.

Rousseau's political theory, therefore, upheld that society is a pact, a convention born from other conventions. Social life is built to deny nature, covering it with a dense net of contractual knots. On the other hand, to define social life as interconnected conventions also means to understand it as an exercise of freedom and will. This is another trait, separating nature from culture. Culture is related to collective and general representations, product of a social will; it is, therefore, the realm of freedom; while nature is repetitive, cyclical, the product of an unchanging order, the eternal expression of the same.

Beyond Rousseau, with Darwin

Historically, Rousseau's thought helped establish the current consensus that freedom is the central mechanism of civil societies. But such commendable achievement is based on a flawed assumption on Rousseau's part. His claim that nature is the domain of necessity is a mistake, unsupported by modern biology. The natural world is not fixed nor permanent and it does not follow a prior plan or a purpose set before the unfolding of natural events. Nature is under relentless change and evolution.

After the avalanche of Darwinian arguments, it is impossible to accept that nature is opposed to another realm of life, reserved and essential to human beings. Darwin's revolutionary understanding of biological processes leads to the recognition that in life 'all past and present organic beings constitute one grand natural system, with group subordinate to group, and with extinct groups falling in between recent groups' (Darwin 1979: 450). Darwin's understanding of nature must be considered a radical departure from Rousseau's apprehension of natural life.

One of the reasons why the metaphysical postulate separating mind and matter remains admissible for so many people is the massive presence in our culture of an essentialist theoretical vocabulary that has been faithfully kept by philosophy, theology, and physics.

Moreover, the illusions of the essentialist tradition seem to be constantly confirmed by how Indo-European languages[5] structure phrases around a subject that functions like a substratum. The grammatical subjects are isolated and separate unities, under which the predicates of the sentence are gathered. The subjects suggest essences, while the predicates would be accidental attributes.[6] The subject *apple* is qualified by variable and non-essential attributes such as *green*, *sweet*, *round*, etc. We talk like that all the time, and end up believing that there is a variety of permanent essences or kinds in the natural world. There should be as many essences as there are names functioning as subject of sentences, and, because God created the things of this world granting them names, each isolated name must indicate a separate set of beings, a species.

In 1831, when boarding the *H.M.S. Beagle* for a trip that would take him during the next five years to South America, Darwin, like all British naturalists, embraced the notion that species were created one by one, and that they were not subjected to change. Darwin then held a form of essentialist thinking. But, in the trip to the Galapagos Islands, the assumption began to erode. He noticed empirical evidence that could contradict the idea of species as stable natural kinds. Back in London, Darwin would present to the ornithologist John Gould samples of mockingbirds collected in different islands of the Galapagos. Gould maintained that they were distinct species. Darwin was not convinced. The variation of the birds was the result of what came to be known as geographic speciation: the mutation of a species living in a separate niche from the one the original species inhabited. Eventually, in one of his notebooks, started around 1837, Darwin (1987: 172) would remark: 'Animals on separate islands ought to have become different if kept long enough. – "apart" with slightly differen[t] circumstances' (*Notebook* B, 7). Two facts about biological life were becoming clearer and clearer: there was evolution and it was gradual (Mayr 1990: 19).

If early British anthropologists diverted their gaze to societies living at the edges of the destruction imposed by the Industrial Revolution, Darwin did just the opposite. As he explicitly stated, the dismal struggle for existence was a reality equally valid in the human and the natural world. In both realms, life is the result of a continuing substitution of solutions aiming at better and better adaptations, without which living organisms would perish. Humans and all other living beings exist at the center of an arena where adaptive solutions would be enacted in confrontation with the environment. The adaptation of an organism to its niche determines its future. In the natural world, the organism incapable of adapting to an environment under constant change is doomed to disappear. For all organisms, life is always a matter of either perishing or surviving; it is a frame limited by ceaseless births and deaths.

Facing the hard countenance of biological existence, Darwin concludes that life is always a delicate state, in which havoc and destruction should be expected. The insight comes from Malthus's gloomy prediction about the fate of Industrial Societies. Malthus (1888) saw the combination of geometric population growth with the steadiness and eventual shortage of housing and food as inevitably spelling disaster. Shortage of housing and food would increase prices, making survival a toss-up in industrial society. Darwin picks up Malthus's prophecy, and extends it to animal species that, incapable of either increasing the production of food or controlling their demography, are under the constant threat of disappearing.

In Darwinian terms, the inherent destruction in life processes receives the name of *natural selection*: in other words, the discarding, the preserving, and the multiplication of adaptive variations in the individual members of a species. The mechanism of natural selection delays evolutionary mutation, keeping organic solutions that have worked in the past and still function in the present, but disposing of them only in the case of change in the environmental conditions bequeathed to the individual members of the species. Again, the term natural selection can be misleading. Natural selection has nothing to do with improvement. In fact, there is nothing in the idea of natural selection to suggest a cumulative progress (Williams 1966: 34). Individual organisms could not care less for the betterment of the species. They just want to survive. The quality of adaptative mutations is measured simply in terms of how long the organism survives. Survival in life is the only objective: 'Animals make a living by eating, avoiding being eaten, and reproducing' (Dawkins 1996: 94).

As life is marked by relentless destruction, the species procreates as much as possible. Under ideal natural conditions, with abundant food and without spatial restriction for multiplication, all species, whether plants or animals, can increase their numbers with each generation (Maynard Smith 1995: 43). But this is not what happens. Why are species limited in the number of their surviving individuals? Certainly because death before full development is the customary fate of many living organisms. Everywhere there is restriction of food sources as well as predation. Another species is just a likely food source. For Darwin (1979: 172), the tree of life covers the surface of Earth with dead bodies and broken twigs. To counter death, though, each new generation of organisms brings with it a new starting point in the gradual process of evolution. Two distinct individual organisms mate and the offspring are altogether new organisms; diversity and variations are cardinal manifestations of life. The evolutionary plasticity that sexual reproduction allows will increase the chances of survival of a species in a mutant environment, owing to a greater genetic variation of its individual members.

The Darwinian conception of life had to reserve a great role for the individual. Individuals carry both the evolution and the adaptative improvement of the species. There are no essences, just individual organisms. Darwinism shows that the arrow of mutation and evolution starts in individual variability and that the most precious trait of life is the variation of their populations. Apparently, with this notion, we find a real alternative to the prevalence of culture as a collective set of representations that precede and conduct the living individuals.

Predatory interaction and the semiotic theater

The chain of living organisms is under the tension of mutual dependence, whose outcome is either survival or extinction. Of course destruction in nature occurs in many forms. It can spring from climate change, causing shortage of food in specific areas due to floods and droughts, or it can result from direct predatory interaction. Community in biological niches is either foraging or outright conflict. The natural world is always under steady competition. Open and generalized predatory pursuit predates any kind of compassion.

Not even the mother and the fetus live in sublime co-operation or lofty compassion, sharing common interests. After Haig's (1993) perceptive paper on genetic conflicts in human pregnancy, the picture is quite different. Harmony between mother and fetus is only occasional, and what defines their relationship is a conflict of non-harmonious interests. Mother and fetus compete for nutritional resources. Fetus cells invade the inner lining of the uterus, through the mother's weakest point: her vessels that cannot defend themselves. The objective of the fetus is to manipulate the mother's physical condition to its advantage. The limit of this manipulation is the fetus's selfish interest: if she dies, the fetus will suffer dire consequences, and the cost of the manipulation will far outweigh its benefits.

The existence of compassion and co-operation is the after-effect, the after-math of erasing or distorting a message that is inscribed biologically in every living organism, that is 'to explore the environment, including friends and relatives, to maximize our proliferation' (Williams 1992: 15).

We must present at this point an explanatory model of the predator–prey link that informs the basic relationship of biological experience. Then, the question is how to describe predatory processes and what conclusions could be extracted for the understanding of human culture and human society.

It is not simple to fathom the mechanics of the predatory processes in the natural world: predation may be universal in biological life, but its concrete strategies are inevitably singular, local, and restricted to specific environments. A successful species in one niche can face extinction in another. As detached observers, human beings cannot know, with ease and without doubt, what goes on in the perceptual process of a species preying on another. Thus, how could we check our hypothesis about other species? How could we build a model common to distinct species when each species has its peculiar mode of percep-tion, not necessarily akin to ours? Moreover, the act of singling out a prey demands more than mere perception. The predator searches for or avoids food sources, because it knows what would match its purpose. How could we cope with such a dazzling variety of cognitive processes when our hypothesis cannot be confirmed or refuted by the testimony of predators and prey?

The grasping of predatory interaction emerges from the consideration of a capacity present across the natural world: the semiotic faculty of representation, in other words, the ability to produce signs. Not only in human societies, but in nature we can see a proliferation of signs resulting from the interaction of living and inanimate beings. Nature is a semiotic theater: just consider what happens when shadows of twigs are projected on a wall; we have indices in direct causal relationship. Indexical signs are unstable. The alteration of the twigs changes the shape of the shadow, or makes it disappear. The sign is completely dependent upon its model.

However, if we move from the inanimate realm to the universe of living organisms, we must take into account that living beings can retain as signs, therefore as representations, what comes indexically to their perceptual systems. The natural world is duplicated. The receptor collects indices which are reinterpreted as visual forms that entertain an analogical relation with what was, an instant ago, a physical event in nature.

In terms of the animal mind, the nervous system of a living organism desig-nates iconically its position facing another organism, possibly its prey. If it is prey, the following will happen: the prey moves and triggers the whole process of capture. The predator then anticipates analogically what is moving in the environment (Thom 1983: 273). We can imagine how the process goes, through a flickering of analogical anticipations. The predator identifies with the prey, loses its analogical bond, for the prey is trying to flee, and concentrates on recapturing through forecasting what the prey would do next. On the other hand, apart from pure and simple flight, the prey is left with two equally analogical alternatives: it can display mimicry and camouflage to deceive the predator or associate itself with other individuals of the species. Analogy is the most fundamental mechanism in biological life; it is the underlining quality of moving predatory interactors as well as the relatively stable environmental scenario where predator and prey get in contact with each other. In any circumstance, both for living organisms and for the environment, analogy drives the natural world.

Predatory interaction and group formation in the natural world

The most obvious mechanisms of defense in predatory interaction are mimetism and camouflage, either through blending with the environment, or else by feigning ferocity. Owen (1982) mentions the case of the frog *Physalaemus netteri* that displays on its back the outline of big, bulging eyes; this allows the frog to point its behind in the direction of the predator, forcing the retreat, or the abandonment of the predatory chase. Another complementary example is the butterfly *Limentis archippus* that mimetically looks not like a predator but a specific kind of prey, *Danaus plexippus*, whose taste is awful to its predators.[7] Besides strict mimetism, there is another option: the prey can associate with analogous individuals of its species with the purpose of protecting itself from predators. We will see that this is the propitious situation for the evolution of social behavior too.

It is naive to presume that conventions precede individuals who are then forced to adapt to the rules of the group. In nature, uniformity is not a given: it is unstable and subject to change. If the most fundamental fact of biological life is individual genetic singularity, the formation of a group is always precarious, thus quite different from the ideal stability that anthropological functionalism used to postulate. All across the natural world, and this includes human cultures, the whole is a relationship made from the individual positions of the interactors; it does not simply follow a prior collective mold.

Undoubtedly, the natural world is perfused with groups. It could not be otherwise: natural life is centered on the transference and the replication of genes within a population; and genetic replication is in itself somewhat a product of co-operation between individual organisms (Trivers 1985: 65). If we look, though, at the gathering of individuals in natural surroundings, we can recognize constant and uniform movements, as if it were the orchestration of a force stronger than any of its parts. Could the regular formation of a school of fish, for example, provide evidence for the claim that a collective mold directly determines the action of each individual organism? If it were so, it would be tempting to give an undue predominance to collective aggregations, therefore suggesting that individuals subsume their selfish interest to the group.

But, considering the phenomenon of group formation, Williams (1964 and 1996) argues that the collective mold of a school of fish evolves from the serial sum of individual behaviors. What seems to be co-ordination is really an illusion of order, quite similar to the impression we get when we see the photograph of a tight crowd trying to escape from a room aflame. From afar, the group seems to behave orderly. But, in the middle of the group, the experience is chaotic: the individual running in the direction of an exit door triggers a response in other individuals that would otherwise run in another direction, or would remain motionless. A new response redirects the movement of the crowd. Group configuration is involuntarily drawn from individual responses.

Fear of predation determines the formation of groups. Inside a group, an individual organism reduces the possibility of being singled out by predators. Zoologists have consistently noticed that groups are more commonly formed by animals that gather in open spaces, whether in plains where herds graze or else in the vastness of waters. Fish inhabiting coral reefs will not form a group: they can hide inside the various crevices around them.[8]

The reason for group formation is simple: the organism in the middle of the group increases its chances of survival. The margins of the group must be avoided. The danger zone between predator and prey must be as large as possible. The organism in the margins and nearer to the predator has more chances of being devoured.

Independently of Williams, and dealing with what he calls the geometry of the selfish herd, Hamilton (1996: 229–52) comes to similar and complementary conclusions. For Williams and Hamilton, predatory interaction marks the evolution of social behavior. Hamilton imagines the behavior of a group of frogs living in a lake where a snake dwells. The snake always attacks at a certain moment of the day. Before the snake emerges from the water, the frogs will move to the edge of the lake, terrified of other predators living in dry land. The frogs run away from the natural habitat of the reptile but they have nowhere to go; they forecast that the snake will eat the one that is closer to it; the snake will feed itself with the least expenditure of energy. The danger zone becomes so small that piling-up is the only solution. The frog in the bottom of the heap tries to escape and jumps to the top, distancing itself from the snake gliding across the surface of the lake. In open or closed spaces, group formation is inevitable. The frogs would avoid grouping only if they could hide individually. In a school of fish, or for panic-stricken frogs, the way out is to be involved analogically with a protective whole.

The individual defends itself by calling attention to the group. It is quite true that in group formation some individuals will inevitably be food for the predator, but it also true that in the company of others the possibility of death is reduced. The more individuals are placed in front of the predator, so much the better. This goes against the interpretation that sociability exists because the group is the central evolutionary unit. A group is formed to protect the individual, not the other way around. For that reason, schools of fish and other gregarious formations became a prevailing adaptive strategy in biological evolution.

Just consider what happens if predation comes from the middle of a gathering, not from its extremes. The prey runs away from the center, with the purpose of enlarging the size of the danger zone separating predator from prey. For instance, a herd of cattle is grazing when attacked by a lion coming not from the margin of the group but from a hiding place in the grass. The group dissolves itself (Hamilton 1996: 247). To avoid concentration, each individual runs in a different direction. The kind of group formed is a direct consequence of what type of predatory attack is unleashed. The group is never formed as a result of a feeling of compassion for the other; it results from a selfish intent for preservation.

Animal groups: co-operation and conflict within species

We must admit, though, that outright selfishness is not the sole type of interaction in nature. Groups are formed for the purpose of avoiding predation, but, in due process, the original selfish sentiment can be modified. There are cases of relationships, in animal groups, that must be described as ones of mutual benefit. In such cases, selfishness is still a vital motive of grouping, but it is not any more its exclusive purpose.

At bottom, mutual benefit is a variation of selfish intent. But there is more than that. I can act in a selfless way because I will also benefit from my deeds: generous charitable contributions will enhance my social status in the community, and will buy me a ticket to the Kingdom of Heaven. It pays off; it is an excellent deal: I buy eternity with a transient donation. I sacrifice myself for my offspring, but my genes will live thereafter. Sociability comes easier to organisms that have genetic links. Social traits are developed in direct proportion to the degree of kinship between organisms. Being good to my sibling, I am also good to myself: we carry common genes.

There are instances, in the natural world, of collaborations between individuals that have no kin relationship, as in the case of the little fish *Labroides dimidiatus*, which cleans up the mouths of bigger ones, and, in return, receives protection from them in the event of a possible predatory attack. Trivers (1971) postulates that, in examples such as this, co-operation occurs after many interactions between specific individuals. Both parties have something to gain in this situation. Trivers (1971) named the phenomenon *reciprocal altruism*. Slowly, and if reciprocal altruism is successful, the number of altruistic organisms in a population will increase. Co-operation and trust are learned and reached; they are not an original legacy of natural life.

Then what to make of the mutual restraint of animals involved in fighting for territory and mates? In an animal conflict between males of the same species, it is easy to see that the contenders are to some extent co-operating with one another; they seem to agree to avoid combats that are completely or treacherously aggressive; they appear to be involved in a form of conventional or ritualized dispute. Why is it that animals – themselves allegedly thoughtless individualists – are involved in conflicts that follow rules and ritualized tactics? Is it not better just to employ any strategy, as long as victory is attained? The fact is that snakes fight without using their fangs; deer interlock antlers but do not hurt each other; fish grasp each other's jaws and the fight is then a sequence of pushing and pulling; antelopes' combats are enacted in a restricting posture, with their knees down; and how about threat displays where physical contact does not occur? To whom is restraint beneficial?

It would seem that the group is the direct beneficiary. But this explanation, like all of those that give credence to groups in natural selection, is blemished. Darwinian interpretation asserts that selection tends to occur at the level of the individual and its genes, not only because each individual is a new and unique evolutionary starting point, but also because it is much more economical for natural selection to weed out particular organisms that cannot cope with an antagonistic environment. A single selective death should be enough to do away with the harmful mutation. And if the mutation is individually beneficial but harmful to the group, it will spread itself through the population, demanding its whole extinction (Maynard Smith 1972: 11). Individual selection is frequently stronger than group selection.

It was with this in mind that Maynard Smith (1972, 1982; see also Maynard Smith and Price 1973) set out to prove that a 'limited war' strategy is beneficial to individuals fighting, and to demonstrate that restrained contact develops into a preferred evolutionary strategy in the natural world.

Consider what happens in the case of three possible strategies to be developed in a conflict. The strategies could be *conventional tactics*, *threat displays*, and *escalating fight*. Conventionalized conflict and threat displays have in common the purpose of avoiding injury through the restriction of physical contact. Escalating fight, on the other hand, would lead to possible injuries. If both contenders employ full escalating fight, the benefits of acquiring reproductive success are impaired by the possibility of extermination or serious debilitating injuries. Reproductive success is certainly desirable, but not at the expense of individual physical integrity. If it is possible to combine the basic strategies, it is evolutionarily more effective to be involved in an initial conventionalized conflict, escalating only if the opponent does so.

A communicative exchange

Imagine now a situation in which the cost is not any form of physical harm but a strategy committed to avoiding injuries, thus consuming exclusively time and energy. That would be the optimal alternative. Evolutionary preference should then be given to conventionalized fighting and threat displays. Communication – the exchange of signs – would take place instead of physical interaction, being beneficial to both contenders. What used to be a belligerent interaction is made into a means of communication. The initial function of all movements of a fight is altered: actions that were exclusively part of fighting mature into a message.

Even in the case of a strategy beginning with conventionalized conflict that escalates to total fight, we would have a communicative scenario. Organism A starts conventionally, in other words, sends a message to its opponent, organism B. If B accepts the message, then the fight will be conventional. But suppose that organism B either distrusts or does not accept the message and escalates fighting. Organism A reacts by escalating, following the received message. Here, we have more than mere conflict. Traded messages determine the kind and scope of animal conflicts.

Threat displays are even more advantageous to the contenders. It is no surprise that so many animals adopt threatening instead of total fight. Animals assume aggressive postures, they emit sounds, they grind teeth, but there is no physical fight. Again they deliver messages. At some point in the conflict, one of the fighters admits defeat, the other wins, but none of them is physically hurt. Maynard Smith (1972) argues that in such ritualized conflicts both sides somehow lose if the dispute goes on endlessly: precious time is wasted that could be devoted to other important activities. So, there is a point at which the persistence in fighting is a loss for both contenders. When must display threats end? Is there a contractual rule binding contestants in ritualized conflicts? If we think that the two fighters cannot have the same physical endurance, owing to distinct genetic legacy or even acquired skills, the rule of ritualized displays is to trick your opponent to its limit.

The whole point of the threat display is, at first, manipulation and deception. Even weaker animals will try to show themselves as stronger than they are. Signs and the behavior that they are supposed to represent are in close analogical relationship. The intensity of a sign indicates intense future fighting. According to Darwin's principle of antithesis (1998), the decrease of intensity of a sign implies its opposite: therefore, it means weakness. There is a tenuous line separating true information about an attack and manipulative deception of an opponent. Organism A must not reveal its limit of endurance, therefore the emission of threat signal must be kept at its highest intensity for the longest period of time. The first to diminish the intensity of the threat is in fact admitting defeat and thus inviting outright attack. From this moment on, it does not pay to persist in the conflict. It is better to leave the dispute.

Viewing the fight as an interaction, where organisms A and B interact on equal terms, we have to recognize that deception is only an occasional strategy. The repetition of deceptive strategies will leave them open to codification on the part of the other contender. Deception can then be seen as a cheat in the future. Evolution selects honesty. In the course of time, deceitful signals would be rarer and rarer. And taking into account that evolution presumes the repetition of strategies over extended periods of time, manipulation has to be temporary. Manipulator and manipulated will be caught in a evolutionary arm-race. Signals evolve to be honest and reliable (Zahavi and Zahavi 1997).

Animal sociability and human groups

To adopt an evolutionary perspective on culture brings with it significant advantages. It overlaps with some of the anthropological claims about human societies, and yet redefines human culture integrating it with biological life.

We saw previously that there are two mechanics in animal grouping, depending on how predation can occur. The result is two different kinds of group formations. If predation comes from the outside, the ideal solution is to form a tight group. But, when the attack comes from inside the group, individual organisms choose to disperse the totality, running each one in a different direction. It is quite the same in human societies. Human groups are organized according to two basic morphologies that ripple across humanity, and recombine themselves in various singular cultures. The singularity of cultural solutions is preceded by a morphology affecting the creation of specific cultural products and messages. In other words, a universal form underlines specific and particular social formations. The two basic social morphologies are supported and created by the 'circulation of complexity, of information, through the social body' (Thom 1975: 318), in short, by communication: a phenomenon not at all different from the definition of fighting strategies in animal conflict resulting from what messages are traded in the interaction.

Superficially, it would seem that the two morphologies are disparate and non-congruent manners of ordering the relationships of individuals and their collection, between the isolated parts and their whole. However, the fact that the morphologies comprise two ways of defining the relationships between individuals is an indication of the dominance of individuality not only among animals but also in human beings, thus following the Darwinian intuition that self-preservation is an active and primary force at the core of life processes. We just have to remember the ruthless action of the fetus over its mother: complete and absolute exhaustion of the mother's nutrient resources could lead to her death. The fetus's selfish interest must be curbed. Her death means its death. In human pregnancy, the alternation of biochemical reactions between mother and fetus can take care of the problem. Outside of the womb, humans create social rules that are shared and must be learned to allow effective interaction.

Human societies are thus organized according to two major structure types with their own rules. One type is based on the subordination of the individual to the group, being therefore hierarchical and holistic. The other type is fluid;

in it, each individual relates to another on an equal basis; its principle and value is autonomy; and only then the individual responds to the aggregation.

Hierarchical and holistic organization

In reply to hierarchical and holistic morphologies, the whole defines the parts and the prevalent rule is that each individual should have a defined place in society. Individuals are expected to occupy a position in a social pattern that is seemingly stable, and that tends to elude change. In the natural world, flocks of birds and beehives are products of a holistic morphology. Among humans, caste formations are underlined by such structure type of subordination.

Bearing in mind that cultures provide the rules that mirror a morphology, and examining Indian culture, we can see an example of an extremely hierarchical and holistic cultural system. In it, one element embraces the other in a relationship of encompassing and encompassed (Dumont 1967 and Khare 1971). The individual social actor does not construct a social identity from scratch. Individuals receive their identity from social personae that antedate and specify their possibilities for life. In Indian society the form of the social frame is like a cusp. At the top of the social gathering, we find Brahmins, or priests, and going down the social slope, we find 'below them the Kshatriya, or warriors, and then the Vaishyas, in modern usage merely merchants, and finally the Shudras, the servants or have-nots' (Dumont 1970: 67). Besides these four social categories, Dumont also identifies a fifth category, composed of the Untouchables, which is outside of the classification. Brahmins and Untouchables are as opposed to one another as purity is to impurity, as high is to low.

The Indian order of castes is a complex cultural system with restrictions placed on food, sex, and rituals. Social order is maintained through the communication of ideas concerning the purity of its members, and through kinship ties that direct endogamous connections, creating binds that anchor 'the Hindu to its place in society and curb the desire to strike out on his own' (Yalman 1969: 125). Therefore, to secure such order, Indian society generates cultural products that emphasize the message of social subordination. Culture creates a constellation of messages powerful enough to act upon individuals. In the case of Indian society, the basic idea of subordinate contrast comes from the distinction between purity and impurity that culminates hierarchically in the figure of the Brahmin priest.

Individualistic organization

The other possible morphology would inevitably invert the idea of hierarchical subordination. In nature, the counterpart is the cloud of mosquitoes (Thom 1975: 319), where the movements of the swarm are oriented from the point of view of the individual organisms interacting in the cloud. The glimpse of other individuals in the swarm corrects the course of the pattern and its constant possibility of disintegration. No totality governs the pattern, the pattern happens. Each individual is linked to another individual organism and all of them, through reciprocity, adjust themselves, avoiding disintegration. In human societies, clear legal definitions of rules respected by each individual can bar disorder.

Equality is the dominant rule in individualistic morphologies. Lévi-Strauss (1946: 643) would say that, in the United States, the chief ideology is that 'what is valuable for the part is equally valid for the whole'. This does not mean that in egalitarian societies there are no rules. With egalitarian relations as its rule, life in America, for instance, moves through a deep and ingrained desire for uniformity. The individualistic streak that this morphology fosters is reduced by a constant demand to conform, to become part of what is considered main-stream. Mediocrity is encouraged. The viewpoint of the common human being is deemed as valid as the extraordinary realizations of the exceptional achievers.

In his trip to America during the 1830s to review its legal system, Alexis de Tocqueville (1994, vol. 1: 254–87) perceived this contradiction in United States society, pointing to the possibility of a tyranny of the majority. The action of an individualistic morphology is present in all areas of American social life. The First Amendment to the Constitution sanctifies the freedom of the press, preventing the government from creating laws that would restrict free speech. It is an amendment against the government, phrased to protect the individual, and to ensure the universal right of free access to individual con-sciousness. All over the social fabric, civil and contractual rights are extended to singular members of the community. Collective entitlements are under con-stant criticism, even if upheld. In personal terms, 'fun', 'pleasure', to be a 'nice person', ways of being cherished by the community as special individuals, are constantly prized in America. In this social setting, entertainment becomes a major industry. The discourse on the social role of individuals is centered more around rights than duties. Hierarchical morphologies are just the opposite: duties come first.

In societies where individualism prevails the purpose of social interaction is easily turned into the pursuit of individual happiness. The economic system is an end in itself, the market is a self-regulating and autonomous sphere (Polanyi 1968, 1975), exactly like the individual social actors. The economy exists to permit and to encourage individual accumulation of wealth. It is very different from traditional societies that bridle economic to social interests.

Conclusion

Whoever accedes to the anthropological concept of culture cannot go much further than identifying the cultural rules of a group. The rest, even dissent and social negotiation, is supposed to come without any other assumption or problem. The traditional conception of culture draws a route to interpret cultural phenomena that moves from the group to the individual, ruling out the alternative that moves from the individual to the group. In cultural anthropology, the group takes precedence over anything; the individual becomes an epiphenomenon.

But from the Darwinian conception of life, the view is different. The set of collective representations defining culture is just a model generalized from the point of view of individuals. Therefore culture cannot completely bind them. At best, culture opens up individual possibilities. The conclusion is that the individual organism will make use of collective rules, subverting them, distorting them, turning them around, deceiving competitors, negotiating relationships, making whatever is necessary, even delivering honest and true signs, just to impose its selfish interest.

The tension between selfish interest and cultural norm is too valuable to be discarded with the unfounded claim that animal societies and human groups are totally excluded from one another. As we have seen in this chapter, it is feasible to interpret human cultures without a rigid line separating nature and culture.

With its emphasis on collective representations, stable, and more or less predeterminant of individual interaction, anthropological theories of culture cannot grasp the individualistic wave that will wash our shores in this age of the global circulation of messages. It is easy to see that there are instances of nationalistic and local resistance or backlashes.[9] But gradually we will recognize that gone are the days when societies could effectively isolate themselves from messages, ideas, influences, and expectations coming from strangers. Soon, there will be no societies flagellated by outside and marginal predation. Predation will just come from within.

Without great cultural chasms around them, like the waters where schools of fish swim, societies will not tighten themselves with organic solidarity, forging the impression of stability and permanence so enchanting to anthropological monographs. Whether we like it or not, singular cultural systems are presently preyed on with information and messages that sprout and leap suddenly not from the rims but from their core. There are no parochial limits to the international media networks, much less to the computerized communication exchanges happening on the Internet. The tendency is to have communication rings that are hopelessly without boundaries.

In this panorama, geographic distance is not a hedge against cultural interaction and influence. Individuals are now able to interact without regard for national boundaries. In fact, global clashes will not be between nations but between conflicting cultural ideas. Perhaps even cultural particularities will be dramatically toned down. Individuals will become more empowered because they have more and more means to choose, with fewer restrictions, what cultural products to consume.

The effect of the action of new communication networks is quite similar to the free-for-all individualistic reaction of a herd running from a predator that appears suddenly in its midst. Individuals will compose transcultural quilts with shreds of what were parts of singular and traditional cultures. As the marginal space between groups is radically reduced, and without frontiers to separate them, we need a theory of culture capable of dealing with the kind of individualism that will spread, like a stain, over contemporary experience.

Notes

1 Malinowski's claim that the fieldworker should take a respectful peek inside the studied culture did not prevent the founding father of anthropology from expressing extreme irritation and contempt for the natives. In his posthumously published diary, Malinowski (1967: 282) would refer to them as niggers: 'In the morning worked for two hours at Teyvava; felt very poorly and very nervous, but I didn't stop for a moment and worked calmly, ignoring the niggers.' To be completely fair, we must mention Stocking's (1983) argument about the difficulty in translating mechanically the original word in Malinoswki's diary, *nigrami*, into the infamous nigger. *Nigrami* as a word composed of the English racial epithet, *nigr.*, plus *ami* from the Polish, could be ambiguous and puzzling. Yet Stocking (1983: 102) believes that this is 'no reason to argue that word did not have derogatory racial meaning'. On the other hand, Leach (1980) defends Malinowski, saying that the *Diary*, as it was published, is an unreliable source of Malinowski's ideas. The *Diary* goes from March 1915 to March 1916, and at this time Malinowski had not started his Trobriand research. That is a reasonable point. But to dismiss, as Leach (1980: 2) does, the translation of *nigrami* for nigger, arguing that *nigrami* 'could not have carried in 1918, the special loaded meaning which the term nigger conveys to American readers of 1970' is an exaggeration. Since the end of the seventeenth century and beginning of the eighteenth century, the term had a contemptuous connotation. The *Oxford English Dictionary* quotes a line from Lord Byron (1788–1824) with this meaning. The same condescending attitude as Malinowski's can be seen in Radcliffe-Brown's (1958) definition of anthropology as 'of practical value in connection with the administration of backward people'.

2 Leopold (1980) provides an excellent detailed description of Tylor's intellectual development and background.

3 Franz Boas was another major force urging the anthropologist to avoid generalizations in favor of detailed studies of particular cultures. For an analysis of the impact of the Boasian approach, see Brown (1991: 54–8).

4 Sahlins (1976) depicts Malinowski's conception of language as the bastardizing effect of a narrow pragmatic idea of meaning. Malinowski's insistence on immediate lived experience created a pernicious division in anthropological thought. We would find conventions and rules that made up cultural dimensions existing in a different realm from the actual behavior of social actors (Sahlins 1976: 80). That division was an obstacle hampering both cultural theory and anthropology as a whole.

5 About half of the world's population is immersed in an Indo-European linguistic universe. Latin, Germanic, Celtic, and Slav languages are part of the Indo-European linguistic tree, as well as Greek, Albanese, Armenian, Iranian, Gypsy, Baltic, and some of the languages spoken in India (Malherbe 1983: 134). Among other traits of the Indo-European languages, such as the fact that words with fixed form (adverbs, prepositions) are less numerous than the ones that suffer some kind of flexion

(nouns, pronouns, verbs), Malherbe (1983: 135) also indicates that the subject determines the conjugation of the verb; the complement plays no role in defining the verbal form. The subject is essential; the predicate will follow it.

6 Refusing to acknowledge that links between language and thought can be reduced to a mere set of superficial distinctions, such as the claim that thought is universal and language particular, Emile Benveniste (1971: 55–64) examined the interaction of language and philosophy. In the Aristotelian system of categories, for instance, the term *ousia* means substance or essence, but it is applicable also to linguistic names signifying a class of objects. Not only essences but all the other Aristotelian categories arise from language itself. Benveniste's point is clear: linguistic categories conduct cognitive assumptions, at least in the case of classical philosophy. The appropriateness of linguistic categories comes mainly from the familiarity of linguistic expressions. Therefore, 'no matter how much validity Aristotelian categories may have as categories of thought, they turn out to be transposed from categories of language' (Benveniste 1971: 61). Earlier on, in *Twilight of Idols* (1990: 48), Friedrich Nietzsche saw that the categories of reason are projections of language. After noticing the influence of philosophical reasoning on theological assumptions, he observed sarcastically: 'I fear we are not getting rid of God because we still believe in grammar.'

7 Wickler (1968) discusses in detail the mechanics of mimetic attack and defense both in the animal world and among plants.

8 Williams's (1964) experiments on the consociation of fish concludes that group formation is an alternative even for fish that, in their original niches, do not exercise this kind of behavior.

9 Many countries including Canada, Israel, China, and France have laws limiting the amount of foreign cultural material, such as music on the radio or movies, that can be presented. For a heated discussion of the French legislation concerning movies, for instance, see L'ARP (1995).

References

Benveniste, E. (1971). *Problems in General Linguistics*. Coral Gables: University of Miami Press.

Brown, D. E. (1991). *Human Universals*. New York: McGraw-Hill.

Darwin, C. (1979). *The Origin of Species*. New York: Gramercy.

—— (1987). *Charles Darwin's Notebooks, 1836–1844: Geology, Transmutation of Species, Metaphysical Enquiries*. Edited by P. H. Barret, P. J. Gautrey, S. Herbert, D. Kohn, and S. Smith. Ithaca and New York: British Museum (Natural History) and Cornell University Press.

—— (1998). *The Expression of the Emotions in Man and Animals*. New York: Oxford University Press.

Dawkins, R. (1996). *Climbing Mount Improbable*. New York: Norton.

Dumont, L. (1967). 'Caste: A phenomenon of social structure or an aspect of Indian culture.' In A. de Rueck and J. Knights (eds), *Caste and Race: Comparative Approaches*. Boston: Little, Brown.

—— (1970). *Homo Hierarchicus: An Essay on the Caste System*. Chicago: The University of Chicago Press.

Gass, W. H. (1989). *Habitations of the Word*. New York: Simon & Schuster.

Haig, D. (1993). Genetic conflicts in human pregnancy. *The Quarterly Review of Biology*, 68: 495–532.

Hamilton, W. D. (1996). *Narrow Roads of Gene Land: The Collected Papers of W. D. Hamilton, vol. 1, Evolution of Social Behavior*. Oxford: W. H. Freeman/Spektrum.

Khare, R. S. (1971). '"Encompassing and encompassed": A deductive theory of caste system'. *The Journal of Asian Studies*, 30: 859–68.

L'ARP (1995). *Quel cinéma pour demain? Cinquièmes rencontres cinématographiques de Beaune, 26–29 Octobre 1995*. Paris: Dixit.

Leach, E. R. (1957). 'The epistemological background to Malinowski's empiricism'. In R. Frith (ed.), *Man and Culture: An Evaluation of the Work of Bronislaw Malinowski*. London: Routledge and Kegan Paul.

—— (1980). 'On reading *A Diary in the Strict Sense of the Term*; or the self-mutilation of Professor Hsu'. *Rain*, 36: 2–3.

—— (1984). 'Glimpses of the unmentionable in the history of British anthropology'. *Annual Review of Anthropology*, 13: 1–23.

Leopold, J. (1980). *Culture in Comparative and Evolutionary Perspective: E. B. Tylor and the making of Primitive Culture*. Berlin: Dietrich Reimer Verlag.

Lévi-Strauss, C. (1946). 'La technique du bonheur'. *Esprit*, 127: 643–57.

—— (1962a). *Totemisme, aujourd'hui*. Paris: Presses Universitaires de France.

—— (1962b). *La pensée sauvage*. Paris: Plon.

—— (1976). *Structural Anthropology, Volume 2*. New York: Basic Books.

—— (1988). *The View From Afar*. New York: Basic Books.

Malherbe, M. (1983). *Les langages de l'humanité*. Paris: Seghers.

Malinowski, B. (1922). *Argonauts of the Western Pacific: An Account of Native Enterprise and Adventure in the Archipelagoes of Melanesian New Guinea*. London: Routledge and Kegan Paul.

—— (1923). 'The problem of meaning in primitive languages'. In C. K. Ogden and I. A. Richards (eds), *The Meaning of Meaning*. New York: Harcourt, Brace, & Co.

—— (1931). 'Culture'. In *Encyclopedia of the Social Sciences*, vol. 6, 621–46. New York: Macmillan.

—— (1967). *A Diary in the Strict Sense of the Term*. New York: Harcourt, Brace, & World.

Malthus, T. R. (1888). *An Essay on the Principle of Population; or a View of its Past and Present Effects on Human Happiness*. London: Reeves and Turner.

Maynard Smith, J. (1972). *On Evolution*. Edinburgh: Edinburgh University Press.

—— (1982). *Evolution and the Theory of Games*. Cambridge: Cambridge University Press.

—— (1995). *The Theory of Evolution*. Cambridge: Cambridge University Press.

Maynard Smith, J. and Price, G. R. (1973). 'The logic of animal conflict'. *Nature*, 246: 15–18.

Mayr, E. (1990). *One Long Argument: Charles Darwin and the Genesis of Modern Evolutionary Thought*. Cambridge, MA: Harvard University Press.

Nietzsche, F. (1990). *Twilight of Idols* and *The Anti-Christ*. Harmondsworth: Penguin Books.

Owen, D. (1982). *Camouflage and Mimicry*. Chicago: The University of Chicago Press.

Piddington, R. (1957). 'Malinowski's theory of needs'. In R. Frith (ed.), *Man and Culture: An Evaluation of the Work of Bronislaw Malinowski*. London: Routledge and Kegan Paul.

Polanyi, K. (1968). *Primitive, Archaic, and Modern Economies*. Garden City, NY: Anchor Books/Doubleday.

—— (1975). *The Great Transformation*. New York: Norton.

Radcliffe-Brown, A. R. (1958). *Method in Social Anthropology*. Chicago: The University of Chicago Press.

Rousseau, J. (1987). *The Social Contract*. New York: Penguin.

Sahlins, M. (1976). *Culture and Practical Reason*. Chicago: The University of Chicago Press.

—— (1977). *The Use and Abuse of Biology: An Anthropological Critique of Sociobiology*. Ann Arbor: Michigan Univerisity Press.

Stocking, G. W. Jr (1983). 'An ethnographer's magic: Fieldwork in British Anthropology from Tylor to Malinowski'. *History of Anthropology*, 1: 70–120. Madison, WI: University of Wisconsin Press.

Thom, R. (1975). *Structural Stabiltity and Morphogenesis: An Outline of a General Theory of Models*. Reading, MA: W. A. Benjamin.

—— (1983). *Mathematical Models of Morphogenesis*. Chichester: Ellis Horwood.

Tocqueville, A. de (1994). *Democracy in America*. New York: Alfred A. Knopf.

Trivers, R. (1971). 'The evolution of reciprocal altruism'. *The Quarterly Review of Biology*, 46: 35–57.

—— (1985). *Social Evolution*. Menlo Park, CA: Benjamins/Cummings.

Tylor, E. B. (1871). *Primitive Culture: Researches into the Developments of Mythology, Philosophy, Religion, Art, and Custom*. London: J. Murray.

Wickler, W. (1968). *Mimicry in Plants and Animals*. New York: McGraw-Hill.

Williams, G. C. (1964). 'Measurement of consocation among fish and comments on the evolution of schooling'. *Publications of the Museum, Michigan State University, Biological Series 2/7*: 349–84.

—— (1996). *Adaptation and Natural Selection: A Critique of Some Current Evolutionary Thought*. Princeton: Princeton University Press.

—— (1992). *Natural Selection: Domains, Levels, and Challenges*. New York: Oxford University Press.

Yalman, N. (1969). 'De Tocqueville in India: An essay on the caste system'. *Man*, 4: 121–31.

Zahavi, A. and Zahavi, A. (1997). *The Handicap Principle: A Missing Piece of Darwin's Puzzle*. New York: Oxford University Press.

3

THINKING ABOUT CULTURE IN A GLOBAL ECUMENE

Ulf Hannerz

Some years ago, we were getting short of storage space in our apartment in Stockholm, so I decided no longer to put off excavating a large closet where I realized a number of things might have accumulated over time which perhaps no longer needed to be there. Far in the back, I recognized a large box, which contained my field notes from my first anthropological research project, in Washington, DC, about twenty years earlier. In the same box, moreover, were several dense pages of more theoretical queries, which clearly I had jotted down for myself on my way home. They were on the stationery of *M/S Kungsholm*, the passenger ship which had taken me back from the USA to Sweden that time (when going by sea was still a very ordinary alternative to flying).

I was a bit amused, and embarrassed, as I looked at that brief summary of some theoretical issues I had identified as worth thinking more about so many years earlier. For it seemed these were the issues with which I was still more or less preoccupied, and one might have thought that in a couple of decades I should have moved on to something else. But then it may not be so unusual among anthropologists that their first fieldwork is such a powerful experience that it puts them on tracks where they will stay for a long time, even as the landscape around the tracks keeps changing.

What those theoretical notes for myself were about was culture – how to understand it, how to describe it. The 'concept of culture' had long been held central to anthropology, but perhaps in truth, at the time, and with a few exceptions, there was not always a whole lot of conceptualizing going on. Many experienced members of the discipline were probably still most inclined to repeat, a bit piously but rather routinely and effortlessly, the sort of definition that would have been on one of the first pages of anthropology textbooks for years: 'a culture is a shared, integrated pattern of modes of thought and action, transmitted from generation to generation'. Or something like that.

In a Washington neighborhood

But then I had made those notes as I had just left a field situation where that view of culture seemed quite problematic. It had been two exciting years in an African-American neighborhood, as I immersed myself in another way of life, at the same time as that way of life was going through important changes, and was also at the center of much public debate. But what was it I had actually been studying? In a way, for 'a culture' it could seem it was not shared enough, as I was inclined rather to distinguish between several co-existing lifestyles, among which individuals might also move as time passed. And people in these lifestyles co-existed, but not always quietly. If some said they preferred to 'walk their walk and talk their talk', there was also intermittent confrontation and continuous debate.

In another way there was too much sharing, extending too far, to allow me to delineate the distinctive culture of the community I had been involved with, for somehow I must do justice to the complicated interweaving between what was in some way more peculiar to a black, largely low-income community, and what was more or less mainstream American – whatever now that could be taken to mean. There was a 'now you see it, now you don't' quality to the cultural boundary, even as the social boundary between races was clearcut enough.

Besides, that notion of culture as 'transmitted from generation to generation' was really far from innocent. In the political climate of the period, such 'trans-mission' could too easily be understood along the lines of an epidemiology of collective maladaptation; a debate raged over whether there was, among low-income black Americans, a 'culture of poverty' which itself maintained poverty.[1] One critical response to such a diagnosis was that, if there were observable modes of action which did not seem properly mainstream American, they were still not 'cultural', just situational responses to extreme circumstances. That seemed like an enlightened line of argument – but did it not take rather lightly the cultural history of a people who had moved, over the generations, from West African village life, through the Atlantic slave trade and plantation slavery, to the rural American South and then to the urban North, mostly without having been really a part of that American mainstream?

So those notes from aboard the *Kungsholm* had to do with the blurred boundaries of my field of study, its striking internal variation, and its ongoing cultural process, in relationship to the changing circumstances of history. In retrospect, one might see that I had come into anthropology in a period when a growing number of its practitioners, like me, were placing themselves, deliberately or rather willy-nilly, in field situations where that culture concept which had perhaps itself been transmitted from generation to generation, within the discipline, did not seem to work very well any more. Probably it had had its weaknesses all the time, but now they could no longer be disregarded.

In an African town

By the time I retrieved those old notes from the depths of my closet at home, I had moved on to thinking about culture in another, wider, context. It was after some travel in West Africa that I had once been drawn into anthropology, and, when I had ended up in Washington instead for my first field study, it was because it had been a very unpromising time for the research I had planned to do in Nigeria – the country was on its way into a civil war. But then in the late 1970s and early 1980s, I spent several periods in central Nigeria, in a town named Kafanchan, built in the colonial era around a new railway junction. I had actually intended to do a study focusing on local social organization, but then the field experience itself had gradually drawn my attention in another direction. It was not only that some of my new acquaintances in Kafanchan would pull my sleeve and suggest that they and I ought to get into an import–export business together; they had lots of ideas about desirable goods to import from overseas (but fewer ideas, it seemed, about what to export). Or that they would propose that I should take a bright and promising young nephew of theirs along when I returned to Europe, to put him into my university where he would get a good education and from which he could come back to Nigeria as a rich and powerful man. Obviously these were people whose horizons did not coincide with Kafanchan's town limits. Nor was it just the intriguing historical fact that this was a community which would not have existed had it not been for the influences from a wider world: the simple logic of space had brought together here one rail line carrying tin with another rail line carrying groundnuts, on their way from northern Nigeria to the port cities on the southern coast. Most strikingly, there was in Kafanchan that young urban culture which was quite basically and dramatically a result of the intricate and shifting blending of West African, European, and by now North American cultures as well. From within Nigeria, and from just about every corner of it, people of a great many ethnic groups ('tribes') – Ibo, Yoruba, Hausa, Tiv, Kaje and others – had arrived in the town to find their places in its life. Even as they brought some parts of their traditions along, however, there were also the meanings and messages from further away. Coming through the loudspeakers of Kafanchan's small record stores was the switching back and forth between American televangelist gospel, Afro-American soul music, Caribbean reggae, and Nigerian popular music genres such as highlife and juju. And because Nigeria had oil and was at least for some time a quite prosperous country, one could now see brand new television antennae being installed over the rusting corrugated zinc roofs of Kafanchan's one-story or two-story houses.

The wider context with which I was engaging was that of 'globalization' – a keyword of our times, although, even when I began to think about some of the things to which it now refers, it was not yet in frequent use. One may take 'globalization' to mean various things, and place it differently in time. Perhaps a few words should be said about its various meanings. Some would use it to refer rather narrowly to the deregulation of capitalist markets in the last decades of the twentieth century. Others might think of it as a more broadly defined process which yet has had much to do with the new technologies of communication and transportation of that same century – with large numbers of people rapidly moving across the surface of the earth by jumbo jets (even moving quickly back and forth), and just as large numbers getting sights and sounds, ideas and images, by way of radio, television, and electronic mail. Certainly, for a great many people, the last few decades have brought major changes along such lines. Yet if (as I do here) we take 'globalization' to refer most generally to a process in which people get increasingly interconnected, in a variety of ways, across national borders and between continents, and in which their awareness of the world and of distant places and regions probably also grows, then it becomes a more multifaceted notion, and one involving a greater historical time depth. It has gone through different phases, with different intensities; it does not proceed inevitably, irreversibly, in one direction, but may sometimes indeed move backwards in the direction of deglobalization. And it can involve different areas of the world in different ways at different times. The centuries of the transatlantic slave trade had been a long period of very traumatic globalization, not so much in the precise area where Kafanchan is now, but in a wide region not so far to the south of it. And among those who thus found themselves forcibly globalized were, of course, the first black Americans – ancestors of the people I had come to know in Washington.

And then, with regard to culture, 'globalization' is also frequently taken to mean global cultural homogenization. In recent times, a certain sweet brown beverage, a certain ground beef sandwich, and a certain stylish, long-haired favorite doll of young girls have turned into powerful and controversial symbols: Coca-Cola, McDonald's, and Barbie together are taken to tell us that we live in a world of increasing sameness, that growing global interconnectedness will lead to the death of cultural diversity. If not always a description of the present, this notion of globalization often involves at least a scenario for the future.

Familiar as I already was with the scenario, it did not correspond to what I saw in Kafanchan (although it is true that Coca-Cola had arrived). What I saw seemed to be rather more of a creation of new culture, even perhaps another civilization, born in the cultural encounters of global connections. This was neither a simple persistence of West African traditions nor the wholesale acceptance of ideas and cultural forms imported from overseas. It was not just a matter of cultural loss, as a necessary consequence of cultural homogenization.

Here once more, then, were questions of a familiar kind coming back at me: what sort of culture was this, really? Who shared what with whom? What really had been transmitted from what generation, when, and where? And, to paraphrase yet further an old formula from communication research, with what effect? The engagement with late twentieth-century, postcolonial African town life made me think about the culture concept again, to see what we can do with it – if actually we can do anything with it.

In the global ecumene

To elaborate a little on that somewhat time-worn concept of culture in anthropology, beyond the brief textbook definition, and to begin to scrutinize it, we can discern several distinct emphases. One has been that culture is learned, acquired in social life; in computer parlance, the software needed for programming the biologically given hardware. We are cultured animals. The second has been that culture is somehow a 'whole'; that is, integrated, neatly fitting together. The third has been that culture is something which comes in varying packages, each with an integrity of its own, and distinctive to different human collectivities, mostly belonging in particular territories. It is with the last of these emphases that culture shifts most clearly into the plural form, as 'cultures'.

It is this particular emphasis, entailing a conception of the organization of cultural diversity as a global mosaic of bounded units, which is most dubious in a world that is to a great extent characterized by mobility and mixture. We need a counter-image to that of the cultural mosaic, one that does not take for granted the boundedness of cultures and their simple relationship to populations and territories, but allows as a point of departure a more open, interconnected world.

Rather hyperbolically, in the 1960s Marshall McLuhan (e.g. 1964) used the term 'global village'. That has stuck in the public mind more than some of his other far-reaching claims about the ways new media were transforming the world and human consciousness. The 'global village', however, is in some ways a quite misleading notion. To many of us, at least, it suggests not only interconnectedness but togetherness, immediacy, and reciprocity in relationships – a large-scale idyll. The world is not really like this. Most directly from one of the classic figures of anthropology, Alfred Kroeber (1945), I want to retrieve instead a concept which Kroeber himself had borrowed from the ancient Greeks – the 'ecumene'. In a lecture given soon after the end of the Second World War, Kroeber noted that the kind of 'culture' anthropologists would usually deal with was 'necessarily in some degree an artificial unit segregated off for expediency'. The ultimate natural unit, on the other hand, must be 'the culture of all humanity'. For the old Greeks, the ecumene, the entire inhabited world as they knew it, stretched from Gibraltar towards India and, just barely, to China. For us now, as an image contrasting to that of a global mosaic, the 'global ecumene' may serve as a way of alluding to the persistent cultural interconnectedness of the world through interactions and exchanges.

With this image in mind, we can return to the three different emphases within an anthropological conception of culture I referred to before. Indeed all three turn out to be contestable – the first of them, with regard to particulars, along the nature/culture divide. Yet in the context of arguing about globalization, in my view, it is this first emphasis, on culture as meanings and meaningful forms which we acquire in social life, that we should take as fundamental. This would define the range of cultural analysis. With regard to the other two emphases, our strategy now may be to reformulate them as core problematics in our thinking comparatively about culture, its variations, and its historical shifts. It is one implication of the interconnectedness of the world that culture may be thought of in the singular, as one combined inventory of the ecumene. As a cultured animal, each one of us now, somehow, has access to more of it – or conversely, more of it has access to us, making claims on our senses and minds. How, and to what degree, do people under such conditions arrange culture into coherent patterns as they go about their lives? How, as they involve themselves with the world, does culture sometimes, in some ways, become organized and subdivided into something resembling the more or less tidy, bounded, collectively held packages we have called 'cultures', and under other circumstances take on other kinds of distribution?

Cultural confluences

One thing that my field studies in Washington and in Kafanchan had in common was that the conception of cultures as clearly delineated place-bound entities did not work. It seemed to be a matter both of the outside 'reaching in' and the inside 'reaching out'. In Washington and other American cities, black people with limited resources, living in the segregated neighborhoods which by the 1960s were routinely referred to as ghettos, could conceivably have shaped their own culture more completely within the prevailing material and political constraints; but in fact their habitat was not segregated enough for that. As far as culture was concerned, something more or less approximating mainstream America, with its beliefs, standards, and ideals, was forever present, represented by schools, social workers, network television, and in a great many other ways, as much part of the accessible cultural inventory as any streetcorner form of meaning and expression. In Kafanchan, the 'reaching out' aspect sometimes seemed more conspicuous, as townspeople played with ideas about what life was like elsewhere; how to get a young kinsman an overseas ticket, perhaps, or what intriguing foreign goods to import. Yet in fact, both 'reaching in' and 'reaching out' are, and have been, present in both cases. Kafanchan, again, had arisen around a railway junction which strangers placed there, and the curiosity and the images of the outside world had in no small part been stimulated originally by Christian missionaries and the churches and schools which they established. Clearly, too, the people of my black Washington neighborhood would often voice interests, hopes, and ideals which were little different from those of most other Americans.

In the book I wrote on the basis of my Washington field experience, I placed on the frontispiece page some eloquent lines by W. E. B. DuBois, the pioneer

African-American scholar and intellectual, from his *The Souls of Black Folk* (1903):

> It is a peculiar sensation, this double-consciousness, this sense of always looking at one's self through the eyes of others, of measuring one's soul by the tape of a world that looks on in amused contempt and pity. One ever feels his twoness, – an American, a Negro; two souls, two thoughts, two unreconciled strivings; two warring ideals in one dark body, whose dogged strength keeps it from being torn asunder.
>
> (1903: 5)

And a recurrent theme in the book was the continuous interweaving in black life between meanings and symbolic forms which are shared by most Americans and those which are more particularly linked with the black experience. As I came around to writing about Kafanchan, about West African urban life, and about globalization as I understood it from a Kafanchan vantage point, the central theme was the overall mixing of cultures and the growth of new culture which came about as people combined and merged ideas, expressions, and organizational forms from sources which had not come together before in history. In a reaction both to the assumption of a cultural mosaic and to the scenario of global homogenization, I borrowed the concept of 'creolization' from sociolinguistics, to refer to a process whereby new culture is born on a significant scale, in the confluence of two or more cultural currents historically separate from one another.[2] What I liked about the metaphor, in relation to my Nigerian experience, was not only its suggestion that mixing and mingling can be creative, but also that a creole culture, like a creole language, can become an elaborate phenomenon which with time acquires its own historical depth, and also that it points toward a more open cultural organization. I saw an internally diverse cultural continuum stretching from European or American metropoles to West African 'bush', where different individuals and groups could engage with partly different ensembles of culture, and yet be in communication with one another through their overlaps.

The use of a creolist vocabulary to conceptualize contemporary cultural phenomena emerging through global interconnectedness has not been mine alone, although it appears I have had a part in drawing attention to it. Meanwhile, in recent years, some number of related notions – 'hybridity', for example, or 'cultural synergy' – have also come into circulation to refer to the innovative force of cultural mixture and recombination. Sometimes they seem to be understood as simply synonymous, although I would argue that creolization entails a more specific, complex relationship between social structure and cultural forms, not just any cultural mixing. This also relates to the broad question of what kind of evaluative stance we take towards cultural entanglements and their results. In the quotation from W. E. B. DuBois above, there is a rather tragic, if at the same time heroic, tone. In recent times, again in response especially to celebrations of cultural 'integrity' and 'purity', the various terms for cultural mixture have undeniably often had more appreciative, favorable connotations. The formulation by the writer Salman Rushdie (1991: 394), describing his most famous novel, has been widely quoted:

> *The Satanic Verses* celebrates hybridity, impurity, intermingling, the transformation that comes of new and unexpected combinations of human beings, cultures, ideas, politics, movies, songs. It rejoices in mongrelization and fears the absolutism of the pure. *Mélange*, hotchpotch, a bit of this and a bit of that is *how newness enters the world.*

Even so, I would suggest that my own understanding of creolization is not really so unqualifiedly enthusiastic. For much as I have enjoyed the vitality of West African urban culture, in Kafanchan and elsewhere, I am aware that creole cultures of the kind I have tried to describe and analyze are extended through structures of transnational as well as national structures of center–periphery relationships, and are far from free of the influences of power inequality also characteristic of such structures.

Actors and relationships

Yet I have lingered here on understandings of contemporary culture which are more particularly tied to my attempts to understand black America, and Nigerian town life. In more general terms, how would I now approach the organization of culture in the global ecumene, in its relative openness?

My point of view comes out of the social anthropological tradition; I return again to the fact that culture is by definition a social phenomenon. Meanings and meaningful forms belong primarily to human relationships, and only derivatively and rather uncertainly to territories. This is an old assumption, but it becomes even more significant when social life for more and more people involves a mix of local and long-distance relationships, drawing on varied patterns of physical mobility as well as media technologies. It is true that when I began my fieldwork in Washington, the emphasis in anthropology was still so exclusively on face-to-face relationships that I was mildly worried by the fact that I was spending so much time just idly watching television in the company of my new acquaintances. Then I gradually realized that the comments they made on what they saw on the screen were themselves a source of insight into their culture. During the years since then, of course, the more or less ethnographic study of media reception has turned into a major genre of media research. By now, we are more inclined to accept that the relational view does not isolate the electronic from the face-to-face, and in principle offers an equal hearing to the migrants and to those who stay put.

The global ecumene then becomes a very large social network – or a 'network of networks', if we also want to allude to its internal diversity, and the clusterings of relationships (cf. Hannerz 1992a). And we need to develop a sense of its variety and density of linkages. The point I want to emphasize here is that a great many kinds of actors now operate, if not literally globally, then at least transnationally. There are more ethnic diasporas than ever before, dispersed kinship groups, multinational business corporations and transnational occupational communities, as well as movements, youth cultures, and other expressive lifestyles with a self-consciously border-crossing orientation; not to speak of media, from the *International Herald Tribune* to CNN and whatever is on the Internet. Each one of them is engaged in its own particular way in the management of some part of contemporary culture. The combined cultural process, and the overall habitat of meanings and practices in which we dwell, can thus be understood as the outcome of the variously deliberate pursuit by a variety of actors of their own agendas, with different power and different reach, and with foreseen or unanticipated consequences.

Consequently, for a more comprehensive study of the cultural implications of globalization, we need a fairly robust sociology of culture, mapping the ways in which these activities come together. As one way of coming to grips with the overall complexity of global cultural organization, I have attempted to conceptualize it as ordered by four main organizational frames, existing in interrelation with one another: state, market, movement, and form of life (see e.g. Hannerz 1992b, 1996). To put it briefly, culture typically flows between rulers and the ruled (citizens, subjects), between buyer and seller, between those converted and those not converted, and between people engaging with one another on a more symmetrical basis in a variety of relationships in going about life, for example as kinspeople, neighbors, friends, or work mates. These frameworks tend to handle meanings and meaningful forms according to different organizational, temporal, and spatial logics. There is probably a greater strain towards innovation and towards spatial expansiveness, for example, in the market framework than in the state framework or in the form of life framework, the former being concerned not least with administrative routines and historical legitimacy, and the latter being in large part preoccupied with daily practicalities.

Particular types of actors and particular kinds of relationships may thus evince some recurrent leanings in the way they deal with culture of whatever kind. (Think, for instance, of the differences between a state religion and the kind of religion propagated in the marketplace by televangelist entrepreneurs.) Yet as we scrutinize cultural processes within the frames further, we may also discern that they are not necessarily entirely homogeneous even within themselves. The global homogenization scenario, for example, is typically most at home in the market framework: there may be a strong tendency on the part of sellers to try and reach the largest possible number of consumers with the same product. It may thus seem to be natural for the market to disregard or subvert boundaries, rather than to respect them or even celebrate them, unless obstacles are placed in its way. None the less, there is also an opposed tendency towards a segmentation of markets, towards finding niches where commodities especially adapted to the needs and desires of particular categories of consumers have a competitive advantage. And such niches may be quite localized. Indeed, what impressed me in Kafanchan was not least the way the cultural entrepreneurs of West African urban life found their place in the market by creating, and offering for sale, their own creolized cultural commodities, attractive to their own compatriots.[3]

What even the simple framework of markets, states, movements, and forms of life shows is that culture is divided into a great many different clusters of meanings and meaningful forms, handled in different ways by different actors in different relationships. Yet while each of the organizational frames may have its own tendencies in the handling of culture, they are also continuously entangled with one another, to the extent that they engage the same people. It is in these entanglements between the frameworks that we find much of what is dynamic in culture today. Through them, that is to say, the flow of culture may shift speed and direction, and meanings and the forms which carry them may be repackaged into new units and combinations. When the 'folk music' of the form of life frame turns into the 'popular music' of the market, for example, the cross-over involves changes in social organization as well as cultural form.

This is the organizational basis, then, for the kind of situation I referred to early in this chapter, where one might think of culture in the singular, as more of a combined inventory of meanings and meaningful forms available to human beings. Yet surely each of us as individuals will not appropriate all that is in this inventory. So what patterns will then emerge? I believe the answer has to be multifaceted.[4] Perhaps as we engage with the cultural flows within and between those main organizational frames – state, market, movement, and form of life – there is nothing in our personal cultural repertoires we do not in some way share with some group of people. There may even be some meanings and practices we share with just about everybody else in the world; and here the global spread of Coca-Cola, McDonald's, and Barbie may actually be less important than for example that of soap, matches, or those blueprints for organized education which mean that a very large part of the world's children go to primary schools with, in principle, a very similar curriculum.

Then there may be other complexes within our cultural repertoires which we share with particular people around us, and by way of which we identify more closely with these people. In such instances we may discern an approximation of that 'cultural mosaic' organization of the world, and it is often here that in the contemporary world the notion of culture is combined with that of identity, to the extent that the shift between 'culture' and 'cultural identity' may occur almost unnoticeably. One might indeed argue that all identities are cultural in so far as they are constructed from meaningful materials acquired through social life. Yet we tend to apply the idea of 'cultural identity' quite selectively, to refer to membership in particular bounded, durable collectivities, frequently with major social and political implications. In such cases, we should be aware that the drawing of cultural boundaries is, not least in the present-day world, often highly selective. People on different sides of the boundary can actually share a great deal, even if what is shared is in large part disregarded for purposes of group formation. The distinctions between ethnic groups in Kafanchan, and between black and white Americans, certainly exemplify this. And so the mosaic metaphor actually turns out to be misleading, except as used in a very selective way.

We may share some of our culture with just about everybody in the world, then, and some of it, more or less self-consciously, with other members of particular groups. But it is also possible that our particular biographies, involving the places and countries we have visited or lived in, the books we have read by authors from anywhere, the television programs we zap between, the websites we visit, the people we have known, may come together as very much our own private, individuated combinations, to be pulled together in coherent perspectives as best we can. Each of us may stand at a particular intersection in that total network of the global ecumene. If there is an 'integrated whole', it may be a quite individual thing. Perhaps we may find our way to some small group, or even a single relationship, where much can be shared in what amounts to a microculture. Yet sometimes, such circumstances may also mean that we are more than ever opaque to one another – and alone in the world.

Such individuation may in some ways be enjoyable, and may even appear liberating. In other ways it can seem quite disturbing, and we may become involved with it only partly by choice, and sometimes through circumstances forced on us. Either way, it does not at all fit with the scenario of global homogenization.

I have already used the metaphor of 'cultural flows'. At this point I should discuss flow a little more fully, because it is also important to the view of culture I have arrived at. In anthropology, its history goes back at least to the same Alfred Kroeber (1952) who reinvented the idea of the ecumene. Flow is basically a processual metaphor, with both temporal and spatial implications. And by now, in some number of disciplines, the general concept of flow has become a favored way of referring to things not staying in their places, to mobility and expansion of many kinds. As far as culture is concerned, there is perhaps some risk that this metaphor makes cultural process seem too easy, too smooth. Certainly we must not just understand a flow of culture as a matter of simple transportation of tangible forms loaded with intrinsic meanings. It is rather to be seen as entailing an infinite series of shifts, in time and sometimes in changing space as well, between external forms available to the senses, interpretations occurring in human minds, and then external forms again – a series continuously fraught with uncertainty, allowing misunderstandings and losses as well as innovation. Even when we deal with durable meanings and meaningful forms, and with culture which stays in place, we must be aware that they can be durable only by being in a way constantly in motion. To keep culture going, people have to invent it, reflect on it, experiment with it, remember it (or store it in some other way), debate it, and pass it on.

Let us come back here to that old-style definition of culture I mentioned earlier, that emphasizing 'transmission', 'from generation to generation'. Such a definition privileges the past as the time when particular cultural forms somehow came into being. Later generations are turned into robots, receptacles. The point of emphasizing process, as I want to do, is not to shift to the opposite bias, and discern only change, change, change. It is rather a matter of destabilizing the privileged assumptions of continuity and timelessness, to make reproduction and change in principle equally problematic, and to direct attention to the part of human agency in it all. When it is understood that human beings are forever cultural, information-handling animals, dealing with their surroundings by way of interpreting and making signs, then culture can be seen as to a degree fluid and permeable, not entirely independent of a variety of practical and material conditions. We may sense that all kinds of interests and pressures in human life take the shape of culture, cultural identity, and cultural difference. Such a view of culture as ongoing, adaptive, collective activity goes a great deal better with my field experience in both Washington and Kafanchan than does that old textbook definition.

Among the foreign correspondents

Recently, I have turned to yet another research project set in the context of the global ecumene. But it is rather different from the two I have described before. The first two could be identified with particular places – an urban neighborhood in the United States, a town in Nigeria. Looking at the world and its organization of culture primarily in relational rather than spatial terms, however, there is no reason why our units of study must always have this kind of territorial anchoring. Indeed we will stand a better chance of eventually getting some grasp of the global whole if we complement such place-bound inquiries with studies of units which themselves somehow extend in space over national boundaries, bridging social and cultural distances.

This is a study of news media foreign correspondents.[5] Turning to a study of an occupation makes sense partly because much of twentieth-century globalization was literally globalization at work. Business people, academics, diplomats, consultants, journalists, artists, athletes; all of them now extend their occupational communities and cultures across borders. And a more specific reason for my curiosity about the foreign correspondents has been that they would seem to be key players in today's globalization of consciousness. People piece together their images of the world from diverse sources: school books, travel brochures, and certainly not least the news media. The reporting of foreign correspondents for newspapers and news magazines, news agencies, radio and television makes up a major part of that flow of information from and about other parts of their world which is a part of the rhythm of many people's daily routine experience.

And then, for me, there is another angle. Foreign correspondents are a sort of anthropologists, or anthropologists are a sort of foreign correspondents, in so far as they both engage in reporting from one part of the world to another. How do the ways media correspondents practice their craft in foreign lands compare with the fieldwork of anthropologists? And what do they report, how do they mediate to their audiences the foreignness of foreign news? Perhaps it follows from this that I am not really equally interested in all foreign correspondents. I have wanted to concentrate on those correspondents who, rather like many anthropologists, specialize in reporting from regions which are not only geo-graphically but also culturally and socially more distant from their audiences. Thus I have paid particular attention to the reporting from Asia, Africa, and the Middle East to Western Europe and North America. So far, by planning or by some degree of serendipity, this has led to meetings with correspondents or ex-correspondents in a variety of places: New York, Los Angeles, Stockholm, Frankfurt, Jerusalem, Johannesburg, Hong Kong. Moreover, of course, I try to keep up with the ongoing flow of news in the press, on radio, and on television. The field can thus be with me in some way even in periods when I cannot venture far from my desk in Stockholm. And after I have had my own encounters with the correspondents in one setting or other, I may continue to read their stories in the papers, hear their voices on the radio, see their faces on television. These informants do not vanish from your horizon the moment you leave the distant field site.

One way in which foreign correspondents are very different from most anthropologists, clearly, is a matter of space. Anthropological fieldwork has conventionally been quite localized, as mine was in Washington and Kafanchan. Foreign correspondents are often 'Africa correspondents', 'Asia correspondents', or 'Middle East correspondents', for example, responsible for reporting on very large regions. It is true that many of the latter whom I met in Jerusalem actually engaged mostly with Israeli and Palestinian affairs, and thus found most of their stories no further than a couple of hours away by car. But the 'Africa correspondents' I talked to in Johannesburg often had to try and deal with the entire continent, at least south of the Sahara. And so the practi-calities of dealing with such a beat have been a major topic of my conversations with correspondents.

Yet this is a research project where the handling of time is equally important, because what foreign correspondents produce is 'news'. There is a connection here to what I said before about a processual point of view towards culture. We may be in the habit of taking culture to be something fairly persistent and stable, but then the flow of meaning in the world may consist in large part of a never-ending stream of quickly forming events and impressions, some of which are repetitive and some not, and from which we perhaps form more enduring ideas. The intriguing relationship between news and culture was also something which I began thinking about during my Washington fieldwork, not least when in early April 1968, after Martin Luther King was assassinated, riots erupted in Washington as in many other cities, and I found my neighborhood surrounded one morning by the National Guard.[6] How does the news of a place reflect its culture?

Indeed the term 'news' is interestingly ambiguous. News can refer to something that has just happened, or something can be news mostly because we simply have not heard of it before, and find it interesting and even surprising. Certainly the news media are primarily oriented to the first of these kinds, to 'hard news', and foreign correspondents tend to take pride in, and be excited by, being present when 'history is made'. But that other kind of news has some particular possibilities for foreign correspondents. A number of things may have a long-term presence in a remote country without our learning of them, until someone tells us. What newspeople describe as 'feature stories' are often of this latter sort, and in this way become most like ethnography, the reporting of anthropologists. I have met correspondents who have done stories on the everyday activities and hardships of Samburu pastoralists in northern Kenya, and on the informal economy of African city streets. These are the kinds of topics anthropologists also choose, even if they report in other formats, to other (smaller) audiences.

We may see that in an era of global interconnectedness, each one of us has ideas of other areas of the world as parts of our personal cultural repertoires, as indeed Kafanchan townspeople had when they brought up possibilities of import–export businesses or study abroad in their conversations with me. But how do we arrive at these ideas? There may be areas about which we form our understandings on the basis of a wide range of sources – we know people from there, we have even been there ourselves, we remember at least a bit of what we may have learned about them in school. And then, in addition, there is the news flow. But as I have become especially aware when I have considered the efforts of foreign correspondents, there are other areas about which many of us know little apart from what that news flow brings; Africa, for many Americans and Europeans, is a major example. And here it becomes particularly important to think about definitions of news, and priorities in reporting. The kind of everyday life I experienced in Kafanchan may get into feature stories occasionally, but much of the time the emphasis is on 'hard news', and 'hard news' tends to be bad news: reporting on conflict, violence, disasters, or other kinds of trouble. There is a classic line by one veteran foreign correspondent which others in the craft are fond of quoting: 'Whenever you find hundreds of thousands of sane people trying to get out of a place and a little bunch of madmen struggling to get in, you know the latter are newspapermen.' (The bureau chief for the Associated Press in Johannesburg said he had had this quotation under a glass cover on his desk for years.)

The correspondents I talked with in Johannesburg have certainly had a number of hard news stories out of Africa to tell the world in recent years. Many of them had witnessed the fall of President Mobutu in Zaire; several had followed the Hutu–Tutsi conflict in Rwanda in different phases; some had reported from the wars in Somalia and in southern Sudan, and the internal upheavals of Liberia and Sierra Leone. And then there had been stories of famines and of AIDS epidemics. The point certainly cannot be that such events should go unreported. It is rather that when this is all we hear, or see, we may get a very biased view of a part of the world. Actually, the situation was not so very different in the case of black America, as portrayed to the world, and by the world, in the late 1960s, when I was in Washington. Again, the 'hard news' involved trouble; those days when the National Guard was in the neighborhood got infinitely more publicity than any other days.

What are the implications of such foreign news reporting for culture in the global ecumene? At times, it may be that the view, on the television screen, of starving children in Ethiopia, or of victims of a grenade thrown into a Sarajevo market, provokes a kind of electronic empathy. The television medium in particular allows a sense of a direct experience of the faces and bodies of other human beings far away, and sometimes an understanding of their terrible circumstances. Yet places defined only by hard news may take on a sort of on-and-off, episodic quality; we do not know what had happened before, and lose track of what happened afterwards. And overall, as conflicts and catastrophes are relentlessly pressed upon us as more or less willing news consumers week after week, year after year, the result may just be a heightened feeling that the world is a dangerous place, and some parts of it particularly so. The foreign news editor of *Dagens Nyheter*, the largest morning newspaper in Stockholm, said to me that she was aware of the possible bias towards trouble and danger, and that her paper tried to avoid supporting such a view of the outside world, as it could foster isolationism and xenophobia among the public. Yet all media organizations may not be so concerned with the issue, and in any case it may be a tendency not so easily counteracted.

Conclusion: cultural analysis as an everyday practice

That leads me to some final reflections. Recently, some of my colleagues in anthropology have become critical of the culture concept itself.[7] For some time, there have been warnings that anthropologists have had a bias toward exoticism: it is more rewarding to report from the field that things are different there than to have to say that they are much the same as at home. And to speak of culture – especially cultures – tends to become a way of underlining, even exaggerating, difference. The critics find it a matter of 'making other', creating distances. In a world of very real greater interconnectedness, this could become more dangerous than ever before. In Europe, characterized in recent decades not only by internal political and economic integration but also by large-scale migration from the outside, what has been described as 'cultural fundamental-ism' now sometimes serves as a convenient substitute for racism (cf. Stolcke 1995).

Some of the critics of the culture concept would therefore avoid using at least the plural form. Others would argue against using the noun form altogether, and use only the adjective, 'cultural', which does not reify culture as a substance but merely draws attention to a quality, a certain aspect of things. Others again, probably not finding such subtlety sufficient, would evidently now prefer to have nothing more to do with the concept at all.

I am afraid this is an ostrich response. Again, anthropologists may feel some special responsibility for the concept of culture, but it is now an idea which is everywhere, and the problem which is certainly not confined to academic usage will not go away just because some rather small group of scholars decides to banish the term from their own vocabulary. In so far as academic scholarship on culture carries any intellectual authority outside our own institutions, we would do better to keep a critical eye on the varieties of culturespeak both among ourselves and in society at large – and try to blow our whistles when a usage seems questionable or even pernicious.

It could seem, moreover, that the personal experiences which many people now have of globalization might well allow them to participate in our rethinking culture. Many of us may find a number of things we enjoy in global interconnectedness, but we must recognize that such pleasures are hardly all there is to it. As meanings and meaningful forms make their ways through time and space, reconfiguring rather than obliterating diversity, conflicts may not just fade away. As people who do not 'share a culture' more or less inevitably come in each other's way, contacts may well appear inconvenient, a bit unpredictable, not quite transparent. Not least importantly, we may need to learn to think of this as a fairly ordinary state of affairs, and simply to cultivate a readiness to cope with much of it as it is – in the same way as one expects mature people to cope with differences and tensions between generations, or between the sexes, or between the parties in a number of other relationships which they also handle on a regular basis. Life may be tough sometimes, but we do not expect to solve problems in such relationships by telling the others to go back to where they came from. Rather, we muddle through; and I suspect that, in daily life in the global ecumene, it will be required of us that we all do a certain amount of cultural muddling through.

But perhaps a kind of cultural analysis as everyday practice could at least make such problems seem less threatening. 'Culture', then, must not be a mysti-fying concept, but must point towards tools to think with. As a reflective stance, everyday cultural analysis would involve a sense of how we know what we know about other people: a sense of our sources of ignorance and misunder-standings as well as of knowledge. It may suggest that differences between people are neither absolute nor eternal. Culture can be viewed in no small part as a matter of cumulative experience, and exchanges about that experience. It is a matter of doing as well as being, it is fluid rather than frozen. And such everyday cultural analysis might also tell us that culture may cut across social distinctions, so as to create at least some areas of sharing, and some possibility of mutual intelligibility.

Notes

1 On the 'culture of poverty' debate, see e.g. Valentine (1968), Leacock (1971), and, for my own interpretation, Hannerz (1969 and 1975).
2 During my study in Washington, I had been associated with linguists studying black American dialects from a creolist perspective, and this later gave me some initial sense of its relevance to my study in Kafanchan.
3 For a detailed discussion of some such products, see Barber and Waterman (1995).
4 See the discussion in Hannerz (1996: 30 ff.).
5 For some discussion of this project see Hannerz (1998a, 1998b).
6 Between my studies in Washington and Kafanchan, I had actually also done a smaller project on politics in the Cayman Islands, in the Caribbean – and, during my fieldwork there, a crisis also briefly drew a British gunboat to an offshore anchorage point (Hannerz 1974).
7 For further comments on this, see Hannez (1996: 30 ff.).

References

Barber, K., and Waterman, C. (1995). 'Traversing the global and the local: fújì music and praise poetry in the production of contemporary Yorùbá popular culture'. In D. Miller (ed.), *Worlds Apart*. London: Routledge.
DuBois, W. E. B. (1903). *The Souls of Black Folk*. Chicago: McClurg.
Hannerz, U. (1969). *Soulside*. New York: Columbia University Press.
—— (1974). *Caymanian Politics*. Stockholm Studies in Social Anthropology, 1. Stockholm: Department of Social Anthropology, Stockholm University.
—— (1975). 'Research in the black ghetto: A review of the sixties'. In R. D. Abrahams and J. F. Szwed (eds), *Discovering Afro-America*. Leiden: Brill.
—— (1987). 'The world in creolisation'. *Africa* 57: 546–59.
—— (1992a). 'The global ecumene as a network of networks'. In Adam Kuper (ed.), *Conceptualizing Society*. London: Routledge.
—— (1992b). *Cultural Complexity: Studies in the Social Organization of Meaning*. New York: Columbia University Press.
—— (1996). *Transnational Connections*. London: Routledge.
—— (1998a). 'Of correspondents and collages'. *Anthropological Journal on European Cultures*, 7: 91–109.
—— (1998b). 'Reporting from Jerusalem'. *Cultural Anthropology*, 13: 548–74.
Kroeber, A. L. (1945). 'The ancient *Oikoumenê* as an historic culture aggregate'. *Journal of the Royal Anthropological Institute*, 75: 9–20.
—— (1952). *The Nature of Culture*. Chicago: University of Chicago Press.
Leacock, E. B. (ed.). (1971). *The Culture of Poverty*. New York: Simon and Schuster.
McLuhan, M. (1964). *Understanding Media*. New York: McGraw-Hill.

Rushdie, S. (1991). *Imaginary Homelands*. London: Granta.
Stolcke, V. (1995). 'Talking culture: new boundaries, new rhetorics of exclusion in Europe'. *Current Anthropology*, 36: 1–24.
Valentine, C. A. (1968). *Culture and Poverty*. Chicago: University of Chicago Press.

Section Two

MAKING SENSE
OF CULTURE

4

FROM WAYS OF LIFE TO LIFESTYLE

Rethinking culture as ideology and sensibility

David C. Chaney

I begin with the proposition that the concept of culture has been a key invention of social thought in the modern era; but I shall argue that, in the course of being extensively used, it has acquired new meanings. I shall further argue that as part of this process implied relationships between cultural forms and social forms have also necessarily changed. I shall argue that the concept of lifestyle is a good example of a new social form. Quite what we mean by lifestyles and some of the implications of this social form will be briefly explored. In particular I will suggest that a key element in the traditional discourse of culture, the value of authenticity, is now being understood less as an inherent quality of objects or actions and more as something produced in lifestyling. I will further suggest that these arguments are more generally an exploration of the implications of recognizing that the discourse of culture has been popularized.

I hope it is uncontroversial to begin by claiming that the concept of culture has been one of the fundamental building blocks of the social sciences. In trying to develop a language of social order and difference, social theorists have found it essential to think of a structure of attitudes, values, and normative expectations that lay behind or were implicit in the patterns of behavior that were characteristic of life in a community.

In order to see the strength of this idea, three points need to be emphasized. The first is that the orientations I have summarized as attitudes, values, and normative expectations were not peculiar to individuals but were shared within a community and formed a more or less coherent structure. That is, they existed somehow independently of actors' minds and persisted through generations. The second point is that, although these orientations primarily determined forms of social interaction, they were also made visible or expressed in other aspects of communal life. These include religious ceremonies and

75

symbolism, patterns of embellishment of elements of material culture such as clothes, food, and utensils, and were celebrated in customary dances, songs, and festivals. Third, what I have called the structure of values that informed behavior, or the sorts of reasons that could be given, was not explicit or self-consciously discussed within the community. Structures of values and inter-pretations might indeed depend upon the analysis of an external observer in order to become apparent.[1]

Culture thus becomes essential to the basic perspective of the human sci-ences. Culture provides a way of framing individual experience and action so that it can be understood indexically (that is actions can be linked to a context). Distinctive patterns in the organization of local customs can be recorded as ways of life that display the persistence of culture through generations; a notion of culture that is 'descriptive of the whole pattern of representations of a recog-nizable and coherent group of people' (Jenks 1993: 159). Cultures and com-munities are therefore mutually constitutive terms – each is established, if need be, by reference to the other. The same process holds true for individuals. Thus we find instances of culture in the performances and artifacts local actors pro-duce, and we are able to explain their productions by reference to a culture that makes sense of what might otherwise seem irrational. Ways or forms of life are an essential bridge between individuals and culture that enable us to tell stories about the diversity and continuity of experience. When I say 'us' here, I do not mean just those of us involved in studying contemporary society, but all of us who are members of modern societies. The idea of culture becomes part of a general modern consciousness so that we all know how to use cultural themes to make sense of a puzzling world.[2]

I will now briefly describe some examples of the use of culture, plucked almost at random, to illustrate how flexibly it can be used. I will then suggest that this very flexibility disguises a crucial movement in the use of culture in an era of mass communication and entertainment.[3] The first concerns a relative of mine who was married for some time to a Nigerian man. The family was distressed to discover that there had been some domestic tension leading to incidents of physical assault by the husband on his wife. In seeking to explain these incidents it was pointed out that the female partner was very indepen-dent. She was used to making her own judgments and then following them. Some family members felt that such independence was foreign to marriage customs in Nigerian culture, in particular the deference due to the status of the male head of household, and therefore that the husband had felt threatened. While it was agreed to be deplorable, his behavior was rendered less alarming, less shameful, by a context of imputed cultural tradition.

A second example concerns the story of an undergraduate student at my university who had been struggling for some time with an eating disorder. She had been unable to maintain her studies, or, more accurately had approached them with too high standards so that she couldn't complete projects. Eventu-ally the tension of struggling to keep up with academic expectations while becoming increasingly seriously undernourished had become so great that she had been forced to withdraw. When I discussed this case with colleagues it was suggested that her problem with food, her obsessional fear of obesity, was a consequence of cultural expectations. Cultural norms of slimness were displayed in advertisements, fashion photographs, and generally in the discourse of magazines so that a gullible reader, as perhaps this student was, felt forced to control and drive down her body weight.

The third example has become very familiar in most European cities. This is the situation of entrepreneurs creating 'Irish' drinking houses, pubs, as places that are attractive particularly to young people. I have put 'Irish' in quotation marks because the pubs are themed environments. They are built, or existing places are adapted, to represent an iconography of a traditional Irish village pub. The simulation is conveyed through seating, decor, signs, drinks, and possibly appropriate music played over a sound system. The pub may employ people who speak with an Irish accent, and occasionally sponsor live performances of traditional Irish songs and dances. These places are then offering a dramatization of a particular strand of Irish culture. While clearly not the real thing, as they are not located in an Irish village, they purport to be authentic. They employ a number of devices to represent or simulate an Irish cultural form that is recognizable and attractive to customers.

Each of these uses of culture can be criticized as not being very sophisticated and indeed could be condemned as superficial or even patronizing. The instances work though, it seems to me, as representative of the sorts of ways culture can be invoked in everyday life as a sense-making resource. Such a practical use is, however, not constrained by the way they also suffer from the more serious flaw that the culture that is invoked in each case has a curious status. It exists as something that is there, recognizable, has an existence – even effects – in the world and yet its power works for some and not others. The culture that is employed in these sorts of situations is a collective entity that is not co-terminous with a distinct social group. The umbilical link between culture and community that I mentioned above has been broken.[4] In mass societies it has become apparent that there are a multiplicity of overlapping cultures with differing relationships with social actors, and with the further consequence that they can make sense in a number of different ways.

What I mean by this is that, as is evident in the examples briefly described, the sorts of 'explanation' culture can provide have different ramifications. For instance, the culture of slimness affecting the anorexic girl operates as a myth of a certain sort of beauty that idealizes largely unattainable norms for a majority of women. It therefore can be seen to have the effect of requiring women to strive against inevitable failure so that they fail to see or understand themselves as they really are. It therefore works as an ideological strategy that underpins male supremacy or patriarchal social relations (on ideology in a culture of mass communications, see Thompson 1990).

In contrast, the conceptualization of Nigerian, or perhaps more widely

African or even black, masculinity trades on traditions of exploitation between white colonial powers and client Third World cultures. In these traditions natives are less civilized, certainly more traditional, than their colonizers so that, although one can pay tribute to the strength and autonomy of their culture, in doing so we are also covertly congratulating ourselves on our superiority. This type of cultural account can also be described as ideological in that it systematically distorts our perception of social relationships, but here we (I am writing as a white, middle-class academic) are not so much victims as beneficiaries – bolstered, rather than threatened, by culture as ideology.

In some respects the case of an Irish pub overlaps with Nigerian masculinity, particularly for a British customer, as it is impossible to separate perceptions of Irish culture from a history of colonial exploitation. That said, though, the international success of these themed environments suggests they are more usefully seen as instances of 'McTourism' (see Ritzer 1997 for his extension of the McDonaldization thesis to tourism). Carefully packaged and sanitized versions of other cultures can be employed, as in theme parks, to give an illusion of difference. Once again I suppose it is a form of ideology except that here the distortions primarily serve commercial ends.

The point I am making here is that the concept of culture acquires further layers of meaning as it is used in a multiplicity of sometimes contradictory ways in mass societies. As we develop and adapt an understanding of culture as something constitutive of a tribal or communal identity, or as equivalent to a national identity, then the idea loses its power to interpret social life as a totality. Culture becomes partial or, more accurately, it goes to work at a number of levels simultaneously. Cultural characteristics have become both how we identify ourselves and members of other social groups, and how those identities are replayed or re-presented in media discourse as prejudices rooted in the competing interests and socio-structural formations of privilege and disadvantage.[5] I do not want to be side-tracked here by the associations of the term 'ideology' with Marxist traditions to concentrate on the extent to which contemporary cultural forms work to stabilize and perpetuate capitalist hegemony. Indeed much of what I am saying about the new social forms of late modernity implicitly rejects the presumptions made in those traditions about competing class interests locked in structural conflict. Instead, I want to emphasize the idea that, in adapting notions of culture to the dramas and entertainment of a mass-mediated environment, culture has become in effect a symbolic repertoire.

What I mean by this is that the signs, symbols, images, and artifacts through which the different cultures of late twentieth-century life are recognized and deployed in mundane interpretations of social life are grouped into genres or repertoires as particular sorts of performance – that is performances associated with particular groups or settings or ways of life. A repertoire is then a set of ways of symbolically representing identity and difference, with implied associations of characteristic attitudes, values, and norms, that form, if you like, a terrain for competing expectations. What is important is that the repertoire exists as a resource at a number of levels (that is individual perceptions as well as group prejudices as well as media stereotypes) simultaneously. It is in the interplay and contrasts between these levels that culture becomes ambiguous; something to be exploited in everyday life and not just used by 'external' analysts.

It may be objected that culture, at least in certain traditions of anthropological theorizing (see, for example, Geertz 1973), has always been understood as a symbolic repertoire. While this humanist interpretive tradition is still a valuable guide to research practice, Geertz could assume that in village societies the culture, or symbolic repertoire, was reasonably homogeneous and the boundaries of culture and community were largely co-terminus. The novelty I seek to describe is that not only are mass societies multicultural but the repertoires are used in different ways in different institutional contexts. The shift in the nature of the repertoire can be clarified by situations when 'traditional' cultures come into contact with the consumption of culture. When Balinese village dancers perform a ceremony not at a traditional location or on a traditional occasion but as a performance for tourists, or even more when they tour Europe and North America staging theatrical performances, the same symbolic event changes its meaning. It becomes a commodity, a source of entertainment, maybe even spiritual enhancement, for anonymous audiences. It becomes part of, or an element in, mass culture possibly appropriated randomly or unpredictably.

If one left it there the conclusion would be that contemporary culture is increasingly dominated by qualities of fragmentation and pastiche in ways that are often condemned as the superficiality of postmodern life. In this account the symbolism of Balinese religious traditions is able to be bracketed with the symbolism of Irish drinking traditions in a virtual cultural supermarket. I will go on to argue though that the burden of the supermarket metaphor is that, as with everyday shopping where people do not buy goods at random but put together distinctive sets of items, cultural choices are put together as styles.

Language and cultural symbolism

In order to bring out more fully what is involved in rethinking culture, I will explore the idea of symbolic repertoires of cultural heterogeneity by turning to an analogy between language and culture. I think it can be argued that throughout the twentieth century theorists used a model of language as a way of understanding how a culture 'works' although the relevance of language has been understood in a number of quite different ways. I have previously suggested (1996) that one can distinguish three main perspectives on how an analogy with language can be used to interpret the use of symbols as cultural artifacts. The first I have called symbolic exchange. From this perspective symbols (including the words of a language) are initially seen as types of representations of meanings and values in much the same way as units of currency are commonly taken to represent economic value. But meanings and values for the social theorist Georg Simmel and those influenced by him have vitality only in networks of relationships. The circulation of fashionable items is a way of marking inclusion as well as exclusion. It is therefore a way of playing with creativity that is equivalent to the creativity of language use (on Simmel and fashion see Gronow 1997).

In the second perspective, most commonly associated with the French social theorist Pierre Bourdieu, a symbolic repertoire is approached as a form of capital (Bourdieu 1984). In the same way that mastery of a language is associated with high status and is a means of aggressively reminding inferiors of their lack of skills, mastery of cultural or symbolic capital enables high-status groups both to display their privileges and to manipulate cultural vocabularies to the continual disadvantage of those with fewer cultural resources. The metaphor of cultural capital can therefore be used to explain the persistence of established structures of privilege through generations, and to illuminate the distinctive expertise of new strata of intellectuals who have been generated by shifts in the dominant modes of production from industrial goods to information and design skills (Lash and Urry 1987, 1994).

The third perspective begins one can say with the deficiencies of language. In the same way that in mass society we do not have a single culture, neither do we speak a single language. Within a general group such as English we are forced to recognize a variety of styles and variants colored by borrowings and adaptations so that English speakers comprise a number of speech communities. And again these communities are no longer clearly distinct or homogeneous. It is clear that whether or not we possess an innate linguistic competence that enables us to grasp rules of grammar and structure, in everyday interaction we display a communicative – or in this context we could say a 'cultural' – competence so that the process of symbolic use is patterned by loose forms or styles (the title of this third perspective is then 'symbolic styles'). The crucial feature of this perspective is that cultural symbols are used more or less self-consciously in the course of which they are adapted and transformed. It follows that meaning is not something 'there' in what we say or do or in the world around us to be appreciated correctly or not, but is something made in the politics of social practice. Although the cultures of mass society frequently concern 'material' entities, for example the goods of mass consumption, in the process of using these entities they are in important ways 'dematerialized', destabilized, made into forms of representation (Chaney 1998).

The perspectives on the analogy with language for cultural symbolism I have just outlined are not mutually exclusive. They are not set out as a set of choices but rather to indicate how we might begin to understand the relationships between culture and society in an era of mass communication and entertainment. On the one hand I have noted how cultural symbols have become commodities marketed as decor and taste as well as experience (the most elaborate and possibly the most developed form this marketing takes is in the various modes of the tourist industry; see for example Rojek and Urry 1997). On the other hand cultural symbolism works to negotiate social processes and structures as a distinctive means of expression. The sort of things we refer to as culture in this account are clearly not representing the social in any epiphenomenal or superstructural sense; with the further implication that the social groups and individuals whose identity is to at least some extent expressed and defined through symbolic repertoires are themselves destabilized. These social groups and individuals lose the coherent integrity of rationalist tradition and lack the stability of more traditional social forms, becoming in effect new social forms articulated through cultural symbolism in the play of association and meaning.

It is common to acknowledge that post-industrial societies are multicultural, and therefore national cultures no longer exist (if they ever did), but I am going further and argue that any idea that these multiple cultures are each a shared framework of norms, values, and expectations is unsustainable because the ways of life exemplifying this framework are no longer stable and clear-cut. In contrast, culture has to be appreciated as a self-conscious repertoire of styles that are constantly being monitored and adapted rather than just forming the unconscious basis of social identity. The approach I seek to make here is to move away from the idea that even within a speech community members speak a common language. Culture is more appropriately imagined as a polyphony of ways of speaking. Rather than just thinking of speech competence as something members have when knowing how to go on, any language is better understood as a family of games. Playing within the spaces they constitute is always and necessarily an ironic performance, much as any other improvisation with the signs of material culture. It is more helpful to think of culture as the sorts of embodied, inscribed skills that enable us to improvise on a musical instrument or draw an image (think here, for instance, of David Sudnow's 1978 self-exploratory study of learning how to improvise on the piano). If all forms of social performance are improvisations, then culture is displayed in characteristic dialogues between actor and resources at hand.

Lifestyle

I have suggested that the ways in which actors in everyday life use notions of culture should make us deduce that traditional conceptions of culture in social theory are no longer sustainable. I have further suggested that the forms of social life (the social institutions) that were given order and meaning in terms of cultural traditions have changed and are being changed by new cultural forms (the circularity here between social and cultural change is inescapable – mutual reciprocity means that one-sided change is impossible). I will go on now to suggest that one example of a new social form, a mode of institutionalization, that exemplifies cultural change has been the development of lifestyles.

Inevitably in ascribing more technical meanings to words used in everyday life one is to some extent arbitrarily juggling with or constraining the looseness of ordinary usage. I want to argue, though, that, first, one can make a meaningful distinction between ways of life and lifestyles; second, it is only in eras of mass entertainment and communication that lifestyles have developed; and, third, lifestyles exhibit some of the characteristics of social forms appropriate to the changing meanings of culture I have described.

I think it is typical to think of lifestyles as a form of social status. They are ways in which members of a group can display their privileges, or, more actively, use their mastery of symbolic capital to control access to desirable status. Following Max Weber's early formulation, it is conventional to think of lifestyles as a form of status that derives from a mastery of expenditure on consumption or leisure time, rather than a structure of stratification based on the ownership and/or organization of means of production. Such displays of conspicuous consumption have in the past been associated with wealth, either inherited or newly acquired. The novelty of mass leisure and consumerism developed in the twentieth century is that the play of status associated with consumption practices is no longer confined to the very rich, but becomes a more widespread focus of social interest.

The development of consumerism in mass society makes it necessary to make a distinction between way of life and lifestyle. I do not want to play with words here but the distinction is useful because it underlies a distinctive type of sociality characteristic of lifestyles. A way of life is typically associated with a more or less stable community. It is therefore displayed in features such as shared norms, rituals, patterns of social order, and probably a distinctive dialect or speech community. A way of life is based in the production and reproduction of stable institutions, and ways of life are therefore grounded in distinctive and specifiable localities. Although in the looseness of ordinary speech we might refer to this way of life as a 'style of life' I think this is misleading. Thus, for example, while Kephart's study (1982) of cultural minorities in the United States uses lifestyles as a central concept, the religious communities he describes are clearly instances of distinctive ways or forms of life.

In contrast, lifestyles are based in consumer choices and leisure patterns. This is significant because, when lifestyles structure social identification, economic practices have to be grasped as representations. As I said above, in the virtual cultural supermarket, choice is not random but coalesces into patterns or styles. In sharing attitudes, values, and tastes which will be characteristic of particular groups, the sensibilities expressed in taste are increasingly imbued with moral and aesthetic seriousness. It becomes accepted that one's tastes are responsibilities by which the person will be judged by others. They are therefore integral to a sense of identity but not as a stable or uni-dimensional characterization. As Bensman and Vidich say in relation to the lifestyles of the new middle classes: 'The existence of artificial life-styles, self-consciously created as if they were works of art, suggests a lack of inevitability in the living patterns that classes adopt' (1995: 239). Ways of life and lifestyles are not mutually exclusive, as they clearly to some extent co-exist in contemporary experience. However, as people increasingly treat their lifestyle as a project articulating who they are, then they will invest it with more significance than ascribed structural expectations associated with gender, age, ethnicity, or religion, for example.

Lifestyles then are ways of categorizing people that could only have developed in an era of modernity or even late-modernity. The distinctiveness of modernity is that access to consumption and leisure is more widely spread in post-industrial societies, both in terms of economic resources and in terms of far-flung distributive networks of communication and entertainment.[6] These networks produce images that make styles and experiences familiar and desirable on an unprecedented scale, but also contextualize those images. What I mean by contextualize is that images are given social location – both historical and cultural. Thus in everyday use symbolic repertoires are both more diverse, and users more self-consciously aware of alternatives. Lifestyles are self-consciously reflexive because actors making cultural choices are necessarily aware that taste could be otherwise. Every aspect of life becomes a matter of style, or we could call it fashion – to wear something or to go somewhere is to be aware of the sort of person who makes that choice and thus the self becomes more clearly an object of cultural mapping.

We must recognize, though, that fashion often has negative connotations. In some accounts it indicates the exploitation of the gullible by those who creatively manipulate images in order to create constantly changing criteria of the desirable.[7] There is, we can note in passing, in this usage at least a suspicion of gender bias in that, as women have traditionally been assumed to be more concerned with fashion, it seems that they have been displaying their irrationality and vulnerability to exploitation (unless protected by men's greater common sense). Although a detailed discussion of the politics of consumerism would take too much space, I should say that recent emphases on audiences' active engagement with cultural choices (e.g. Lull 2000) have been a welcome corrective to the paternalism of many accounts stressing exploitation. I have, however, already emphasized that cultural symbolism has become a commodity marketed as image and it is then clearly true that fashion is a key adjunct of the marketing of consumer culture. It is therefore unsurprising that lifestyles have been used as frameworks for marketing – whether it is the audience delineation of market research organizations or the identification of social variables associated with positive or negative 'health behaviors' (e.g. Blaxter 1990).

To write then of lifestyles as new social forms does not mean that they are being portrayed as untrammelled avenues of emancipation – although it is important to acknowledge the number of ways in which fashion, and other associated aspects of lifestyle, have acted as the means of contesting orthodox moralities and stimulating change (see for example some of the ambiguities in interpreting a figure such as Madonna in Schwichtenberg 1993). I accept that as the instability and capriciousness of fashion have come to characterize values in all areas of social life, not just dress, so those concerned to sell us images, whether it is politicians, mass media executives, soft drink manufacturers, or icons of adolescent rebellion will strive to find ever more effective ways of manipulating audience values. In the reflexive consciousness of mass media-dominated social formations the sorts of social categories that are being formed and re-formed around cultural values and choices cannot be 'innocent'. The shifts of fashion are endlessly fascinating to social commentators in the media as well as to marketing entrepreneurs, social policy managers, and those who are both audiences and social actors.

Authenticity, sensibility

The significance of fashion as a process characteristic of lifestyle as social form is twofold. In one respect it brings out how lifestyles are caught up in strategies of manipulation. Although people invest their lifestyle with personal signifi-cance, they should be aware that at the least they do not have complete control over the terms that lifestyle employs. The second important aspect of fashion is closely related to the first in that it concerns the authenticity of cultural objects and actions. Because fashion is inherently unstable, being bound in with cycles of change and arbitrary shifts in meaning, the elements of a fashionable system, in whatever sphere it is, could be argued to have a tendency to lose any intrinsic meaning or authenticity and be purely defined 'externally' through the context of their use (that has been one of the lessons taken from Hebdige's classic study of youth culture fashions in Britain: 1979). I believe that the mean-ing or authenticity of cultural choices in lifestyle politics is more complex than such a view would allow.

I have noted that such a process of uprooting meanings (turning signs into arbitrary signifiers) has been taken to be a defining characteristic of post-modern sociality – whether condemned or celebrated. I do not want to be led into the issue of periodizing cultural change, but the issue of whether authen-ticity (in any respect) has become impossible or superfluous in the process of the shifting meanings of culture that is our topic is important. Authenticity has been one of the defining metaphors of traditional notions of culture. To be authentic is to be true to (consistent with) tradition, or locale, or one's self. Thus something is authentic when it corresponds to how it would have been in its original state or before it had been significantly affected by external influences. One frequently speaks of a way of dancing or playing music as authentic to a region or to the characteristics of a style. It follows that in-authenticity is a way of being duplicitous so that, returning to the theme of manipulation, organizations, such as food manufacturers and politicians – both of whom we often intuitively feel to be very inauthentic – may use a rhetoric of authenticity to make themselves more convincing.

Authenticity is important because it concerns the possibility of ethical choices. If it was an implication of cultural change that an ethic of authenticity became impossible or irrelevant, that would clearly be a cause of great concern. Not least because in making cultural choices ordinary members of society, at least some of the time and in some respects, will be seeking out authenticity. Whether it is in tourist destinations or home decorations or types of restaurants, and so on, the fact of some place or thing being authentic or not is clearly a relevant concern for some consumers (I have discussed elsewhere some of the reasons for a quest for authenticity in musical choices amongst British suburban residents; see Chaney 1997). The idea of postmodernity therefore matters because it draws attention to the proliferation of choices in what I have called virtual cultural supermarkets; we are forced to ask whether a blanket condemnation of the impossibility of meaningful judgments in mass consumerism is another way of reiterating elitist despair at the popularization of cultural discourse.

I suggest that much of the confusion over authenticity has arisen because in the connection with traditional notions of culture it implies an essential truth or rightness. The self-evident totality of 'a' culture is exemplified through judgments that certain ways of acting or using symbols are authentic. As we recognize that we use culture now not as a complete entity but as a symbolic repertoire, our expectations of authenticity should shift from what is intrinsically true to the ways in which cultures are made. Authenticity is a cultural value because it seems that when it is invoked people are talking about *how* something is being done rather than *what* is being done. Authenticity concerns representation and performance. That is why it should concern the extent to which social actors are able to use symbolic repertoires in creative and consistent ways.

In seeking to elucidate the distinctiveness of lifestyles as a social form I have touched at several points on the reflexive character of the decisions they embody. Now when drawing this chapter to a close, I should be more explicit about what is meant by this idea. Clearly when people choose (or are allowed to choose) whether or not to be married to their sexual partner, or what sort of vacations they will take, or whether they accept a responsibility to maintain a youthful body, they are making decisions about the organization of their life. At varying levels of seriousness they are shaping or styling both *who* they are and the *way* they are. Decisions about choosing from symbolic repertoires, in the context of endless recursive discourse about the options and meanings of symbolic discourse, are helping to constitute new accents and themes in those repertoires. In all these ways lifestyle choices are reflexive. They constitute lines of affiliation and association to form patterns that can be recognized and used by others as well as themselves.

I suggest then that it is in a self-conscious commitment to sensibility as the grounds of affiliative association that the novelty of lifestyle as social form becomes clear. By sensibility I mean an attitude or perspective which enables disparate activities or choices to be seen as consonant or consistent. A sensibility is therefore a constellation of tastes that 'hang together': they form a

85

pattern that is recognizable to those who share it and probably to outsiders. Of course sensibilities are vague, amorphous orientations that do not lend themselves to precise definition but crucially they do enable actors to know how to keep going. I wrote above of the practice of improvisation being embodied – it is a creative practice that employs a sensibility as the grounds of expression. I began by saying that cultures for communities were invisible, unconscious. The difference with the idea of sensibility is that while in everyday terms it is largely taken for granted by actors in the instability of lifestyle practice, sensibilities are continually being foregrounded, made self-conscious, so that the improvisations of everyday life are being rethought as genres or styles.

The central roles of sensibility and reflexivity in lifestyle formation mean that as social groups lifestyles are loose agglomerations. Any attempt to map them is chasing after a vague and constantly changing constellation of attitudes. I have therefore previously suggested that this new social form can best be characterized by distinctive focal concerns with sites and strategies (Chaney 1996). Sites are the sorts of places and spaces that lifeworlds inhabit, and strategies are the sorts of projects that are pursued – whether it is maximizing child growth, or spiritual development, or acquisition of certain types of expensive consumer goods. Sites are meaningful not because they are necessarily identifiable places in a physical environment but because they are physical metaphors for the spaces that actors can appropriate or control. And strategies must be acknowledged because lifestyles are best understood as characteristic modes of social engagement, or narratives of identity, in which the actors concerned can embed the metaphors at hand. Sites and strategies work together then because lifestyles are creative projects – they are forms of enactment in which actors make judgments in delineating an environment.

In conclusion, I hope it will be apparent that I am trying to offer an interpretation of cultural and social change as it is happening – a form of contemporary history. Cultures are now so much a routine part of the conceptual furniture of contemporary social discourse that they cannot be abolished. Indeed one cannot legislate for how the term should be used and, like many other social concepts, it will doubtless continue to accumulate layers of confusing, possibly contradictory, usage. I have not tried to 'clean up' this conceptual confusion, but in responding to perceived shifts in meaning I have pointed to congruent changes in social forms that help to make sense of the 'cultures' of post-industrial societies at the beginning of the third millennium.

Notes

Fragments of this chapter have been presented to a graduate seminar in communications at the University of Oslo, and to the *Theory, Culture and Society* conference in Berlin in 1996. I am grateful for the opportunities to have made these presentations, and for the comments made by members of the audiences. I am also very grateful to James Lull for his help and support in the preparation of this chapter.

1 For an elegant interrogation of the need for a concept of culture in social theory, see Carrithers (1992).
2 I have discussed how the study of culture has been diffused in more general social consciousness in greater detail in Chaney (1994: chapter 2).
3 I will from here on refer without further elaboration to the social world in an era of mass communication and entertainment as a mass society.
4 I will go on to argue that culture becomes something that is more or less self-consciously invented, with the result that it can been as artificial – a perception that probably underlies much of the hostility shown by intellectuals to suburban ways of life (e.g. Silverstone 1997).
5 Again I have previously discussed how notions of culture and ideology have been elided in the development of cultural studies, in the first chapter of Chaney (1994).
6 On the development of lifestyles in the context of consumer culture, see Chaney (1996) and Lury (1996).
7 Different versions of this exploitation thesis can be found in Haug (1986) and Cross (1993), and it clearly still troubles a book on fashion by Davis (1992).

References

Bensman, J. and Vidich, A. J. (1995). 'Changes in the life-styles of American classes'. In A. J. Vidich (ed.), *The New Middle Classes: Life-styles, Status Claims and Political Orientations.* London: Macmillan.

Blaxter, M. (1990). *Health and Lifestyles.* London: Tavistock Press.

Bourdieu, P. (1984). *Distinction: A Social Critique of the Judgement of Taste.* London: Routledge.

Carrithers, M. (1992). *Why Humans Have Cultures: Explaining Anthropology and Social Diversity.* Oxford: Oxford University Press.

Chaney, D. (1994). *The Cultural Turn: Scene-setting Essays on Contemporary Cultural History.* London: Routledge.

—— (1996). *Lifestyles.* London: Routledge.

—— (1997). 'Authenticity and suburbia'. In S. Westwood and J. Williams (eds), *Imagining Cities.* London: Routledge.

—— (1998). 'The new materialism? The challenge of consumption'. *Work, Employment and Society*, 12(3), 533–44.

Cross, G. (1993). *Time and Money: The Making of Consumer Culture.* London: Routledge.

Davis, F. (1992). *Fashion, Culture and Identity.* London: University of Chicago Press.

Geertz, C. (1973). *The Interpretation of Cultures.* London: Hutchinson; New York: Basic Books.

Gronow, J. (1997). *The Sociology of Taste.* London: Routledge.

Haug, W. (1986). *The Critique of Commodity Aesthetics: Appearance, Sexuality and Advertising in Capitalist Society.* Cambridge: Polity Press.

Hebdige, D. (1979). *Subculture: The Meaning of Style.* London: Methuen.

Jenks, C. (1993). *Culture.* London: Routledge.

Kephart, W. M. (1982). *Extraordinary Groups: The Sociology of Unconventional Life-styles.* New York: St Martin's Press.

Lash, S. and Urry, J. (1987). *The End of Organized Capitalism.* Cambridge: Polity Press.

—— (1994). *Economies of Signs and Spaces.* London: Sage.

Lull, J. (2000). *Media, Communication, Culture: A Global Approach* (second ed.). Cambridge: Polity Press; New York: Columbia University Press.

Lury, C. (1996). *Consumer Culture.* Cambridge: Polity Press; New Brunswick, NJ: Rutgers University Press.

Ritzer, G. (1997). *The McDonaldization Thesis.* London: Sage.

Rojek, C. and Urry, J. (eds) (1997). *Touring Cultures: Transformations of Travel and Theory.* London: Routledge.

Schwichtenberg, C. (ed.) (1993). *The Madonna Connection: Representational Politics, Subcultural Identities and Cultural Theory.* Boulder, CO: Westview Press.

Silverstone, R. (ed.) (1997). *Visions of Suburbia.* London: Routledge.

Sudnow, D. (1978). *Ways of the Hand.* Cambridge, MA: Harvard University Press.

Thompson, J. (1990). *Ideology and Modern Culture: Critical Social Theory in the Era of Mass Communication.* Cambridge: Polity Press.

5

THE QUESTION OF CULTURAL GENDER

Mirja Liikkanen

At each moment in time throughout our lives we are all gendered bodies. Yet, despite the massive, penetrating presence of gender, there is no original pure body, no original pure gender. The processes by which gender is produced and reproduced are never-ending. Even when gender is not a conscious identity, it is constantly being constructed in relation to messages and meaning structures in our environment – in the media, the workplace, the home. Gender is socially constructed as it is built into our very selves. And, because our very selves are all historically and geographically located in real places, gender is necessarily experienced through the complex matrices of culture. This omnipresence of gender makes it a very diffuse object of study.

We all face situations in which we become acutely aware of our gender. Sitting in a theater in Helsinki, Finland, for example, I may remember that 'culture' (of the 'high culture' variety) in my country, Finland, is supposed to appeal mainly to middle-aged women like me. Sometimes when I am shopping or traveling on my own I am reminded of my gender because of threatening or derogatory gestures or words directed my way. I seldom go down dark streets. I go into the wooded area near my home in the daytime only when I know other people are around. Indeed, like all women, I must deal with fear of the cruelest of all forms of gendered violence: rape. The scars that culture imprints on the gendered body affect women in ways that are quite different from the ways men experience their gendered bodies. That's the main reason women seem to worry about gender more than men do.

I often find myself, with my female body, in the wrong place. Sometimes my body is of the wrong type, sometimes of the wrong age. That's when I remember so clearly how culture has gendered me, enveloped my body, and entered my head. We produce and reproduce gender through our conscious and unconscious behavior, across the whole genealogy that influences how gender is defined and etched in our minds, in our emotions, on our bodies. We create our gender, but it also grows upon us.

Gender is constructed in and through every societal space, including the institutional spaces of the public domain, and it is in these public spaces that men and women are sorted into hierarchies. Yet it is also precisely in the public spaces – when I am traveling or shopping, for instance, or when I attend an art exhibition or go to a theater – where I can feel free, where I am coasting (without a body?), that I am safe (from what?). Are these truly the moments when I forget the restricting marks that culture has imprinted on my body, when I feel I part of a universal humanity, when I am a free and autonomous individual?

And what about home, the private spaces? Is that the domain where women have the necessary and appropriate 'cultural competence', where we can escape the critical evaluations we face elsewhere? Or is the private space really just the 'golden cage' that history inscribes as 'the female domain', where we again feel guilty and inadequate?

Generations of women everywhere have shared, and continue to share, common experience. Almost everywhere in the world women remain subordinated in their social groups. But to understand the phenomenon more deeply, we must also take into account how culture mediates gender as well as the different histories between groups of women according to race, ethnicity, age, and social class.

Everything in culture – geographical places, social institutions, work settings, everyday habits, leisure-time hobbies, and all the rest – is gendered. In most societies, everything connected to the feminine carries certain negative qualities, while the masculine is embedded with numerous positive qualities. This troubling, systemic complex of discrimination derives from the fact that, while gender is a structural and ideological question, it also exists as a highly personalized, intimate system of everyday practises in public and in private, to which every one of us has a personal position and relationship. Gender articulates deeply into our emotions, love, affection, dependency, and sexuality.

In this chapter I take up two main themes: how gender is represented and lived in Western culture, especially in my cultural homeland, Finland, and, second, how gender has been evaluated and theorized in women's research. Gender as a public discourse is created in concrete professional practices and discussions. That is why this chapter will deal rather extensively with the politics of knowing about gender and culture, in particular the practices of research on gender, and the representations of gender that such research produces. (See also Widerberg 1995.)

I will stress the central point that, despite having a biological appearance, gender as a sociocultural phenomenon is an *ideological* issue that is directly connected to questions of dominance and power in society – both in the symbolic and in the more formal senses.

Moreover, like gender itself, research on gender is greatly influenced by the cultures that produce it. Consequently, when research and theory on gender travels around the world it does not necessarily harmonize with the cultural traditions and practises of the places where it is read. Such is the case of British feminist theory arriving in Finland, for instance. In the Nordic countries it is taken for granted that normal people go to work and that women are normal people. Women expect to be able to combine work and family, and the 'official' society supports them in this far more than is the case in most other parts of the world, including Britain. Societal conflicts over gender and analyses of these conflicts, therefore, emerge from differing cultural histories and understandings. Furthermore, normal distinctions that are made between high culture and popular culture do not carry the same gender-related cultural meanings in the Nordic region as they do in the Anglo-Saxon world.

Given these contingencies, when discussing any international trend in theory and research on gender, I participate from a geographical and cultural margin. In one sense I share that experience with any other non-Anglo-Saxon intellectual. But as a Nordic woman I come to the table with expectations of gender equality, independence, and societal support that are far more democratic than those in most other parts of the world.

Cultural representations of gender

To make this chapter as concrete and meaningful as possible, I will provide examples of cultural gender from the cultural zone I know best – the Nordic countries generally, and Finland in particular. Let me begin with an interview (R. Liikkanen 1999) that appeared in *Helsingin Sanomat*, the leading daily newspaper in Finland. The interview was conducted with the Finnish sociologist Jari Aro. In the article, Aro describes himself and his colleagues as a rather bland lot:

> Sociologists . . . are quite dull and uninteresting people, almost like talking heads. They used to wear Marimekko shirts, but now they sport a beard or spectacles and a striped jacket . . . not a Matti & Teppo jacket, but the kind you see in television interviews. Seated behind a desk scattered with assorted papers, and a computer screen rolling in the background, the sociologist will be leafing through some book or other. If the sociologist happens to stand up, it will always be with hand in pocket.

The cultural space that is created in this extract is distinctly very Finnish. The Marimekko shirt is almost a national institution; in its heyday the company that invented it achieved cult status and became known internationally for fashion design. The Marimekko-style shirt hinted at a bohemian lifestyle that was very closely associated with intellectuals in the 1960s and 1970s. The Matti & Teppo jacket also has very strong national and male undertones. Matti & Teppo is a duo of male singers who were very popular in Finland in the late 1970s and early 1980s. So, the Marimekko shirt represents left-wing intellectuals and Marxist critical theorists of the Vietnam War era. The Matti & Teppo jacket reminds Finns of the transition from the 1970s to the 1980s, and to the rehabilitation of research in popular culture. The third piece of clothing mentioned in the interview refers to a contemporary situation – the pin-striped jacket you often see in television interviews in northern Europe. This last reference underscores the recent transformation of sociologists, among many other professions in modern society, into 'mediatized experts'. The characterizations of the professional researcher described by Jari Aro explicitly make clear the gender of 'the sociologist'.

Being a Finnish sociologist myself, my feelings were contradictory when I read this newspaper article. My bodily figure, my gendered style, is certainly different from what I was reading. I do not have a beard. I have never had a Marimekko shirt, a Matti & Teppo jacket, or a striped jacket I keep handy for television appearances. If I were to be interviewed, I am not at all sure that I would sit behind a desk, and I would not put my hand in my pocket if I stood up. All this leads me to ask: do I really belong to the community of European sociologists? Is the Finnish feminist author Suvi Ronkainen right when she claims that the 'place of the abodily and placeless expert is not open to all bodily subjects. It rejects the female body (or female experience), and favors the male body (human experience) of the androcentric tradition' (Ronkainen 1999: 156)? Then again, could it be that there is also something inherently Finnish in this setting, perhaps something quite exceptional? Would a male sociologist from Britain, for instance, or Japan, or the United States define his profession in the same sort of national and masculine terms?

About the same time in 1999 *Helsingin Sanomat* also published a series of women's diaries in celebration of Mother's Day (Aaltonen and Härkönen 1999). The invited writers were well-educated women of different ages with varying feminist commitments. Below I will re-present some extracts from their published diaries. None of the writers appears to be non-heterosexual. Most of them speak in one way or another about families that are made up of a woman, a man, and children, or about childless heterosexual couples. The writers are clearly in touch with the present day, and are well aware of the norms for 'gender definition':

> *Riikka Kaihovaara (eighteen years old, student, Anarcho-feminist Union, Friends of the Earth):* It seems that again the Parliamentary elections are a battlefield for middle-aged men. I suppose to me it makes no difference whether the candidates are men or women, I'm just annoyed that all women candidates are just that in these elections: women. Womanhood defines their existence. They're there as beautiful young women, as competent women, as mothers, etc. Why don't men have to justify their candidacy in any way?. . .

To me as an anarcho-feminist it is important that the structures of society should be thoroughly changed. No managers or directors, even if they are women . . .

I know many people who represent various sexual minorities. Sexual equality is a natural thing to me, I haven't questioned it for years. On the other hand excessive freedom and openness can put you under pressure to be something other than what you really are . . . I like to put on make-up. I don't do it to emphasize my femininity (at least that's what I say to myself), but my individuality. To neglect your looks serves no purpose. Some feminists or lesbians dress like men or differently to make a statement and detach themselves from gender roles. But when you do the opposite of what's expected, that's like admitting that the expectations are there and in a sense you reinforce them. But the gender roles will not go away even if women grew beards and men started to wear miniskirts.

For the writer above, gender appears at once as performative and essentialist. Womanhood and manhood are self-evident qualities, and at the same time gender appears in the shape of different performative sexual minority roles. But this cultural openness also causes personal pressure. The excerpt reflects an awareness that heterosexuality is a 'given' identity.

Now, two other views:

Suvi Ronkainen (thirty-six years old, social psychologist and feminist): Personally I feel more comfortable under the label of feminist than under the label of woman. Woman somehow coaxes you into a self-evident category. And yet women are very different; we're a very heterogeneous group. Within the category of 'us women' there are groups with whom I might not even want to be in the same room! That's why sisterhood is not global, unless it is consciously, politically, made into a global issue.

Sirpa Pietikäinen (forty years old, Member of the Finnish Parliament, founding member of For Women network): My own relationship to feminism and to the feminist perspective has been somewhat ambiguous. I know women whose values are much more macho than many men's, but also women who are so bunny-girl that it makes me feel sick. I don't think we have anything else in common apart from our ovaries except of course the stereotypical treatment we receive. Womanhood is always present, furnishing us with labels in a completely different way to manhood. Manhood is more often 'genderless', as if it were somehow neutral and objective.

The two short excerpts above exhibit a keen awareness of the diversity of womanhood. The researcher makes a very strong and conscious statement in favor of the postmodern feminist line by refusing to commit herself to the identity of 'womanhood'. The politician also underlines the diversity of womanhood, but in accord with the very first writer's stress on its 'social' nature.

Another Finnish woman's voice:

> *Katja Krohn (thirty-two years old, director-scriptwriter):* What is the first thing that comes to mind from the word feminist? Someone who wants to change the status quo, a minority representative, bitter, angry, injustice, victim. Victim. I need to make clear my position to this concept of victim straightaway. The word WOMAN, in my mind, is much less valuable; it carries a negative meaning. I often feel victimized. I am annoyed and get angry when I feel I am not treated fairly. And during the past year I have been working on my career like a maniac. I am very sensitive. I'm sure I'll lose my turn and my opportunity unless I defend myself furiously. On the one hand I am torn by the most painful sense of guilt if I am not home in the evening when my sons, who are now aged two and three, come home from kindergarten. On the other hand I am not a victim at all. I love my life, I feel I can really influence my life, do the work I want to do. The only thing that annoys me is that the job is not a steady one and that I haven't managed to get a regular salary. So in reality my husband is supporting me. That really hurts my self-esteem. Is the problem that I am a woman, or is it the quality of my art?
>
> Thanks to the efforts of our mothers, the women of my generation have been able to enjoy a very equal existence. When I was young I thought you can get and you can do what you believe you can. Gender was no obstacle. My children, however, have brought along some harsh facts. I am no longer so sure that I am just the same as 'men' . . . I have always felt that others exercise some sort of power over my body. There's always been an outside eye there to assess my body, and by now that eye has intruded my mind as well.

This interesting excerpt shows very clearly the late modern ambiguities of womanhood in a society like democratic Finland, which regards itself as egalitarian in all social aspects. As in the remarks made by one of the other commentators, the person quoted above exhibits a strong desire to stand apart from earlier generations of women. Both endeavor to represent 'humanity in general', and express an overall repugnance at how women's bodies are treated – that is at how we are treated as female bodies. This excerpt shows the strong female value in Finnish culture to be economically independent. It is indeed a shame to be supported by the husband, even for a short while.

And finally, another culturally gendered voice:

Hilkka Pietilä (sixty-eight years old, former Secretary General of the UN Association, active in international women's networks): How can you tell from how I lead my life that I am a feminist? Nowadays it's from the fact that I prefer to work with other women, in women's movements, in women's studies, in women's networks. In joint projects with men over the past decades I have time and time again run into a glass wall. No one has wanted to listen to my thoughts and suggestions, regardless of whether or not they have been sensible.

The great diversity of female identities and definitions of womanhood can be seen clearly in these few excerpts. One can find in these passages many levels of the overall problematic: how the public sphere and expertise are gendered, the hierarchy of gender in culture, and how gender manifests in the emotions. The passages show how gender is produced as a personal identity, but is also constructed through political action. Furthermore, we can see how vulnerable we are with our gender in the most private and intimate sphere – at home with our families.

The excerpts also illustrate how these women have incorporated different elements from the highly visible international debates on womanhood and gender into their own identities. The excerpts manifest a vague, shared sense of some external cultural force which continues to define 'woman' as a 'gender', the category of woman as non-neutral and non-autonomous. Although there is a clear and firm commitment to women's unity in just the last excerpt, a universal experience of some external force with restrictive or preventive power pervades the assumptions which underlie the women's comments. The possibility of what could be considered a culturally 'feminine' voice is reduced to a quiet whimper. Gender definition becomes interwoven within the suppressed female body.

One element that is particularly Finnish in these diary excerpts is the importance attached to waged employment as a natural, self-evident, building block of identity. Closely related to this is the fear or lived reality that work will be, or already is, infected by 'womanhood', relegating the central public activity in society to the lowest end of the gendered social hierarchy. As I will describe in more detail later, it is precisely to the importance of work in the Nordic region that a strong ambivalence about womanhood is attached, creating a severe pain of ultimate injustice.

We find striking differences when we compare the image of the male, made-for-television sociologist who appeared earlier in this chapter and the women whose diary extracts were printed in the same newspaper. The coherent, self-evident, and universal scholar appears as a male bodily figure. In contrast, female subjectivity appears in the diary excerpts as ambivalent and contradictory, even painful. Matters of such subjectivities – women's subjectivities in particular – have been discussed quite extensively in women's studies and feminist research. As Pulkkinen (1998: 230) observes, the search within different disciplines for what is often assumed to be a 'neutral subject' has in fact often uncovered a hegemonic 'male, Western, heterosexual, white, and middle-class' subject. Masculine domination is naturalized in the form of profound biologization. The 'superiority' is traced boldly on the masculine body.

The 'dead end' of empirical gender research

The last twenty or thirty years have seen an enormous amount of empirical and theoretical research produced on gender issues, especially on women and femininity. The starting point in all stages of research has been the observation that women and femininity are subordinated throughout society. Not until recently have serious discussions about masculinity and its role in society and personal identity appeared (e.g. Connell 1995). One can say that feminist research represents one of the most forceful and significant lines of scholarly inquiry in the social sciences of the last century. It has moved out of the margin on to center stage and can no longer be bypassed in any scientific discussion of gender. A number of different schools have grown out of this work which promote alternative views on the categories of woman, the feminine, gender, and gender relations. Feminist research has developed along a linear trajectory, moving from structural and egalitarian feminism through a gynocentric (female-centered) stage, to the post-structuralist stage (Anttonen 1997). The story is very similar to what has happened generally in cultural studies theory and research. Indeed, feminist research and cultural studies research are closely related. Both reflect a distinct turn from (male-dominated) normative scientific research, through anthropological debates, literary studies, and philosophically oriented deliberations.

The female-centered research stage – which was especially prevalent in the late 1970s and 1980s – highlighted the importance of women's shared experiences, which had been sidelined, to make 'women's culture' more visible and to acknowledge women's special competencies. The only way to reach the genuine sources of women's realities was to listen to the authentic voices of women themselves. Consequently, a sharp turn towards qualitative and ethnographic research was made. Cultural and media studies showed marked growth during this period, producing a large number of reception and audience studies where the accent was on popular media genres like soap operas and romance novels, and on processes of signification in media reception. Through their broadly ethnographic work, Ien Ang, Janice Radway, Charlotte Brunsdon, and Dorothy Hobson among others became important voices at this stage.

In the words of British scholar Charlotte Brunsdon reflecting on this stage of research:

> it is in relation to soap opera and audience that feminist critical work on television has made a distinctive contribution which is recognized as such in wider arena. In the late 1970s there began to spring up a

research tradition which re-evaluates traditional feminine genres and forms, like the women's picture, romantic fiction, the diary and the magazine, and either by implication or directly, investigates audience engagement. Soap opera, as a genre, including US prime-time shows as well as much more localized national serials, has moved from being a ridiculed object of study to a mainstay of many syllabuses.

(Brunsdon 1997: 190).

The Anglo-American research tradition introduced the term 'female genre'. On the one hand, the tradition wanted to make visible what had been suppressed. On the other hand it also tried to identify the distinctive feminine features of cultural products – links among women's empirical choices, the 'feminine essence', 'female space', and the 'feminine experience', for example.

But something has happened since the days of the groundbreaking ethnographic research and theorizing of the late 1970s and 1980s. Empirical work on women's cultural issues has receded into oblivion. As Angela McRobbie writes:

While there has been an enormous output of feminist poststructuralist writing of late, there has been some resistance to looking outside 'theory' and asking some practical questions about the world we live in. At every point the spectre of 'humanism' haunts the practise of those who align themselves with the 'anti-Es'. Ethnography? That truth-seeking activity reliant on the (often literary) narratives of exoticism and difference? Can't do it, except as a deconstructive exercise. Empiricism? The 'representation' of results, the narrative of numbers? Can't do it either, except as part of a critical genealogy of sociology and its role in the project of modernity and science. Experience? That cornerstone of human authenticity, that essential core of individuality, the spoken voice of evidence of being and the coincidence of consciousness with identity? Can't do it, other than as a psychoanalytic venture.

(McRobbie 1997: 170)

This quotation neatly captures the feelings of many researchers interested in gender issues, and in particular social scientists who do empirical research, including me. Many scholars who started their academic careers with great enthusiasm for women's studies have moved on to less philosophically troubled waters and more manageable research topics. Many scholars seem to feel now that it is impossible to say anything specific or concrete about gender without being labeled a hopelessly outdated essentialist. Even a young female university student can refuse to answer a question concerning women, claiming that it is impossible to answer because, after all, 'women don't exist' (a claim made recently by a University of Helsinki student). From this viewpoint, all empirical knowledge is said to be inherently contaminated, or said not to be legitimate knowledge in the first place. Unfortunately, such abstract philosophical claims have too often unproductively clouded empirical possibilities that could lead to policy discussions and social change that would benefit women (and men too).

The first empirical symbols to be attacked were numbers and statistics, which were said to distort women's 'real' reality. At that point some years ago it was argued that the only way to obtain true knowledge about women's experiences was to engage ethnography and various related qualitative empirical research methods. But quite soon, and located within broad discussions that questioned whether any common womanhood exists in the first place, ethnographic empiricism was also argued to be hopelessly contaminated.

The implications of this brief history are monumental, and by no means all positive. As Angela McRobbie correctly points out, the anti-empirical turn 'leaves us feminists who are concerned with the politics of culture high and dry when it comes to contributing to political debates outside the academy' (McRobbie 1997: 171). The 'dead end' in empirical research therefore comes at the end of a long road, and the 'politically correct' consequences of the anti-empirical movement will not be easy to overcome. This strict exclusion/inclusion mentality effectively inhibits free-flowing debate. Moreover, many empirically minded scholars now steer clear of women's research because they feel uncomfortable with the self-absorbed, overly poetic discussions that now dominate the debate. Such abstract discussions seem to many to be simply too far removed from the realities, and the possibilities, of the complex, undetermined, empirical world.

Feminists and ordinary women: research as powerful practise

Charlotte Brunsdon (1997) has productively explored the category of 'ordinary women' produced by feminist research. She distinguishes between categories of 'feminist' and 'ordinary woman' created by shifts in research on women and has constructed a three-part typology reflecting stages of this research: (1) *transparent* – no others; (2) *hegemonic* – non-feminist women others, and (3) *fragmented* – everyone an other.

Brunsdon describes the first stage (*transparent*) as utopian. There was a belief in a shared sisterhood of all women, in a common consciousness of women as a group subordinated by a global patriarchy and thus sharing gender-specific experiences.

The next relationship (*hegemonic*) is described by Brunsdon as the most common within her own sphere of interest – media criticism. She says that this stage can also be described as 'the impulse to transform the feminine identifications of women to feminist ones'. She continues, 'the construction of feminist identity through this relation involves the differentiation of the feminist from her other, the ordinary woman, the housewife, the woman she might have become, but at the same time, a compulsive engagement with this figure. The position is often profoundly contradictory, involving both the repudiation and defense of traditional femininity' (Brunsdon 1997: 194).

Brunsdon puts forward the interesting argument that 'well-intended' feminist research has arrested 'woman' into 'tradition'. But here we can really see how culture mediates not only gender, but academic discussions about it. The question one must ask here is, therefore, into *which tradition* has 'woman' been arrested by feminist research? I come from an environment, for example, where the 'ordinary woman' is definitively *not* a 'housewife'. And while women have been studied specifically as media audiences, and almost entirely as audiences for popular genres like soap operas, this intellectual history actually serves to anchor 'women' more firmly than ever to Western traditions. Ever since ancient Greece and early Christian times womanhood has been associated with passivity and the status of audience, while manhood is thought of in terms of activity and subjectivity.

Indeed, both these categories of 'ordinary woman' produced by feminist research – the transparent and the hegemonic – have been and should be criticized for their failure to take into account ethnic, sexual, cultural, and other differences among women.

Brunsdon labels the third stage of how women have been theorized by researchers as *fragmented*, 'because it is founded on the possibility that there is no necessary relationship between the first two categories'. At this stage, 'woman becomes a profoundly problematic category, and ironically "feminist" becomes rather more stable' (Brunsdon 1997: 196). The third stage is closely related to the postmodern and anti-essentialist critique, which reminds us not only that women are gendered but that other social and cultural differences among them (such as class and ethnicity) may be more significant. The critique stresses that knowledge is always situated and partial. Although 'a fragmented feminist identity' undoes the 'symbiotic' relationship between 'feminist' and 'woman', it is still threatened by a 'potential solipsis' (Brunsdon 1997: 198), referring to the very impossibility of empirical research discussed earlier.

International feminist research of course is closely interwoven with the evolution of the political feminist movement worldwide. But by creating the 'right' kind of view on womanhood, and in speaking up for the 'ordinary woman', feminism has produced a link between 'womanhood' and 'empirical women', and ultimately, through a critique of empirical research, has called into question the very possibility of knowing women.

Towards better understanding gender and culture

In many recent discussions gender is associated with sexual desire and its diverse objects, which is then represented by external symbols, especially by dress, and by a modifiable body. In these discussions notions of style and performativity are central. To extend the point somewhat, gendering easily appears as a performative role-playing game in which the roles can be constantly re-elected. Dress appears as an important marker of gender. Moya Lloyd (1999), for instance, argues (quoting Bell *et al.* 1994: 34–5) that the 'skinhead look' became 'fashionable in gay London' in the 1990s and evolved into 'one form of gay "uniform"'. It was not only a style of dress, but represented a politically affirmative way of life: 'the gay skinhead can be seen as a progressive identity' (Lloyd 1999: 199). Gender identities that challenge the heterosexual presumption seem to appear often as progressive and changeable fashion. In this use of gender, performativity and style are associated with identity politics and are connected to political action. Lloyd sees shortcomings in the concept of performativity, however, in that 'it is comprehensible primarily as an account of individuation: the historicity of a particular subject's construction as a gendered being . . . What is occluded, as a consequence, is the space within which performance occurs, the others involved in or implicated by the production, and how they receive and interpret what they see' (Lloyd 1999: 210).

Although the individual subject and the construction of individual identities is an important and interesting angle, even in the sense of identity politics it is also possible to take a broader view. I am specifically interested, therefore, in what may be described as *cultural gender*, a distinctive 'mode of being' (Veijola 1996). One can begin by asking a simple question: why is it that female- and male-appearing human beings tend to behave the way they do? This would be the most simple of sociological questions, perhaps, if gender were not embedded in a profoundly hierarchical relationship. 'Cultural womanhood', therefore, also comprises the cultural signs of womanhood, the repetition of these signs, and their consequences. Given the hegemonic and cultural coercion that inheres in these signs of womanhood, they can exercise a very cruel form of power over individuals and groups. But of course, that is not *all* they are.

Performativity and style are associated with much more than gendered identities. Many social scientists regard performativity and style as central features of postmodern, mediatized societies, and as parts of the current movement away from steady ways of life to more flexible and individualized lifestyles. Abercrombie and Longhurst (1998), for example, connect style and performativity with the 'diffuse audience' of contemporary media and society. Ronkainen (1999) uses the concept of style as an analytical tool to describe and explore 'cultural, contextual womanhood'. In this application, style coalesces the conscious identity – the subjectivity accumulated during the individual's lifetime in the shared culture. Sociologically, this seems to be a very interesting approach. Style as an analytical concept is extremely useful for uncovering contextual differences related to gender and culture (e.g. Hebdige 1979; McRobbie 1991, 1994; Lull 2000). It might be helpful for deconstructing the historical and contemporary contextuality of gender construction, for instance, or for highlighting the 'modes' of gender construction and reproduction in different cultures and social contexts. For many women, cultural images of gender – such as culture-specific views on women's mental endurance, their special competencies and inabilities, their great moral responsibilities, and their symbolic and social domains – could be more important indicators than the typical focus on sexuality and desire.

David Chaney's idea of 'sensibility' comes quite close to this. By sensibility he means 'a way of referring to a perceived affiliation for an identifiable group with, for instance, certain ideas, or values, or tastes in music, food, or dress. A shared sensibility is not mandatory for all members, and may . . . vary between genders within a particular community so that sensibilities play across other more established ways of life . . . The theme of sensibility is then another aspect of delineating identities' (Chaney 1996: 126).

Chaney refers to research reported by Csikszentmihalyi and Rochberg-Halton (1981). When asked to nominate their most cherished objects, 'Males mention significantly more TV, stereo sets, sports equipment, vehicles, and trophies. Females more often mention photographs, sculpture, plants, plates, glass, and textiles' (Csikszentmihalyi and Rochberg-Halton: 106). These gendered domains of media, popular culture, and everyday life are clearly very important in producing and maintaining gender traditions. Studies of cultural behavior in Brazil (Tufte 1999), Sweden (Jansson 1999), China (Lull 1991), and Finland (Liikkanen 1996b) all indicate that men tend to choose action, and sports-oriented activities, while women prefer different media genres – drama and music, for instance. Furthermore, it is easier for women to step over into male cultural domains than it is for males to enter the female cultural spheres.

More cultural sensitivity

Deconstructing the history of feminist and gender research, and how gender has been theorized, reveals its powerful contextualities and situatedness. International debates about women have always reflected a very strong Anglo-American bias, which in turn has influenced a great deal of theoretical and empirical work outside the United Kingdom and the United States. Indeed, to some extent Anglo-American feminist traditions have even colonized localities *inside* the Western hemisphere. This is especially true of feminist-oriented research undertaken in the fields of media and cultural studies.

However, as Angela McRobbie (1997) points out, major differences inside the Anglo-American world have also arisen. In her own British intellectual trajectory from the 1970s onward, the accent initially was on 'feminist material-ism'. McRobbie says that what is perhaps most relevant to later feminist cul-tural studies, however, is the fact that research combined a culturalist and materialist perspective, and was very much focused on 'the history and culture of working-class women and girls at home, in the community, in school, in leisure, and at work' (McRobbie 1997: 171). Comparing the various turns of feminist research, McRobbie argues that 'in the UK feminist intellectual work has grown out of a more socialist tradition. There has been much less concern to assert gender over and above class and race; instead the emphasis has been on thinking through these relations of difference' (McRobbie 1997: 175).

As the different debates drift from one country and culture to the next, they land in different intellectual fields of force; a critique that in its original context and discipline had a clearly identifiable target may suddenly lose that objective altogether. Within the Scandinavian and Finnish context, for example, hegemonic masculinity and femininity no doubt have created a story of gender relations that differs from those in the United States or Britain, though many hegemonic and less hegemonic femininities and masculinities exist in the Nordic region as well. And what about the relationship between center and margin; is that as clear as it used to be?

Feminist research arrived in Finland partly as a counterforce to Marxist structuralist research and was not directly attached to any political movement. To the contrary, it was specifically stressed that the feminist movement would be kept separate from women's studies, a turn of events which served to set feminism apart from the orthodox political Marxism of the 1970s. Feminist research in fact became depoliticized in Finland. Still, feminist media and cultural studies were imported to Finland and the other Nordic countries. The international debates concentrated mainly on forms of 'women's entertainment', which is not a big issue in the Nordic region, where women have been historically involved in cultural politics that carry a distinct ethos of enlightenment (Liikkanen 1996a and 1999). Womanhood and highbrow culture, manhood and popular culture, have gone hand and hand in Finland. High culture, however, does not signify only 'high-class culture' in Finland, and does not carry the same strong discriminatory meanings as it does in many other Western countries.

In the Nordic countries, then, feminist research on the use of media and culture helped deconstruct the literary, intellectual, highbrow atmosphere while it freed middle-class women, intellectual women, and feminists alike to enjoy and study popular culture without their having to feel guilty. However, this development did not produce an 'other' category of 'ordinary woman' as Charlotte Brunsdon claims took place in the Anglo-American context. In addition to enjoying 'female' media genres, Finnish women from all social classes read newspapers on a daily basis, follow news and information programs as often as men, read fiction and non-fiction to a far greater extent than men, don't watch much television overall, go out to the theater and other cultural events alone or with female friends, and constitute the majority of public audiences for cultural fare generally (Liikkanen 1996b, Eskola 1999). Certain public spaces traditionally have been more open to Finnish women than elsewhere.

There is a long tradition of gender neutrality in Finnish culture. It can be seen, for instance, in the Finnish language, which has just one non-gendered pronoun for 'she' or 'he.' Nouns likewise have no gender in Finnish, and the terms 'sex' and 'gender' are not differentiated. Several explanations have been offered for this egalitarian profile: a tradition of separate, equal, autonomous lifeworlds for women and men, the autonomic traditions of peasantry, the legacy system, welfare arrangements which offer a wide range of work opportunities for women, and the wake of the Enlightenment period are among them. Clearly, Nordic social structures and sex/gender systems differ greatly from Anglo-American traditions, and this greatly influences our understanding of 'woman', 'gender', and 'gender relations'.[1]

I do not believe in theories which proclaim deterministic, genetic explanations for differing female and male modes of thought and behavior. However, the gender system and the cultural memory of our bodies persists longer than we imagine. The cultural sphere where I come from – situated geographically as it is between East and West – draws its heritage from both sides. When I watch a television program on Karelian lamenters, or when I go to an exhibition on Siberian women shamans, for instance, deep memories are evoked in my body and I once again *know* that I belong not only to a Western but also to an ancient Eastern cultural circle of women (Apo 1999).

Perhaps we don't take seriously enough the power of the emotions and the mental pictures we produce. Through them perhaps we can better understand, after all, why things change so slowly, or how the gendered 'hierarchical iron cage' (Heiskanen and Rantalaiho 1997) intertwines so closely with the 'golden cages' of everyday life – our emotions and privacy.

In trying to understand the processes of 'doing gender', many different levels must be taken into consideration: the deep memory of culture, traditional cultural beliefs with their gendered, hierarchical dualities, formal gender structures that are visible in societal institutions (such as legal systems, the division of labor, and so on), and, of course, the wide variety of vital personal and micro-social contexts and experiences. And, too, it must be made clear that, in the era of globalization, cultural images of gender and gendered practises, like all culturally loaded representations, travel very fast and enter new surroundings with unpredictable results. All these cultural processes are negotiated thorough the matrices of human emotionality and rationality, and take empirical shape in the range of gendered social processes and choices that people make in the routine undertakings of their everyday lives.

Notes

Special thanks to Lotta Kratz, Liisa Rantalaiho, and Anna-Maija Lehto for very useful comments on previous drafts of this chapter, and to James Lull for his careful editing and support throughout the project.

1 A surprising fact, however, emerges from the Nordic countries. Despite the fact that Finland, Norway, Sweden, and Denmark have reached what many consider to be the world's highest standards of gender equality, occupational segregation is extremely high in the Nordic countries, and persists mightily today (Lehto 1999: 8). A gender hierarchy tends to be reproduced again and again in working life (Heiskanen and Rantalaiho 1997). Paradoxically, the national ideology of gender equality tends to

make the gender hierarchy more invisible. These structures and modes of being and doing things are deep-seated and extremely slow to change. The sociocultural site of all this gender work, of course, is *everyday life*, where the gendered modes of being are reproduced and broken through the most ordinary of communication practises (Liikkanen 1996b, Rantalaiho 1997).

References

Aaltonen, S. and Härkönen, R. (eds) (1999). 'Naisasiaa vai ei'. *Helsingin Sanomat*, Kuukausiliite, May.

Abercrombie, N. and Longhurst, B. (1998). *Audiences: A Sociological Theory of Imagination*. London, Thousand Oaks and New Delhi: Sage Publications.

Anttonen, A. (1997). *Feminismi ja sosiaalipolitiikka: Miten sukupuolesta tehtiin yhteiskunta-teoreettinen ja sosiaalipoliittinen avainkäsite.* Tampere: Tampere University Press.

Apo, S. (1999). *Women in Finland*. Helsinki: Otava Publishing Co. Ltd.

Bell, D., Binnie, J., Cream, J., and Valentine, G. (1994). 'All hyped up and no place to go'. *Gender, Place and Culture: A Journal of Feminist Geography*, 1 /1: 31–47.

Brunsdon, C. (1997). *Screen Tastes: Soap Opera to Satellite Dishes*. London: Routledge.

Chaney, D. (1996). *Lifestyles*. London: Routledge.

Connell, R. W. (1995). *Masculinities.* Berkeley, CA: University of California Press.

Csikszentmihalyi, M. and Rochberg-Halton, E. (1981). *The Meaning of Things: Domestic Symbols and the Self*. Cambridge: Cambridge University Press.

Eskola, K. (1999). 'Culture – the empowerment of women's lives'. In *Women in Finland*. Helsinki: Otava Publishing Co. Ltd.

Hebdige, D. (1979). *Subculture: The Meaning of Style*. London: Methuen.

Heiskanen, T. and Rantalaiho, L. (1997). 'Persistence and change of gendered practises'. In L. Rantalaiho and T. Heiskanen (eds), *Gendered Practices in Working Life*. London: Macmillan.

Jansson, A. (1999). *A Matter of Attitude – Outline to a Phenomenology of Media Culture*. Presented to the 14th Nordic Conference of Media and Communication Research, Kungälv, Sweden.

Lehto, A.-M. (1999). 'Women in working life in Finland'. In *Women in Finland*. Helsinki: Otava Publishing Co. Ltd.

Liikkanen, M. (1996a). 'Culture consumption in Finland: Distinctive characteristics'. *The Nordicom Review of Nordic Research on Media & Communication*. Special issue.

—— (1996b). *Culture Consumption and Leisure Meanings in Cultural Change of Society*. Licentiate dissertation. Department of Sociology, University of Helsinki.

—— (1998). 'Taideyleisöpuhe ja suomalaisuus'. In Pertti Alasuutari and Petri Ruuska (eds), *Elävänä Euroopassa: Muuttuva suomalainen identiteetti*. Tampere: Osuuskunta Vastapaino.

Liikkanen, R. (1999). 'Sosiologia on arjen taikureiden tiede'. *Helsingin Sanomat*. C6 (Kulttuuri). 10 May.

Lloyd, M. (1999). 'Performativity, parody, politics'. *Theory, Culture & Society* 16: 195–213.

Lull, J. (1991). *China Turned On: Television, Reform, and Resistance*. London: Routledge.

—— (2000). *Media, Communication, Culture: A Global Approach* (revised ed.). Cambridge: Polity Press; New York: Columbia University Press.

McRobbie, A. (1991). *Feminism and Youth Culture. From Jackie to Just Seventeen*. London: Macmillan.

McRobbie, A. (1994). *Postmodernism and Popular Culture*. London: Routledge.

McRobbie, A. (1997). 'The Es and anti-Es: New questions for feminism and cultural studies'. In M. Ferguson and P. Golding (eds), *Cultural Studies in Question*. London: Sage Publications.

Pulkkinen, T. (1998). *Postmoderni politiikan filosofia*. Tampere: Gaudeamus.

Rantalaiho, L. (1997). 'Contextualizing gender'. In L. Rantalaiho and T. Heiskanen (eds), *Gendered Practices in Working Life*. London: Macmillan.

Ronkainen, S. (1999). *Ajan ja paikan merkitsemät: Subjektiviteetti, tieto ja toimijuus.* Helsinki: Gaudeamus.

Tufte, T. (1999). *Gauchos going Global — Mobile Privatisation and Ritualized Media Use*. Presented to the 14th Nordic Conference of Media and Communication Research in Kungälv, Sweden.

Veijola, S. (1996). 'Naisen asema urheilussa: Kenkäsosiologisia ajatuksia sukupuolista, ruumiinkulttuureista ja yhteiskunnallisista olosuhteista 90-luvun Suomessa'. In *Piikkareilla pintaa syvemmältä*. Helsinki: Opetusministeriö.

Widerberg, K. (1995). *Kunskapens kön: Minnen, reflektioner och teori*. Stockholm: Norstedts Förlag, Falun: ScandBook AB.

6

CULTURAL FRONTS: TOWARDS A DIALOGICAL UNDERSTANDING OF CONTEMPORARY CULTURES

Jorge A. González

Every single day since birth we have been forced to situate ourselves inside a vast number of different discursive environments and social situations that touch what we consider necessary to 'live well', that help us construct the meaning of 'who we are', and that introduce and reinforce the 'common values' we share and pursue. As we produce material life in order to survive (food, housing, clothing), we also find ways to exist in the middle of an intricate, dynamic, and constant flow of social discourses. Some of these discourses come from professional organizations whose very job is to define, regulate, and concentrate the meanings of common needs, identities, and values considered worth achieving and preserving. These tendencies are the *centripetal forces* in society.

We will see through the *cultural fronts* approach, however, that what is considered and lived as normal, taken for granted, evident, given, truthful, and obvious at any one time should be understood as a collective, but provisory and momentary, symbolic order. This precarious arrangement and organization of meaning is always subject to endless symbolic organizational counter-flows between cultural institutions (for example, schools versus churches on sexual information; scientists versus journalists on 'objective' interpretations of events; 'good' physicians versus 'healers' on the treatment of a simple cold; 'true' artists versus 'popular' singers, and so on). This precarious order is also submitted (or should be!) to other kinds of counter-flows and definitions coming constantly from 'bottom-up', that is, material deployed from the unspecialized zones of everyday life. These counter-flows can be seen as *centrifugal* forces, which not only escape from the centralizing tendencies of institutions but take form as cultural dialogues that can eventually change the 'normal' definitions of life.

Among the most important consequences of modernity have been the processes in which institutional specialists in the symbolic elaboration of the world have appeared, changed, and sometimes disappeared. Through intense discursive work, these cultural institutions, their agents, and their practices have reshaped the meaning of the public sphere. But the craft of redefining public life (in a centripetal direction) never occurs without other influences. It has had to conquer a *symbolic occupied territory*, filled and threatened by competing centrifugal interpretations, in a constant struggle. The study of such cultural dynamics as cultural fronts permits us to know how our dearest commonalties and most beloved feelings have been created. Cultural fronts therefore opens up possibilities for understanding the development and construction of diverse modes of symbolic convergence and integration.

Hegemony and cultural fronts

When symbolic convergence and integration depend on the discursive work of a more or less allied social group, in social science we often say that we have a relative state of hegemony (Fossaert 1983). Whether active or passive, hegemony implies the recognition of authority and cultural legitimacy of a certain group. But the traditional concept of hegemony as it was used by V. I. Lenin in Russia, and later by Antonio Gramsci in Italy (González 1994), generally has been applied in a rather limited way and without sufficient theoretical and methodological connections to the experiences of everyday life; that is, without clear and plausible links to the forces that shape the concrete and actual meanings of our lives. Thus hegemony has remained a highly abstract concept. Typically it has been understood as something that happens at the macro-scale of the nation-state or the world system: all social classes fall under the command of a certain block of dominants. The concept often has been theorized to overlap with political domination and economic exploitation.

We need a less confining understanding of hegemony to serve us well. I'm thinking here more in terms of the way the concept is discussed by Stuart Hall (1979) and James Lull (1995, 2000), where hegemony is considered not a direct stimulation of thought or action but a framing of competing definitions of reality to fit within the dominant class's range.

This useful concept, hegemony, permits us to analyze how collective social agents have established historical and specific symbolic relationships with each other. Hegemony lets us identify the totality of relationships in society from a cultural perspective; that is, from the point of view of all the representations of the 'world' and 'life' that are skillfully elaborated, either by social institutions or by social agents, in an endless dialogical way. Because the tensional and dynamic construction of the common meanings that are created between ordering and dissipating social forces have not been well described, hegemony has been under-utilized or poorly utilized in empirical accounts of the very production of life (Bertaux 1977).

Cultural fronts: the fundamentally human formations at stake

Because of this poor implementation of hegemony in theory and research, the core role of a number of fundamentally human elements or transclass cultural formations has been neglected. What is missing, as the Italian anthropologist Alberto Cirese has brilliantly pointed out (1984), is a discussion of the plausible creation of diverse and expansive commonalties. Similarly, the space of position-taking in the search for 'distinction' (Bourdieu 1984) is established precisely from the actions of competing contestants operating on symbolic transclass formations. These fundamentally human elements should never be taken as immanent essences or as 'natural'. They all have been historically generated in relation to primary needs to survive as a biological species – feeding, housing, caring, loving, believing, eating, gendering, aging, trusting, honoring, and so on – and all of them have been generated and molded through the long term of history. Crucial contemporary issues like gender definition, ecology, economic development, and ethnicity have been shaped into discursive formations that are shared across social divisions: women have been subjugated mercilessly in every social stratum; ecological movements cannot be expanded as the exclusive property of any particular nation; economic policies over migration affect post-national realities, and so on. Transclass elements are constructed, not given, and owe their actual shape and symbolic existence to the tensional forces of different sociohistoric contingencies and contestants.

Hegemony is the name given to the *momentum*[1] of the objective relationships of forces that exist between different collective social agents (for example, classes, groups, regions, and nations) situated in a determined social space which we observe from a *symbolic* point of view – that is, where the creation and recreation of meanings take form in the enactment of all social relations.

I find myself more comfortable, therefore, not conceiving of hegemony as a negative given fact like a syndrome of class control or a cancer to extirpate. Instead, I believe we can create a dialogical understanding of our common symbolic existence if we ask questions about how, from where, and between whom specific relations of symbolic authority have been structured, deconstructed, and re-created across a specific history. By history I mean changes and movements that are prompted by social agency and symbolic force performed both by specialized cultural institutions (acting as centralizing or 'centripetal' strengths), and by networks of social agents (the dissipative or 'centrifugal' forces).

Viewed within this framework, no society can organize its everyday production of life without hegemony. Thought of in a positive way, we can study any society as an integrated, structured set of objective relationships that emphasizes symbolic interaction. The cultural fronts approach, therefore, should be considered a kind of methodological intervention that permits us to interrogate the totality of social relations from different but complementary points of view (Fossaert 1983). Following Fossaert's elaboration of three dimensions of Karl Marx's ideas, if we interrogate a society as a whole based on the way it produces economic value, then the representation of the totality of relations appears to be a system of exploitation. We can also analyze society in terms of the ways power is organized and exercised; then, the society will appear as a system of domination. Third, when we analyze society by focusing on how that society creates its ideologies as representations of the world, we observe the totality of structured social relationships as a system of hegemony. Moreover, economic value, power, and ideology are dimensions of all social relationships and should by no means be understood as isolated levels or crystallized stages. Gramsci's notion of hegemony (1975) in fact deals well with the specificity of this complex relation. He was clear that hegemony should not be mistaken for simple domination (González 1994: 21–53).

Because of its specific 'signicity' (Cirese 1984) and the implicit elementally human potential to create and recreate multiple possible worlds, hegemony should therefore *not* be necessarily linked in some rigid way to class domination and exploitation. The social relations of hegemony, unlike its dialectical relatives economic exploitation and political domination, imply not just two human components (exploited in one case, dominant in the other), but a triad of elements: the hegemonic (centralizing) pole, the subaltern (centralized) or subordinated pole, and the other (dissipative) possible element in the midst of an occupied symbolic territory.

In any hegemonic relationship the possibility always exists for a social agent to become no longer 'subordinated' when specific configurations of common meanings indicate that efficacy over this 'other' no longer exists. At the same time, the 'other' status opens a range of possible new configurations of meaning, still not yet 'hegemonic' (as another centralizing force), because it has not yet articulated the *collective will* of allied social agents or enemies around its symbolic framing enterprise (Gramsci 1975). Thus, we can think of hegemony productively as a framed space of possibilities, as an expansive space of multiple convergences. It should be noted in this regard that hegemony depends not only on the work of anticipation and elaboration, but also on the potential to articulate meanings and actions as centrifugal forces in strategies of social interpretation.

In contrast to crude explanations of social relations that are limited to discourses of political-economic exploitation and domination, hegemony can be built and destroyed only through communication.

Centralized order and reflexivity

Part of the symbolic efficacy of the sort of hegemony we actually know and experience resides in the fact that we don't know what we don't know (Maturana and Varela 1992). The opacity of our relations is mainly caused by a lack of self and social reflexivity. Acquiring reflexivity means to empower oneself, at least to the point where some significant degree of self-determination can be achieved. That is at least part of the reason why the study of contemporary culture through the cultural fronts approach can be useful, not only in terms of the creation of scientific knowledge but in grassroots terms of getting involved in the reflexive reconstruction of self and society.

Identity: always dialogical, always plural

Identity is a rather rigid concept frequently used by social theorists to describe the ways different symbolic universes are constructed and used. In the contemporary world, however, the complexity of systems of self-reference has increased enormously. Accordingly, I will address questions of 'identities' rather than 'identity'. Furthermore, it is the everyday experience of the structured social worlds that brings about differentiated and differentiating representations and perceptions of these increasingly multi-dimensional social worlds. Thus, we recognize and talk about ourselves as 'being part of' a number of imagined communities (Anderson 1983). For instance, a single person can feel 'Latino', 'Mexican-American', or just 'Mexican' depending on the kinds of complex cultural tools the person employs in a specific social context (Werscht 1998). The person may feel proudly Latino when Ricky Martin, Selena, or Carlos Santana is launched to the top of entertainment business by the media. The same person can also feel deeply touched as a Mexican-American in the midst of a demonstration against an anti-immigration law. That same individual may feel simply Mexican through family and *barrio* memories when eating enchiladas, drinking Corona beer, and 'listening' (singing, shouting, dancing, crying) at a massive live concert when Los Tigres del Norte performs 'El otro México' or 'Los Hijos de Hernández'.[2] This person certainly will never meet either the 'Latino Community' as a whole, or the 'Mexican-American minority' in person. But through contact with various cultural texts and complex narratives, a man or woman, boy or girl, can have the sensation – the deep feeling of being part of something bigger – in which he or she is included in one way or another.

The concepts of *cultural field* and *social network* will now be introduced to help understand the two main forces (order and chaos, centripetal and centrifugal energy) merging in those intertwined symbolic zones I call cultural fronts.

Facing plural identities: communication between cultural fields and social networks

We know that any kind of identity is constructed into a determined situation, and that any construction is a selection of traits that fit particular social situations. Beyond this, we must recognize that each situational construction has a trajectory; it is built up historically. Consequently, we have a very complex system of different 'we's' and 'others', of selfness and otherness. All these symbolic universes are constantly created and recreated with tremendous invested human energy. They are moving forces going in different directions. Their equilibria are precarious. Human behavior of all types is always linked with, and constructed in relation to, the material dimensions of these symbolic spaces which we can refer to as cultural fields:

> In analytic terms, a field may be defined as a network, or configuration, of objective relations between positions. These positions are object-ively defined, in their existence and in the determinations they impose upon their occupants, agents or institutions, by their present and poten-tial situation (situs) in the structure of distribution of species of power (or capital) whose possession commands access to the specific profits that are at stake in the field, as well as by their objective relation to other positions (domination, subordination, homology, etc.).
>
> (Bourdieu 1993: 97)

The cultural fields are wide; they must be understood as complex structures of relations connecting institutions, agents, and practices that have been divided into varieties of specialized discursive formations coinciding with the structured social division of labor.

The cultural fields always evolve into crucial dynamics with *social networks* in which non-ideological specialists – families, folk, common people – read, interpret, interact with, and negotiate any specialized discursive production. Furthermore, the resulting symbolic universes are always constructed in a dialogical way; specialized valenced vectors intercross with the discursive con-ditions of everyday life. For example, churches, schools, hospitals, museums, restaurants, dance halls, broadcasting organizations, and many other institutions play a strong role in shaping our very selves from birth. All these institutions operate not only as vectors in the construction of 'our selves' but also in the construction of 'our differences' with others. This increasingly complex world of subjective differences also becomes a site where plural identities are perpetu-ally constructed as systems of classification, and where attendant social practices take form.

But how can those very different and contradictory systems of classification be solidified, articulated, and merged? They can be shared only through com-munication. Since the beginning of the modern world, but especially since the advent of technologically mediated communication (Thompson 1995), cul-tural fields have been intertwined in a very specific kind of metasymbolic work. This process can be understood as a *second-order*, specialized, discursive, societal elaboration of pre-elaborated meanings.[3] It is only through symbolic work and elaboration that elementally human events (birth, death, feeding, healing, believing, expressing, amusing, learning, consuming, and so on) are labeled, narrated, and metabolized – symbolically 'centralized' from a socio-historical and skillful elaboration, designed precisely to conquer and occupy symbolically the semantic space of those deeply human events. This process of symbolic occupation involves both the quality and quantity of people whose space of possible meanings has been shaped and centralized around the particular definitions of a certain social group. We can find a good illustration of this in the work of Jane Tompkins (1985), for instance, who shows how stereotyped female characters and melodramatic plots in literature were designed to touch large audiences between the years 1790 and 1860. These are precisely the years of the formation of a national identity in the USA, embracing such central notions as independence and westward expansion. Tompkins brilliantly shows how sentimental novels of that period, such as *Uncle Tom's Cabin*, operated 'as a political enterprise, halfway between sermon and social theory, that both codifies and attempts to mold the values of its time' (Tompkins 1985: 126). This kind of literature was either not taken seriously or deplored by most literary critics, but it immediately appealed to thousands of readers. Instead of disappearing, it has endured for generations.

In such cases, all the specialized discursive vectors are in constant interaction with an infinite number of non-specialized discursive elaborations that together create and sustain the common social discourse. This dynamic interplay gives us our first sketch of the total social discourse of any society (Fossaert 1983). In order to understand this complexity, we can invoke the familiar example of any society's 'gross national product' – the sum of the total economic value produced by a population within a concrete nation-state. In a similar way, the total social discourse should be the 'sum' of the total symbolic value generated within the confines of a particular geo-human location. As we can imagine, it is endless, always in arborescence, and cannot be quantified. It looks infinite because it really is.

These constellations of objective differences and positions can be connected only via an intensive discursive production whose precarious equilibrium can be interpreted as the momentum of hegemony. However, I do not consider hegemony to be the sum of the circulating dominant ideology. Hegemony as considered here does not have a measurable, fixed, or deterministic character. Hegemonic consensus and all its junctures must be considered to be very unstable. Every situated hegemony is always subject to a variety of symbolic struggles in which various social agents – corporations, institutions, classes, groups – invest mightily in the hard work of discursive elaboration of possible links and commonalities. Those conflicted crossings of precarious equilibrium are what I call cultural fronts.

Cultural fronts can be used both as a theoretical construct in cultural studies and social science generally, and as a methodological strategy for making observable and understanding the complexity of symbolic power in everyday life. In order to understand this complexity, we need a complex approach. The study of a cultural front can be accomplished only by constructing multi-dimensional configurations of empirical information.

112

Borders and arenas: open concepts

The meaning of a 'cultural front' has itself been polysemic from the beginning. The term has been used mainly in Marxist lines of critical theory as a way to link political struggles with mass mobilization (Mattelart 1977). More recently, Michael Denning (1997) has studied in detail the proletarian avant-garde that shaped American culture in the wake of the General Strikes of 1934; the cultural front came of age in the labor movement, in New Deal art projects, and in the emerging media industries. New York University Press has launched a book series named 'cultural fronts' with the same radical commitment across a range of cultural issues (Nelson 1997; Linton 1998). As a theoretical tool, cultural fronts should therefore be understood as an open systemic concept. It cannot be applied separately from its relations within other theoretical constructions: hegemony, cultural field, social network, and so on. As Bourdieu points out, 'concepts have no definition other than systemic ones, and are designed to be put to work empirically in systematic fashion' (Bourdieu 1993: 96).

I use the term 'cultural fronts' to refer to some key ways for organizing such critical social analyzes. Variously located symbolic universes constantly produce 'borders', cultural boundaries that are determined by the objective positions of social agents. The borders must be considered as porous limits constructed under terms that represent and express the interests and strategies of various sociocultural formations and collective entities – nations, classes, groups, and regions.

Cultural fronts can be understood also as sites or struggling 'arenas', versions of which are constructed through elaborate discursive work which traces the dynamics of situated conflicts and tensions. For example, a regional sanctuary of Catholic devotion can be understood as a cultural front (González 1994: 97–157) because its physical space operates like a border between at least two ways of understanding and practising the Catholic religion. The cultural front is the arena in which popular religion – that of poor peasants and the urban proletariat – intertwines and mixes in micro spaces with the 'official' and 'legitimate' definitions of faith, deities, and saints that occupy the religious discourse of the field claimed by the upper socioeconomic classes and by the religious hierarchy. We can empirically document and describe that discursive co-existence as relatively peaceful, but at the same time traces of intensive and sometimes passionate cultural struggles emerge too. These spaces are the sites of symbolic struggles around the meaning of 'divine images' and their relationship with humans. We can find the same symbolic borders and arenas in the midst of a public ritual like a local celebration or feast. There, the 'regional identity' of an imagined community is created through the process of connecting and dismissing cultural traits as the public limits of 'amusement' are elaborated through discourses and practices that differ among social classes (González 1994: 185–225). We might also think of cultural fronts in terms of the crossover appeal of some television genres such as the Mexican soap operas (*telenovelas*), and the range of meanings that can be constructed over the same cultural experience of viewing (González 1998).

The transclass nature of cultural fronts

The work of cultural fronts thus consists of constantly defining and redefining what is constructed as socially shared meanings. Cultural fronts are transclass symbolic formations because they are by no means exclusive to any single portion of the society. Even more, they can potentially be shared across all social sectors and strata, groups and regions. Within this dynamic, communication-based process, what has to be constructed historically is the 'true' meaning of specific common needs for everybody.

Think, for instance, of the 'commonsense' need for technology like a truck, which is regarded as a basic tool to survive, as films like *Hands on a Hard Body* have shown us.[4] Trucks are transclass discursive concepts because inclusive identities are created over them ('We are Texans', 'Don't mess with Texas!'), as a number of bumper stickers and advertisements clearly remind outsiders and insiders of the Lone Star state, regardless of social differences. Trucks are transclass because, extending from their functional specificity, they have been elaborated to represent common values, like the meaning of 'democracy' and 'freedom' for all Americans, despite the wide range of political and religious differences that Americans actually have.

We can also substantiate the transclass nature of cultural fronts by looking critically at *Culture Wars*, an interesting book by James Hunter (1991). Departing from Gramsci's ideas about hegemony and the role of intellectuals in society, Hunter focuses on contemporary everyday battles for making sense of American institutions like family, art, education, law, and politics as key and conflictive issues for the moral definition of the nation. He focuses on a number of common issues that resonate with our concept of cultural fronts. For Hunter, the 'culture wars' that the United States is experiencing these days are linked to structural changes of modernity: in particular, the growth of people with higher education since 1960, and the strong competition between different religious and non-religious institutions for the establishment of moral authority. He also claims that contemporary (transclass) American culture wars represent the most important event since the Civil War for defining national identity: 'the culture wars intersect the lives of most Americans, even those who are or would like to be totally indifferent' (Hunter 1991: 50). Hunter identifies five sites of conflict at stake:

> this conflict has a decisive impact on the *family* – not just on the critical issues of reproduction and abortion but on a wide range of other issues such as the limits (if any) of legitimate sexuality, the public and private role of women, questions of child raising, and even the definition of

114

what constitutes a family in the first place. The cultural conflict concerns the structure and content of public *education* – how and what American children will learn. Also affected is the content of the popular *media* – from the films that are shown to the television shows that are aired to the books that are read and to the art that is exhibited. It has a critical effect on the conduct of *law* particularly in the ways in which Americans define rights – who should have them and who should not and with whose interests the state should be aligned. Not least, this cultural clash has tremendous consequences for electoral *politics*, the way in which Americans choose their leaders.

(Hunter 1991: 50–1; emphasis mine)

Those created symbolic configurations in the everyday social world engender different appropriations that help produce the construction of sets of different cultural 'selves'.

Entering the cultural fronts

Cultural fronts are multi-dimensional configurations produced within the dynamics of multiple historical changes and symbolic structures. These processes take place precisely at the vortex of a tense and uncertain equilibrium. We can use the case of the different readings and social uses of the liturgy in the class-divided religious behavior of Mexican Catholics to show how this works. Here, we see how contrasting, even directly opposite versions of the liturgy have undergone tremendous symbolic negotiations and changes over time. In sum, varying social agents have very different perceptions of what a religious practice should be. The upper classes and the Church hierarchy embrace a 'status justification' religion. At the same time, the lower classes and peasants are more likely to have strong feelings and expressions of their relationship with mighty powers that take the form of 'salvation religion', as the classical work of Max Weber has shown (1978). Both sides of the society share the same images and temples, but create very different meanings from the symbolism that characterizes the Catholic Church in Mexico. Such struggles over meaning represent the dynamics of one cultural front.

On the one hand cultural fronts are structural, making up a set of relationships. On the other hand cultural fronts constantly move, refract, and help produce a pot of boiling cultural conflicts and tensions. The tentative structure and order made up of multidirectional, non-linear flows and trajectories of meaning creates chaotic conditions. The stability of such constructed symbolic universes is constantly subject to the variable actions, interactions, and negotiations of many symbolic forces. We can think of a cultural front as a whirling space of motion that, once arrived at a critical bifurcation, suddenly crystallizes into recognizable, yet still unfixed, structures and semblances of symbolic order. In this scenario we can locate the particular sites of concrete cultural struggles.

Cultural fronts: sub-processes, processes, and meta-processes

We find tension, instability, and precarious order at different levels of analysis. Following the suggestions of Piaget and Garcia (1989), any cultural front can be established and studied at three levels. First, at the level of *sub-processes*, we have to describe the intra-object relations between each one of the front's own elements. Normally, this stage implies a thick description and phenomenological approach to the specificity of each component. For instance, an accurate description of the key spaces of interaction during a regional fair can satisfy this level. Or, in our study of the production of Mexican television soap operas (González 1998: 90–1), the intra-object level was concentrated in relations and activities of the production crews.

At the second level, the *processes*, we identify the inter-object relations that link components or elements. We enter this level only when we establish sets of differing relations between, for instance, the components of a regional fair (marketplace, expositions, ballroom, cockfighting arena, and so on). The level of processes in the soap opera study arrived when we established relations between all the production crews and the organizational structure of the broadcasting corporation, Televisa.

Finally, the highest level of complexity comes when we study the *meta-processes*, in which we have to establish the trans-object relations between our analytical components. Meta-processes can be interpreted as third-order relations, that is, relations concerning the meta-relations of phenomena. They actually operate as, and should be considered to be, contour conditions, or external perturbations, for second-level processes. That is why Piaget and Garcia (1989) use the expression 'trans-object relationships'. For example, the symbolic structures of the regional fairs interact with the cultural entertainment industries through icons, objects, artists, messages, and broadcasting practices. In the case of Mexican soap operas, the meta–process level is the structure of the field of entertainment and the world market of fiction. With these tools we can set forth very different levels of cultural conflagration and conflict: *intra*-cultural front (first-order relations), *inter*-cultural fronts (second-order relations between different cultural fronts), and *trans*-cultural fronts (third-order relations). That is what I mean by the systemic construction of cultural fronts as an analytical framework and methodological instrument.

Constructing cultural fronts: the methodological strategies

The kind of methodological strategy that complex social processes implies and merits is at the same time itself multiple. It includes the use of various research questions and techniques for an adequate construction of observables, and the employment of complementary methods of analysis for processing and handling the information in order to make our theoretical objectives plausible. The construction and analysis of any cultural front requires at least four kinds of information sources and a format that can facilitate analysis at the three levels specified above.

The first information source is *structural information*, regarding the multi-dimensionality of any social space. The second is *historical information*, mapping the different social trajectories of the various agents and strategies at play. The third kind of data needed for constructing a cultural fronts approach is *situational information*, which can be used to describe the ethnographic contexts in which the conflicts, struggles, and merging results are located in terms of time, space, and activities. The fourth type we need is directly *symbolic information*, requiring a social semiotic strategy that can make detailed descriptions of the located social construction of meaning in detail. Let me now elaborate on these entry points.

Structure

Any attempt to study the cultural dynamics of a given society as cultural fronts should be situated in a broad spectrum of objective social relations. 'Objective', in this sense, refers to the existence of different social relationships in a wide range that is independent of individual human will and knowledge: the structure beyond the social agent. These are by no means only economic relations. They are at the same time political and symbolic relationships resembling what the French ethnologist Marcel Mauss (1974) called a 'total social fact'. These relations are the philosophical principles and the practical bases for the configuration of any social space where we find different loci – positions, sites, or places. These loci are defined both by the relative distances between them and by the struggles between them. Any attitude, action, practice, or interaction depends, in principle, on the social position of the actors or the institution. The observation and description of any feature or characteristic of a social agent therefore must be related in a non-mechanistic way to these social relations.

Let's put forward a couple of examples here. It is because of their position in the subfield of popular music entertainment that the Mexican *ranchero* band, Los Tigres del Norte, sing certain kinds of songs, use particular traditional customs, and express a sort of easy, simple thinking in their television interviews. Once a cultural entity occupies a key position in the cultural field, the social forces that have been created 'talk', 'perform', and 'make sounds' through their individual actions. So, the recognized characteristics of (in this case) Los Tigres del Norte (lyrics, melodies, rhythms, and virtuoso playing of the accordion) lie beyond any individual thought or action of its individual members. Fame – the symbolic recognition of situated cultural properties for specific audiences – derives more from a structural position than from any 'freewill individuals'.

The same principle operates in the public behavior and performances of

Puerto Rican singing sensation Ricky Martin. Martin may or may not like *ranchero* music, but, because of his objective place in the field of entertainment, he will never sing or dance a *ranchero* song. Even the shape of band members' and singers' bodies and their techniques of self-presentation are not individual choices. If the biological Hernández brothers and their group (Los Tigres del Norte), or Enrique Martín Morales (Ricky Martin) never existed, another social agent would cover and occupy the structural position in which they are located. That agent would generate, cultivate, and show the properties created and required from the given structural position. Personal style or 'flavor', therefore, exists only if it is recognized within the strict limits of a given symbolic market. The market is the structure that gives or withdraws relative value to specific performances. Any given structure operates as a set of objective constraints, with or without the awareness of the social agent. We need to generate appropriate information about the structure and about the composition of the social space in which we wish to study particular cultural fronts. We can construct this information by using several techniques that help us identify and describe the social distribution of 'valid' resources operating in that specific field. We are already used to describing the structure and composition of the economic, social, and cultural 'capitals' at play (Bourdieu 1993). But we must keep in mind that capital is not a thing, but a social energy – an objective, active relationship. The dynamic quality of culture creates serious analytical problems with some theoretical approaches, for instance the 'culture wars' perspective of James Hunter (1991) mentioned earlier. Hunter locates very well the conflicts, attitudes, and performances of cultural contestants, but he doesn't offer the structural analysis we need to explore the processes and meta-processes of conflicts in modern societies.

History

Images produced by structural descriptions of social space should be understood as a point (or a momentary state) of a larger trajectory. That trajectory should be traced through a detailed historiography that is elaborated from a variety of documents and other sources. When possible, it should include oral testimonies (Bertaux and Thompson 1993).

From these sources we can trace and elaborate the long-term positional changes of the cultural elements, agents, places, and relationships we observe. That constructed history must *not* be understood as linear. The historical creation and re-creation of social settings can be delineated well only by analyzing multiple threads of social and cultural experiences. Following and reconstructing the long-term formation of cultural fronts gives us the perspective needed to understand the intertwined footprints, traces, and paths of the symbolic struggles and strategies that have converged and merged into 'normal' or commonly shared understandings of socially differentiated groups. The claim behind the cultural fronts approach is that what we experience today as obvious, taken for granted, normal, everlasting, and so on, derives tentatively from a series of cultural confrontations. These struggles can be located in how social agents 'in their own way' define and elaborate basic transclass elements: needs, identities, values. It is upon these fundamentally human elements (Cirese 1984; González 1994: 62), that meaning – shared commonly across social positions, but always unstable – is constructed. Only by interrogating historically specific cultural sites can we delineate in some detail the nature of this instability.

We can follow the sociocultural trajectory of the aforementioned Los Tigres del Norte or Ricky Martin, for instance, by moving from their actual positions backwards. We can see them as placed in different positions in the field, and we can get information regarding their entrance into the specialized social space of entertainment. Both Los Tigres and Martin necessarily had to learn their 'place' from their interactions with other situated agents. Thus, we find, for example, stories of their 'discovery' and the ways they began to gain media visibility, and from that point, we learn of the taste of large audiences. Good historiographies would also the trace the different stages of the musicans' physical transformations. In the case of Martin (Figure 6.1), this includes body-building in order to become more generally admired and sexually attractive. In the case of Los Tigres del Norte (Figure 6.2), they must achieve the stylized look of the folkloric *norteño*. They must really look like 'Mexicans'. To meet this structural requirement, the movements and bodies of Los Tigres

Figure 6.1 Ricky Martin (Max Becherer: San José Mercury News ©1999)

119

Figure 6.2 Los Tigres del Norte (by permission of Fonovisa)

don't have to fulfill the aesthetic design imposed on Ricky Martin or other performers of his genre. Here we can clearly see the constructed and edited image of these 'stars', and how the structure is sensitive to the tastes of their particular publics. The body building of Ricky Martin and his racial traits (a white, Caucasian look), as well as good organizational image management through public rituals and media events such as the Grammy Awards on television, made his 'discovery' possible. So, a specific structural momentum and an adequate launch platform permitted the kind of quantic spin of Martin's performance abilities to be valued from the still-marginalized Spanish market (that is, a specific dominated position in the global social space), to the 'big leagues', the global entertainment industry.[5]

Ricky Martin can transcend some constraints (voice, choreography, clothing, external appearance) that never would be structurally allowed to Los Tigres del Norte. The *ranchero* band has been formed historically and structurally to satisfy another taste, which is hard to swallow outside the structural position and properties they actually fulfill: the musical and aesthetic taste of lower social classes in Mexico and the same classes of Mexican immigrants living in the USA. The songs of Los Tigres have been formatted to follow a very long narrative tradition known as *corridos*. In that genre, lyrics are always sung in Spanish. They tell stories of the pain, suffering, discrimination, and pride of being Mexican in the truly difficult, marginalized position outside their home-land. For more than twenty years, the songs of Los Tigres del Norte have functioned as a memory reservoir for hundreds of thousands of poor Mexican immigrants – one of the lowest positions in the American socioeconomy (Trueba 1998). With only gradual transformations of their physical appearance, musical skills, and performances, Los Tigres del Norte, like Ricky Martin, are products of big cultural organizations. Sony Music is making very good profits in the global market from both. A large share of the total sales of 'Latin music' is linked to the growing buying power of the 'Latino community' in the USA. Los Tigres del Norte were in fact quite 'famous' long before Ricky Martin, but they still share one thing with him: they are famous in their respective dominated zones in the cultural field of popular music.

To help illustrate the point I am making here, I will now quote some readers' reactions to a *Time* magazine (24 May 1999) cover story about Ricky Martin and the Latino pop music explosion. First, two opinions from the 'top':

> I don't know about Martin's music (I'm a Mozartian), but it's nice for a change to see a pop singer who doesn't look as if he came out of a garbage dump.
>
> (Ray Damskey, California)

> I recall reading in *Time* about Bob Dylan, John Lennon, and other trend-setting singers, but somehow Martin just doesn't fit into the same class as these cultural icons. I saw Martin's 'break-through' per-formance at the Grammys and I found it repulsive. Is this where music is today? Can I become a musically successful by wearing tight clothes and dancing? I think we're being fooled.
>
> (Ben DuPriest, Atlanta)

And one from the 'bottom':

> Martin is an example of a person who persevered and worked hard to attain his dreams. But most important, he and singers Jennifer Lopez and Marc Anthony are examples of the duality of cultures that His-panic youngsters face every day as they grow up in a bilingual and bicultural environment. I'm glad that my kids have several role models.
>
> (Vivian Alejandro, Tucson)

Studying cultural fronts implies a search for and construction of successive changes and transformations of cultural agents and the modulating stakes of different positions they occupy over time. Construction of a cultural front can operate as a useful methodological strategy once we define the limits of the study. For instance, the focus could be the transformation of specific, localized musical tastes of Mexican immigrants into fandom for nationally renown artists for the lower classes all over Mexico. Or if we are interested in an even broader arena, we could study the reconstruction of different strategies for creation of a transnational icon extracted from the dominated cultural field of industrial entertainment that was made originally for the lower positions in the social space. Along both trajectories we could find a number of different struggles (at levels *intra*, *inter*, and *trans*) for the construction of a common symbolic platform in which all the social agents involved could recognize, at least in part, something of their own. When this higher level of organizing cultural meanings fails, however, we confront a critical shift of momentum in which the precarious equilibrium that defines some phase of hegemony is threatened and the possibility of change opens up structurally.

With these two first approaches – which resemble *genetic structuralism*, as Bourdieu has said – we must identify the space of objective relations that is largely independent of the consciousness and will of the agents (Bourdieu 1993). In the next two sections of this chapter – on situational and symbolic considerations – we will focus on the space of such position-takings. We will go first to everyday life in order to understand and describe the systems of classification and actions operating in specific social settings and public rituals, and then we will move to the symbolic specificity of cultural fronts.

Situation

Once we have studied the structural representations and historical trajectories that configure the processes we want to analyze as a cultural front, we have to deal with the quotidian circumstances and negotiations of a given situation, context, and interaction in which real social actors communicate and otherwise interact. This is the place where social actors and activities merge in specific, 'natural', everyday settings. As we have seen before, all these settings must be understood as components of a structure of relationships that take their actual forms through trajectories of historical change. However, by no means can the contexts in which different social actors produce different social activities be simply deduced from the structural organization of the social space. In order to study a cultural front in detail, we must locate specific social activities in a web of social coordinates (space, time, people, actions, goals). Such work can best be accomplished ethnographically (see, for example, Goffman 1967: 47–95; Mauss 1974; Spradley 1980; Babbie 1997: 202–30; Galindo 1998: 347–83; González 1998: 233–53; Werscht 1998; Jensen and Jankowski 1991; Lindlof 1995).

Descriptions of cultural contexts usually produce a number of observations that can be integrated into taxonomies through which we can make observable locally situated systems of classification from the 'insider's' or 'native's' point of view. Becoming crucial at this stage is the *second-order reflexivity* of the 'observer' who monitors the very production of his or her own observation (Maturana and Varela 1992). The cultural fronts approach thus intends to understand the creation of precarious consensus in complex societies in which the researcher participates as an active and skillful social agent, and not just as a non-intrusive subjective presence making 'clean' observations. So, for example, we can make several ethnographic descriptions in different settings that could lead us to catch slight nuances, or even explicit clashes, about what really 'good music' is and is not. We can observe live presentations, visit retail music stores, listen to schoolyard chats, attend to radio and television shows, study musicians' organizations, and watch bands and singers participating in various public rituals, for instance. Erving Goffman (1967) is among those who stressed the importance of societal rituals for the construction and social recognition of the self. It is the situational context that makes possible the construction and display of specific systems for classifying cultural phenomena in real and vivid confrontations (for instance, discriminating between the 'real' good performer Ricky Martin, and the 'evident' bad taste and poor musical abilities of Los Tigres del Norte).

We can observe also that in the case of the Catholic religion in Mexico, lower-class believers communicate in their own indigenized, ritualized ways with mighty entities like Sanjuanita or El Santo Señor de Chalma, while others affiliate with the higher powers of the Church – God, the saints, the virgin – by means of *ex voto* narrative paintings, discursive displays of 'god's grace' embraced sentimentally by the faithful (González 1990: 97–157). We can then compare religious practices of the popular classes such as these with the far more conventional actions performed and valorizations given by the upper classes and by the Church hierarchy responding to the 'commoners' traditional, naive, and irrational' practices. This way the upper classes differentiate themselves from 'low taste' and 'idolatrous misbehavior'. In situational analysis, we give analytical emphasis to multiple clashes of such rituals and narratives, showing and linking alternative identities with the pre-eminence of those that actually (that is, structurally and historically) control and manage the rules, spaces, objects, and collective icons (for instance, the sanctuaries).

The aim of the situational entry, therefore, is to identify the symbolic taxonomies[6] actually operating in natural settings and in public rituals where different social positions are expressed and confront mobilizing sociocultural resources and forces such as religious icons, musical genres, or communications technology. Here we can actually see how deep transclass factors like gender, race, and age shape the ways we experience fundamental human activities such as loving, caring, believing, healing, expressing, feeding, thinking, consuming, amusing, and being visible in society (Cirese 1984). Through a detailed elaboration in which several semiotic and discursive operations are made possible, these symbolic constructions can be designed, shaped, and modulated to cross over the limits imposed by social space positions and the class-originated *habitus*. The relationships which take form within these cultural performances make possible the 'social space of stances' (Bourdieu 1993), in which different cultural fronts are created, deployed, and eventually clash. In musical terms, for instance, these operations could imply modification of a style to appeal to a larger, more differentiated audience. This brings about the constant reshaping of complex symbolic forms (Thompson 1995) to anticipate a more expansive passive or active consensus. That consensus or ideological agreement is linked to a first-order elaboration, designed to evoke either passive or active recognition of an elaborated hierarchy of meanings and narratives as a more complex form of organizing and transmitting symbolic vectors across time and space.

The role of the public ritual as a cultural front in the construction of consensus narratives in this process has already been highlighted (White 1990, 1991) as key to understanding how hegemony works. In the contextualized study of the cultural fronts, therefore, we can identify various strategies to compose, limit, and occupy common symbolic territory by analyzing how social powers frame discourses. But we can also identify the polysemic portrayal of rhetorics which have the potential for diverse and even contradictory interpretations of the very same community of symbols. No exerted power can exist without multiple resistances, and, similarly, no discourse goes forward without counter-discourses. That takes us now to the symbolic dimension of the cultural fronts.

Symbolism

The study of cultural fronts must always be connected with historical and social determination, but at the same time it must resist any kind of reductionism. We are contemplating meaningful actors, actions, relationships, and processes, so we need to be able to describe in some detail the dynamics of how meanings take form in actual social settings and public rituals. Certainly we cannot deduce directly and mechanically any determination of meanings from structural and historical conditions. We must work in detail with the symbolic specificity that underlies and permeates the constant and complex discursive elaboration of experience. In fact, that specificity operates as a sort of *second reality*, as cultural semioticians sometimes say, but it is as real as the first-order reality of human beings. Any struggle or conflict in which we can locate structure, history, and contexts has its own symbolic specificity, and is in no way secondary. Symbolic specificity is thus crucial for understanding cultural fronts.

On the one hand, there is a complex structure of specialized organizations (cultural fields) occupied in the creation, preservation, and delivery of complex symbolic forms. Throughout world history these fields have produced their own specialists – priests, scientists, educators, philosophers, journalists, singers, painters, and many others. All these symbolic producers have supervised the creation and recreation of multiple specialized and complex discourses and practices known as religions, sciences, pedagogy, philosophies, journalism, arts, and so on. They have their own internal stakes, rules, and struggles to preserve or change, maintain or challenge, the specific relations that define a field. All cultural fields have a variable degree of autonomy with respect to other social constraints and meta-processes coming from the 'fields of power' (Bourdieu 1993). What Bourdieu calls a 'field of power' should be understood as an objective frame of meta-processes in which trans-object relations operate; that is, relations across all the different fields that establish, for certain periods, a type of hierarchy among them. So we can find 'trans-fields' levels of struggle for the exercise of symbolic power.

We must therefore understand the fields of power like the 'field of fields', a global social space in which every field and element occupies a position that is in constant tension. In order to preserve the fields and operate with maximum symbolic efficacy, each cultural institution must generate and maintain a public, an audience, a clientele, or followers over time. The audiences are placed, but arrive in constant motion, in a determined state of distribution and access to the specific social energy of this very field. The specialized institutions must be able to obtain and focus people's attention; that is their bio-time (Romano 1998). These institutions must design multiple, flexible, symbolic strategies to anticipate the potential audience for their productions (a book, song, sermon, news story, scientific paper, and so on). The core of these organizational strategies should always feature some discursive elaboration upon an elementally human theme. That way the public should be able to identify, select, and attend to the symbolic productions of the specialized agents. Thus we find ourselves to be 'Christians, fans, followers, amateurs, members, consumers, or militants'. This symbolic efficacy is then translated into *habitus* and into a kind of 'distributed self'. Clearly, nothing like pure individuality or isolated taste exists. Thinking this way, the non-subjective approach to subjectivity (Bourdieu 1993) can be reinforced with the notion of 'distributed cognition' (Salomon 1993), to create a productive dialogue with the neo-Vygotskian developments of the mind as action (Werscht 1998).

The ideological livelihood of modern societies implies, on the one hand, the specialized discursive elaboration of meaning by a set of specific institutions and agents, and, on the other hand, non-specialized social agents living in a pre-interpreted social world (Giddens 1989). The persistence and prevalence of large-scale discursive formations is constructed through a process of gaining and losing ideological efficacy. When a constructed symbolic configuration can no longer be part of our 'selves', that is, when it is no longer embodied in social agents, then a process of dilution and decay begins. This is the moment in which the elements of its composition can be disembedded, reordered, and reorganized around a different kind of symbolic and discursive axis. As human beings we cannot stop producing meanings. We are ourselves meaningful entities. We dwell not only in the material world but inside discursive, symbolic universes too.

This question of discourse, therefore, is crucial. Any discourse implies a tensional, specific composition of meaning. The specificity of that composition, however, is always linked to counter-compositions and counter-discourses that make up discursive social space, a kind of discursive market in which any entry generates, gains, or loses value. That is the space of position-taking. These processes occur as time passes through the actions of social agents, whether specialized or not. We thus need a social semiotic and discourse analysis to make observable the porous borders and symbolic confrontations that are constructed between different positions. The symbolic space created in between discursive elements should always be considered as an occupied territory. Mikhail Bakhtin has described these territories in linguistic and symbolic terms: 'Language is not a neutral medium that passes freely and easily into the private property of the speaker's intentions; it is populated – overpopulated – with the intentions of others' (Bakhtin 1996: 294).

Bakhtin's insight can be perfectly applied to a dialogical understanding of culture as well. Indeed, Bakhtin's seminal work and the dialogical influences it contributes to cultural fronts merit a full discussion that is not possible here. None the less, let me use some of Bakhtin's thinking to help explain the forces that are deeply embedded in our finest mediational tool for creating social worlds – language:

> Unitary language constitutes the theoretical expression of the historical processes of linguistic unification and centralization, an expression of the centripetal forces of language. A unitary language is not something given but is always in essence posited – and at every moment of its linguistic life it is opposed to the realities of heteroglossia. But at the same time it makes its real presence felt as a force for overcoming this heteroglossia, imposing specific limits to it, guaranteeing a certain maximum of mutual understanding and crystallizing into real, although still relative, unity – the unity of the reigning conversational (everyday) and literary language, 'correct' language.
>
> (Bakhtin 1996: 270)

We can approach the study of cultural fronts by analyzing different cultural 'voices' or languages ('cultural *heteroglossia*') that converge and clash in this precarious order, this 'unity' we call hegemony. To do so, we must reconstruct the detailed and conflictive history of symbolic confrontations, observing how 'legitimate' cultural fields ('literary language'), try to impose unity and order – the *centripetal* vectors and strength – in the middle of a multiple and chaotic space of dissipative social networks – the *centrifugal* forces (Figure 6.3).

The cognitive target of the cultural fronts is exactly that provisional unity, trajectory, and composition of symbolic social space generated in the clash of contradictory cultural forces. My claim is that through the detailed internal (*intra*) study of the construction of different cultural fronts, we can establish and identify a number of non-linear symbolic flows and fluctuations that create in other scales (*inter* and *trans*) the sort of dissipative structure of hegemony. From this perspective, hegemony can be understood as a complex attractor[7] of different forces that forms a structure that stays far from equilibrium. Originating in physics and the biological sciences, the idea of non-linear flows, fluctuations, and dissiptative structures is increasingly being applied in a number of domains

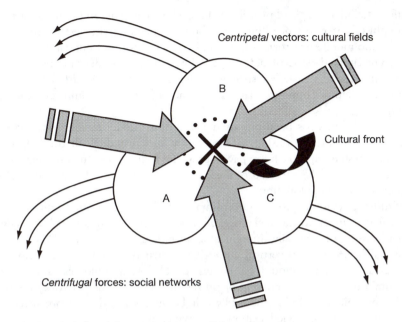

Figure 6.3 Cultural fronts as order out of chaos

like economics, sociology, anthropology, and linguistics because they are useful to describe and understand the dissipative structures that compose any relational framework (Prigogine 1984).

Conclusion: cultural fronts, grounded reflexivity, and empowerment

A key issue in the study of the cultural dynamics of modern societies is the construction of commonalities of meaning within disputed symbolic spaces between different social agents who are loaded with different skills and resources. Cultural fronts has been proposed as an open concept that rejects any positivistic definition, advocating instead a systemic understanding through interacting, differential levels of complexity. Each level needs its own kind of observables, understood as a relation established between *information* coming from the object and *meaning* coming from the subject. In order to analyze symbolic processes as cultural fronts, we must elaborate and deal with four different types of related observables: structural, historical, situational, and symbolic information.

Through these complementary configurations we can understand from a well-grounded standpoint that any possible common meanings can only be constructed from intense, contested, discursive elaborations of a variety of transclass cultural elements, or basic human themes, normally linked to needs, differential identities, and plausible values. These elements and themes must be thought of not as 'essences' but as symbolic occupied territories. Those meaningful and mobile territories can be understood as porous boundaries between different situated ways of defining possible common understandings. At the same time the territories are struggling arenas, even cultural battlefields, where diverse, sometimes opposite, elaborations and definitions of common meanings interact.

Cultural fronts has been proposed as a tool for understanding how, where, and when social relationships of hegemony are created. With the help of a dynamic systems approach, we have a powerful tool for the study of hegemony as a *space of possibilities* instead of a *negative fact* that is inevitably linked to class domination and exploitation.

Studying symbolic processes as cultural fronts has another important implication that is linked to the social organization for the generation of knowledge. Social research is typically thought of as an individualized, isolated task that is normally performed in vertical, authoritarian structures. That social definition of research activity should be contested. The methodological strategy of cultural fronts implies a different organization – a horizontal network in which different voices, abilities, and skills can be merged and auto-organized to produce reflexive knowledge about our own common sense.

For this reason, the cultural fronts approach suggests second-order reflexivity in the sense that, as the research project goes on, the research team can deeply ponder the relationship between observer and observed. Unlike a positivistic approach in which subject and object are to be kept separate, and where the project shouldn't be 'contaminated' with the subjectivity of the researcher, a cultural fronts approach deals squarely with the critical reflexivity of those who produce the knowledge (the research team or network). The process and results of the work can be used in action research as a critical tool for the empowerment of social agents and researchers. The very act of dismantling and making observable the trajectories, structures, contexts, and symbolic specificity of pre-constructed social meanings can be used as a tool for increasing the degree of our own self-determination.

One ongoing attempt to do what I am describing here is a national research project that is producing a system of cultural information in Mexico (*La Formación de las Ofertas Culturales y sus Públicos*: FOCYP). A group of researchers connected by information technology throughout Mexico is mapping the differential development of eight cultural fields in the country spanning the past hundred years. For us, perhaps even more important than the cultural knowledge this project is producing, is the creation of new, more democratic research communities, a dialogical reconstruction of Mexican people's collective memories, and a thoughtful reflection on our most beloved dreams and expectations (González 1997). The challenge therefore is to create a wider space for those who have been historically conquered, excluded, and expelled from their own symbolic territories to be able to reflect and confront, define and identify, that which they believe is dead and alive in their own culture. These are all steps along an infinite path of symbolic activity and dialogical reflexivity in which meaningful encounters with the 'other' are crucial. Indeed, a complex cultural attitude is surely needed as we navigate the turbulences of the Communication Age.

Notes

Special thanks to James Lull for his constant encouragement and extensive editorial work in Colima and California, and for procuring the photos of Ricky Martin and *Los Tigres del Norte*. Thanks also to Henry Trueba for his donation of space, time, and resources in support of this work.

1 I use 'momentum' (quantity of motion of a moving object) instead of 'state' (condition) to name such complex and mobile symbolic relations.
2 Los Tigres del Norte are probably the most important *ranchero* band, both in Mexico and the United States, mainly because of the traditional flavor of their music and lyrics, and because of the appropriation of the music by Mexican workers in the USA. Through their music, the lived experience of millions of Mexican immigrants has been elaborated into a musical narrative that has enormous appeal and meaning.
3 I use the expression 'second-order elaboration' to describe a more complex level of discursive work upon first-order interpretations of the world, all of them taken for granted, or *doxa* (Bourdieu 1993).
4 This film has been shown for a complete year in Austin, Texas.
5 Ricky Martin gained world visibility through a combination of public ritual and television, first in July 1998 when his song, ' La Copa de la Vida' was selected for the opening ceremony of the World Cup in France. His performance was well received (mainly in terms of economic profits), and he was invited to the Grammy Awards Ceremony in 1999 (another combination of public ritual and broadcasting), in which his song and style were received as 'fresh air'. Suddenly, 'Livin' the Vida Loca' became a big hit. Martin then went straight to the cover of various magazines and the most popular prime-time American television shows.
6 A taxonomy implies making explicit some principle of the hierarchization of relations and symbolic objects.
7 An 'attractor' is a concentration point in which all trajectories converge in equi-librium. The social relations of hegemony can be attracted as a complex attractor if the convergence point functions to draw and frame different trajectories of meaning as an ideological 'center' (see Coveney and Highfield 1996).

References

Anderson, B. (1983). *Imagined Communities: Reflections on the Origin and Spread of Nationalism*. London: Verso.
Babbie, E. (1997). *The Practice of Social Research*. Belmont: Wadsworth.
Bakhtin, M. (1996). *The Dialogical Imagination*. Austin: University of Texas Press.
Bertaux, D. (1977). *Destines Personnels et Structure de Classes. Pour une Critique de L'Anthroponomie Politique*. Paris: PUF.
Bertaux, D. and Thompson, P. (eds) (1993). *Between Generations: Family Models, Myths and Memories*. New York: Oxford University Press.

Bourdieu, P. (1984). *Distinction: A Social Critique of the Judgement of Taste.* Cambridge, MA: Harvard University Press.

—— (1993). *The Field of Cultural Production.* Cambridge: Polity Press.

Bourdieu, P. and Wacquant, L. (1992). *An Invitation to Reflexive Sociology.* Cambridge: Polity Press.

Cirese, A. M. (1977). *Oggetti, segni, musei.* Torino: Einaudi.

—— (1984). *Segnicitá, Fabrilitá, Procreazione: Appunti Etnoantropologici.* Roma: CISU.

Cole, M. (1993). 'A cultural-historical approach to distributed cognition'. In G. Salomon (1993).

Coveney, P. and Highfield, R. (1996). *Frontiers of Complexity.* Astoria, NY: Fawcett Book Group.

Denning, M. (1998). *Cultural Front: The Laboring of American Culture in the Twentieth Century.* London: Verso.

Durkheim, E. (1954). *The Elementary Forms of the Religious Life.* Illinois: Free Press.

Fossaert, R. (1983). *La société (VI). Les Structures Ideologiques.* Paris: Seuil.

Galindo, J. (1998). *Técnicas de Investigación en Sociedad, Cultura y Comunicación.* Mexico City: Pearson.

Giddens, A. (1989). *Las Nuevas Reglas del Metodo Sociológico.* Buenos Aires: Amorrortu.

Goffman, E. (1967). *Interaction Ritual. Essays on Face to Face Behaviour.* New York: Anchor.

González, J. (1994). *Mas(+) Cultura(s): Ensayos sobre Realidades Plurales.* Mexico City: CNCA.

—— (1996). *La cultura en Mexico City (I) Cifras clave.* Mexico City: Universidad de Colima y CNCA.

—— (1997). 'The willingness to weave: cultural analysis, cultural fronts and networks for the future'. *Media Development,* 44/1: 30–6.

—— (1998). *La Cofradía de las Emociones (in)Terminables. Miradas sobre Telenovelas en México.* Mexico City: Universidad de Guadalajara.

Gramsci, A. (1975). *Quaderni del Carcere.* Torino: Istituto Gramsci/Einaudi.

Hall, S. (1979). 'Culture, media and the "ideological effect" '. In J. Curran, M. Gurevitch, and J. Woolacott (eds), *Mass Communication and Society.* London: Hutchinson.

Hunter, J. (1991). *Culture Wars. Struggles to Define America.* New York: Basic Books.

Jensen, K. B. and Jankowski, N. (eds) (1991). *A Handbook of Qualitative Methodologies for Mass Communication Research.* London: Routledge.

Lindlof, T. (1995). *Qualitative Communication Research Methods.* Thousand Oaks, CA: Sage.

Linton, S. (1998). *Claiming Disability. Knowledge and Identity.* New York: New York University Press.

Lull, J. (1995, 2000). *Media, Communication, Culture.* Cambridge: Polity Press; New York: Columbia University Press.

Mattelart, A. (1977). *Frentes Culturales y Movilización de Masas.* Barcelona: Anagrama.

Maturana, H. and Varela, F. (1992). *The Tree of Knowledge: The Biological Roots of Human Understanding.* Boston: Shambhala.

Mauss, M. (1974). *Introducción a la Etnografía.* Madrid: Kairos.

Nelson, C. (1997). *Manifesto of a Tenured Radical.* New York: New York University Press.

Piaget, J. and Garcia, R. (1989). *Psychogenesis and the History of Science.* New York: Columbia University Press.

Prigogine, I. (1984). *Order out of Chaos.* New York: Constable.

Romano, V. (1998). *El Tiempo y el Espacio en la Comunicación: La Razón Pervertida.* Guipúzcoa, Spain: Argitaletxe.

Salomon, G. (ed.) (1993). *Distributed Cognitions: Psychological and Educational Considerations.* New York: Cambridge University Press.

Spradley, J. (1980). *Participant Observation.* New York: Holt, Reinhart and Winston.

Thompson, J. (1995). *The Media and Modernity: A Social Theory of the Media.* Cambridge: Polity Press.

Tompkins, J. (1985). *Sensational Designs. The Cultural Work of American Fiction, 1790–1860.* Oxford: Oxford University Press.

Trueba, E. (1998). *Latinos Unidos: From Cultural Diversity to the Politics of Solidarity.* Lanham and New York: Rowman and Littlefield.

Weber, M. (1978). *Economy and Society.* Berkeley: University of California Press.

Werscht, J. (1998). *Mind as Action.* New York: Oxford University Press.

White, R. (1990). 'Cultural analysis in communication for development: The role of cultural dramaturgy in the creation of a public sphere'. *Development,* 2, Journal of SID: 23–31.

White, R. (1991). 'Media reception theory: Emerging perspectives'. Paper presented in *Le program pluriannuel en sciences humaines* Rhône-Alpes: société et communication, Lyon, France.

7

SUPERCULTURE FOR THE COMMUNICATION AGE

James Lull

How can people find their way in a world where the stabilizing influence of culture as a communal project is being transformed into a far more symbolic, personalized panorama of images and dreams, fantasies and illusions, journeys and retreats? The historically unparalleled development of communications technology and the sweep of globalization that surrounds us today are changing the very nature and meaning of culture. Although 'community' remains a key characteristic, culture is becoming more an individualistic and highly discursive enterprise now. Moreover, cultural communities themselves are being formed in new ways, signaling a fundamental transformation of human experience. The empirical and imaginary space between the communal and the individual is precisely where much cultural work is undertaken in the Communication Age. A discussion of how that work is accomplished, and what some of the major consequences are, is the main purpose of this writing.

The focus of this chapter is a concept I call the superculture. As the name implies, the superculture transcends traditional categories of culture and cultural analysis. It continues to reflect culture as community, taking form even at the global level, but it is based primarily on the idea of culture as personal orientation and experience and on the dynamic ways that meaningful social interaction, activities, and identities are constructed by people through contemporary modes, codes, and processes of human communication. Supercultures are customized clusters, grids, and networks of personal relevance – intricate cultural multiplexes that promote self-understanding, belonging, and identity while they grant opportunities for personal growth, pleasure, and social influence.

The superculture is the cultural matrix that individuals create for themselves in a world where access to 'distant' cultural resources has expanded enormously. At the same time, however, the superculture embodies traditional or 'close' cultural resources too – the values and social practices characteristic of 'local' cultures as they are learned and reproduced by individuals and groups. The essence of the superculture resides in the dynamic interfaces that link and mediate the available cultural spheres. People today routinely fuse the near with the far, the traditional with the new, and the relatively unmediated with the multimediated, to create expansive material and discursive worlds that transform life experience and radically reconfigure the meaning of cultural space.

The global explosion of symbolic forms makes patterns of cultural thought and behavior much more fragmented and generative than integrated and limiting, and the role of individual persons in shaping cultural styles and patterns more original and labor-intensive than ever before. Individual persons today no longer live in all-embracing, 'full-time' cultures (of course they never did in any complete sense); instead they invent multiple, simultaneous, 'part-time' polycultural composites made up of accessible cultural resources in order to construct their impermanent 'parallel lives' (Tomlinson 1999: 169). The superculture in some respects resembles what David Chaney refers to in Chapter 4 as 'lifestyle' (a 'repertoire of styles' and 'constellation of tastes') that is driven more and more by global commercial forces and a rapidly increasing consumerist mentality, rather than the more encompassing 'ways of life', which typify culture in far more static and provincial terms.

Why 'superculture'?

By modifying 'culture' with 'super' I hope to capture the magnitude, freshness, and uniqueness of current developments. There are related precedents in cultural theory. Some years ago Michael Real applied the term 'super' not to culture but to mass media (Real 1989). Real wanted to stress the extraordinary influence of media and popular culture in cultural analysis at the very time when information technology, the Internet, and personal communication devices were just beginning to pervade American society. According to Real, 'super' can refer to 'the position of a thing physically above or on top of another', can indicate 'a thing's higher rank, quality, amount, or degree', and can also mean 'the highest degree, in excess of a norm, as in superabundant' (Real 1989: 18). Like super media, superculture refers to a cultural mode that is above other modes, has a higher rank, quality, and abundance than is reflected in other conceptions of culture, and certainly exceeds the norms which typify and limit traditional ways of thinking about culture. Moreover, supercultures are composed in part of symbolic content that is made available by super media.

Superculture also fits well theoretically with what the French anthropologist Marc Augé calls 'supermodernity' (1995). In contrast to the more concrete, material contours of late modernity, supermodernity refers to an era in social history characterized by generic 'non places' such as ATM machines, international airports, high-speed trains, and supermarkets more than the '"anthropological places" of the organically social' (see Tomlinson 1999: 109). Supercultures embody features from this seemingly anonymous 'supermodern' world, and from cultural debris scattered about in what is often called the 'postmodern' world, but they are also made up of more enduring, substantive cultural traits and traditions.

Superculture also corresponds closely with what Manuel Castells calls a 'supertext'. In his discussion of 'the network society', Castells uses the expression 'supertext' to refer to hybrid symbolic products that are created through the reflexive mixing of various 'realities' by 'blending in the same discourse . . . messages emitted from [various] levels of existence' (Castells 1996: 373). Castells employs an extended example from American commercial television to demonstrate how supertexts are routinely produced industrially by folding various cultural fragments and narratives into media productions. The example he uses is the famous *Murphy Brown* episode where a videotaped segment of former Vice President Dan Quayle's criticism of the show's controversial and well-publicized story development (lead actress Candice Bergen was about to become an unwed mother) was itself edited into an upcoming installment of the program. This visual and narrative blending of 'reality' and fiction produced a supertext – 'a new text of the real and the imaginary . . . from [different] levels of experience' (Castells 1996: 373). Sophisticated technology and creative editing techniques make such cultural sampling and fusions possible. The scene in the film *Forrest Gump* where Tom Hanks shakes hands with deceased former US president Lyndon Johnson, or the routine recycling of television commercials and pop music oldies into contemporary hip-hop music are other kinds of supertexts. Such syntheses have become commonplace in media production.

These striking examples of media mixing and matching reveal once again how symbolic resources can be used in very creative ways. But we must not restrict our understanding of cultural invention to the world of industrial pop culture production. Ordinary people from all walks of life regularly and skillfully infuse their relatively unmediated cultural worlds with far more 'distant' (novel, mediated, symbolic) cultural resources to shape the multiple trajectories of their daily lives. These creative exercises produce positive outcomes for their 'authors'. They represent complex cultural applications of 'symbolic power' (Thompson 1995; Lull 2000). Thus, if we redirect our theoretical emphasis from text to context, from symbolic forms in and of themselves to processes of cultural construction, we can move productively from the semiotic sphere of symbolic representation to the more theoretically rich contexts and contingencies of everyday life.

Technology and cultural programming

'The fact that people aren't only empowered to make music, but to publish it and broadcast it almost instantly is just tremendous . . . this democratization of the whole pop-star process is a healthy thing' (recording artist and software pioneer Thomas Dolby commenting on how computers and the Internet make it possible for anyone to make and distribute music globally).

Although the Internet revolution contributes enormously to the construction of contemporary supercultures and will be a main focus of this chapter, the trends that underlie the superculture have been shaping up for quite some time. The explosion in the 1970s in the United States (and later around the world) of cable television and videocassette recorders, the advent of the remote control device, and the quickly growing popularity of direct broadcast satellite systems all work together to expand tremendously the number and range of program options and their cultural content, encouraging people to customize their media experiences according to their individual interests and tastes. User control has also increased through zipping, zapping, grazing, blocking, time-shifting, and the like. In addition, the marketplace success of the audio compact disc and the digital video disc, digital still and video cameras, personal communications gadgets such as fax machines, telephone answering machines, beepers and mobile phones, portable music systems, palm pilots, and digital planners have all helped prepare the ground for a radical transformation of culture by giving individuals more control over the way they communicate and construct routine experience. In Silicon Valley parlance, the flow of today's technologically mediated interaction now emphasizes 'pull' (by consumers from information sources) more than 'push' (by information sources on to consumers). The ensemble of expanded options and consumer-friendly communications devices further interacts with the monster of the midway – the personal computer, and all its attendant hardware, software, and connectivity. Contemporary communications media further converge in the form of multimedia configurations, integrated home entertainment centers, WebTV systems, mobile communications apparatuses, and microcomputer networks of various kinds.

The technological revolution is characterized overall by modular integration, miniaturization, interactivity, portability, utility, multipurposivity, increasing user-friendliness, commercialization, and relative affordability. Because of their widespread attractiveness, abundant and diverse symbolic content, and ease of use, new media technologies help change the locus of 'cultural programming' from institutional sources of information and entertainment to individual persons, small groups, and growing numbers of 'virtual cultures'. Doing so, the very nature of contemporary communication and culture is being transformed so that complex cultural decision-making and communications multi-tasking have become routine human activities. Such developments render absurd any idea of culture as a monolithic force that acts on people or somehow 'programs' their minds (Hofstede 1984). Moreover, because of the strong decentralizing tendencies of contemporary cultural life, and the increasingly evident role of new media in everyday life, we certainly can no longer think of 'media audiences' in traditional ways either. The technological and symbolic conditions that give rise to supercultural construction emphasize the motivated ambitions of people as initiators and creators of cultural experience through communication processes, not some notion of 'passive' or even 'active' receivers. The person himself or herself is now a 'cultural programmer' (Lull 2000: 268) rather than just a 'cultural member', 'audience member', or 'consumer'. For this reason, social science research traditions in mass communication and media studies such as 'direct effects' or 'cultivation' have been mightily relativized by the recent trends in technology and society.[1]

The global divide

Constructing a robust superculture presumes the abundant availability of symbolic forms that can be appropriated and orchestrated as cultural resources. Such cultural activity requires 'complex connectivity' (Tomlinson 1999) in order to access the 'multidimensional circuits' of communication and culture (Castells 1996: 371). But because access to technology and to symbolic resources is by no means distributed equally across social groups in any nation, or across national cultures on a global scale, supercultural construction does not take form in any uniform or egalitarian way. Consequently, cultural construction in the global context continues to sort human beings into categories of extreme difference related to social class, race, age, gender, and country – a tendency that was of course well in place long before the current era.

What has changed is that people and symbolic forms move about today as never before in an atmosphere that is nourished and accelerated by the spectacular, irreversible explosion of mass and micro communication technology and, for the economically (and therefore culturally) privileged – the international middle class – by convenient, relatively unregulated access to constantly multiplying sources of information and emotional stimulation – an expanded array of cultural resources. As available symbolic universes become more robust and extreme, so navigation, experimentation, and symbolic creativity – the keys to contemporary cultural construction – increase greatly. People combine local cultural traditions and practises with the pertinent and attractive fields of more distant cultural information to which they have access – the cultural 'galleries', 'malls', or 'supermarkets', we might call them to reflect their predominantly commercial nature – in order to construct their signature, customized cultural hybrids – their supercultures.

Connectivity and community

People don't do all this just for fun. I am not just talking here about 'surfing the Net', for instance, as a hobby or simple pastime, although 'cultural surfing' is not a bad metaphor for what's going on. Supercultural construction underscores the ability of human beings to transform the mundane cultural worlds they inherit through birth and physical presence in particular locales of time and space in order to explore the unknown, and to overcome limits while creating new modes of personal stability and belonging. Indeed, the construction of a superculture is a contemporary way to organize cultural elements into patterns that help people make sense, manage their lives, and feel more secure. The interplay between varying levels of cultural 'reality' becomes the core of cultural activity. Technologically mediated 'distant' cultural impulses are integrated into more physically 'close' cultural scenes and situations through supercultural construction in order to gratify fundamental human needs, particularly the emotional and expressive necessities.

Life for many members of the international middle class at the outset of the third millennium is characterized by short-term jobs, changing partners and families, anonymous neighborhoods, throwaway material goods, and societies that feature constant distractions and sensations, promises of pleasure, and opportunities for immediate personal gratification. Although supercultural construction clearly contributes in some ways to such impermanence and hedonism, it does more than that. The 'networking of cultural practices and experiences across the world' (Tomlinson 1999: 71) may not create a McLuhanesque global village, but the transition to imagined cultural collectivities and discourses attracts and pleases people, especially computer-literate young people who generally construct the most complex and technologically sophisticated supercultures. The superculture's creativity, hybridity, and interactivity open up possibilities for establishing, maintaining, and linking meaningful 'virtual cultural communities', and for inventing and managing other new encounters and mediations in ways that are positive and productive (Martín-Barbero 1997). The new technologies have indeed transformed the way we create and communicate (Johnson 1997).

Symbolic variety and cultural discursivity

The concept of the superculture is based on the central idea that culture is symbolic and synthetic, and that contemporary syntheses today can be constructed from symbolic and material resources that originate almost anywhere on Earth. In this regard, one crucial point must be stressed: the discursive qualities of contemporary culture have become central components of cultural construction. This doesn't mean that the foundational axes of social interaction and organization have become less important, authentic, or intimate, however. As John Tomlinson points out, 'The point is to think of tele-mediated [or computer-mediated] intimacy not as a shortfall from the fullness of presence, but as a different *order* of closeness, not replacing (or failing to replace) embodied intimacy, but increasingly integrated with it in everyday lived experience' (Tomlinson 1999: 165; inserts mine). Likewise, the respected and still-meaningful term 'culture' persists in the nomenclature used here in order to avoid fetishizing or diminishing the sociopolitical significance of diverse, historically situated human experience. The concept of the superculture simply reframes common understandings of culture to fit the current era better. Moreover, because customized supercultures draw from the rich, distinctive discursive features of traditional cultures, they often help preserve those mythical ways of life as celebrated, visible dimensions of the new hybrids.

Just as technological trends in electronic communications have been developing since the end of the nineteenth century, the principle of creative cultural synthesis likewise long predates the current era. Cultural construction has always involved material and symbolic melding and mediation. A basic premise of the superculture is that today the fundamental nature of this synthetic cultural construction operates with far greater symbolic variety and much more speed than ever before. As we know, mass and micro media communications technologies and the distributive capacity and reach of globalized economies are at the heart of this dramatic elevation of cultural complexity and movement. The challenge for people today is to navigate and combine an unprecedented range of cultural territories and resources ranging from relatively unfamiliar terrain imported to the self through technological mediations and human migrations of various types, to territory that is far more familiar and stable, such as that offered by religion, nation, and family, in order to invent combinations that satisfy individuals' changing needs and preferences. Because culture is largely symbolic, and is therefore open to unlimited possible interpretations and uses, and because culture and cultural identity are so intimately connected to the human imagination, the actual physical origins of cultural information have become less obvious but also less important.

The consequences of this transformation are profound. Traditional power agents such as Church and state suffer an unprecedented challenge to their cultural and political authority because the nature of modern technologies decentralizes sources of cultural information, and the symbolic forms which circulate today can easily be reproduced, edited, and retransmitted in ways that provoke a range of possible interpretations and ideological conversions. At the same time, various forms of popular culture rise to unprecedented levels of exposure and influence, a tendency which further disrupts and relativizes the hegemony of more traditional, institutionalized varieties of political, economic, and cultural power (Thompson 1995; Lull 2000).

The cultural spheres

Supercultures draw from the entire range of cultural resources, including universal values and imported international materials, civilizational and national cultures, and the more geographically proximate regional influences and local circumstances that make up the most mundane features of everyday life (see Figure 7.1). In the discussion which follows, I will concentrate on the discursive relevance of the more 'distant' resources for supercultural construction – universal values, international media, civilizations, and nations.

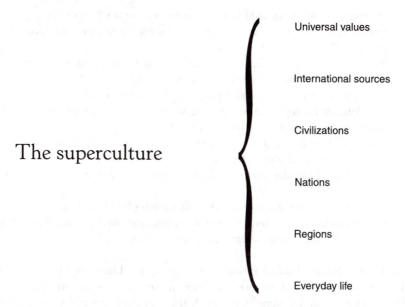

The superculture

Universal values

International sources

Civilizations

Nations

Regions

Everyday life

Figure 7.1 The superculture

Universal values

'We may have different religions, different languages, different colored skins, but we all belong to one human race. We all share the same basic values'.

Kofi Annan, General Secretary of the United Nations (Annan 1998)

Annan's claim that we all share the same basic values can easily be criticized, but that obvious gesture would obscure an important point: discursively the notion of universal values has considerable currency. Universalist discourses represent the first cultural sphere to be considered here in our brief presentation of the superculture.

The very idea of universal values was codified in the Universal Declaration of Human Rights adopted by the UN General Assembly in 1948. That document speaks of the 'equal and inalienable rights of all members of the human family' and prescribes 'a common standard of achievement for all peoples and all nations' (Office of the United Nations High Commissioner for Human Rights 2000: 1). The Declaration contains thirty articles. Among the 'universal' assumptions and rights prescribed by the United Nations relevant to this cultural analysis are the following:

- All human beings are born free and equal (Article 1).
- Everyone has the right to life, liberty, and security of the person (Article 3).
- No slavery (Article 4), torture, inhuman, or degrading treatment (Article 5).

- Everyone to be recognized as a person before the law (Article 6).
- No arbitrary interference with privacy, family, home, or correspondence (Article 12).
- Right to marry with free and full consent of intending spouses; family is natural and fundamental group unit of society (Article 16).
- Everyone has the right to own property alone (Article 17).
- Freedom of thought, conscience, religion, opinion, expression, peaceful assembly, and association (Articles 18–20).
- Everyone has the right to work, and to free choice of employment, and equal pay for equal work (Article 23).
- All people have the right to leisure and adequate standard of living (Article 25).
- Everyone has the right to basic, free education (Article 26).
- All the world's people have the right to participate in the cultural life of the community, including the arts and sciences (Article 27).

The United Nations' stated intention for issuing the Universal Declaration of Human Rights is to promote freedom, justice, and peace in the world. Whether or not global compliance with the requirements of the Declaration would achieve such objectives cannot be said with confidence. In fact the Declaration – with its explicit emphasis on marriage, family, property ownership, individuality, freedom, rule of law, even the right to leisure – reads like a laundry list of basic Western, middle-class, heterosexual values and lifestyles.

With the United Nations organization as its high-profile launching mechanism and public relations arm, news of the Universal Declaration of Human Rights has traveled widely and entered the consciousness of many people in most parts of the world over the years. How the document has been interpreted and acted upon by diverse populations, though, is by no means uniform. In fact, the universalist moral posturing of the United Nations is frequently considered to be little more than a tool of American-led, Western global hegemony. Many Westerners themselves tend to be blind to or not interested in what's happening globally, however. As the American political scientist Samuel P. Huntington points out:

> The West, and especially the United States . . . believe that non-Western peoples should commit themselves to the Western values of democracy, free markets, limited government, human rights, individualism, [and] the rule of law . . . the dominant attitude toward [these values] in non-Western cultures ranges from widespread skepticism to intense opposition. What is universalism to the West is imperialism to the rest.
> (Huntington 1996: 184)

Universalism, it seems, is hardly universal. It emerges from a partisan political-economic space, promotes some values and interests over others, and is put to work discursively in global politics, especially foreign policy discussions. Within those political discourses universalism has even been appropriated by the West in a quasi-religious way. Former American President George Bush claimed to speak on behalf of the entire global population in the early 1990s, for instance, when he referred to a post-Cold-War 'new world order' in defense of his military intervention in Iraq. In a world of 'shared principles', Bush told the American public in his 1991 State of the Union address, 'America has selflessly confronted evil for the sake of good in a land so far away'. Universalist discourses have become a stamp of American political imaging, a strategy that tries to mainstream global consciousness into an American perspective. For example, former President Bill Clinton told a televised gathering at Beijing University in 1998 that the right to free expression, association, and religion 'are not American rights or European rights or developed world rights . . . these are the birthrights of people everywhere'. The triumph of global capitalism over communism in the late twentieth century is often said to validate the belief that Western values are universal, or at least they should be.

We need not further berate American foreign policy (though that's never a completely bad idea). In practise, 'universal values' will never materialize as globally standardized cultural values. They will however remain highly visible discursive themes. Mass media play a crucial role. The widespread visibility of universalist themes derives in considerable measure from the fact that (mainly Western) international news media create stories that are framed around a sensationalized moral tension concerning abuses of 'human rights', the best example of which may be the persistent accusations of the People's Republic of China. Organizations such as Amnesty International help to arrange the agenda for news coverage of such stories, perhaps most famously the reports about the plight of the indigenous population in Chiapas, Mexico.

Human rights may be the most visible of the universal domains, but people also have a sense of shared standards of aesthetics and physical beauty, of basic sexual and survival needs, and of common forms of emotion and expression. Media play a major role in bringing these rather abstract commonalities out too. In his cautiously optimistic assessment of television's influence on culture, for example, Ulf Hannerz points out that 'the sight of starving children in Ethiopia, or of victims of a grenade thrown into a Sarajevo market . . . seems capable of provoking a kind of electronic empathy, a view of the other which has more to do with notions of shared human nature than with cultivated differences' (Hannerz 1996: 121).

Universalism is itself not a cultural effect, result, or conclusion but a process of global recognition that resonates with the ideologies and cultural values of major societal institutions – religious organizations, political treaties, national constitutions, and the international mass media among them. What matters in construction of the superculture is the discursive presence of the universal cultural themes, not any pretense of essential truth or global consensus. Universal themes enter human experience discursively where they encourage reflection and evaluation, and symbolically represent real human concerns as part of the cultural imagination. The pivotal role of media in such processes will now be explored in greater detail.

International cultural imagery

'We live in a time of fractures and heterogeneity, of segmentations inside each nation and of fluid communications with transnational orders of information, style, and knowledge. In the middle of this heterogeneity we find codes that unify us, or at least permit us to understand ourselves . . . these codes are less and less of ethnicity, class, or the nation into which we were born'.

(García Canclini 1995: 49)

Especially for the global middle class, supercultural construction increasingly reflects exposure to the abundant symbolic resources and discourses that occupy international media and information technology. Global knowledge of universal human rights, aesthetic standards and preferences, basic psychological needs, and emotions, as we have just briefly discussed, reverberate widely. Their visibility has been facilitated by advances in communication technology and use of that technology by persons all over the world. These are not the only global cultural phenomena. Some media genres and narrative forms – action, romance, science fiction, sports, and music, for example – appeal widely, though differentially, according to gender. As the Mexican cultural anthropologist Néstor García Canclini points out, certain 'spectacular narratives' such as the movies of Steven Spielberg and George Lucas are based on myths that 'are intelligible to everyone, independent of their culture, educational level, national history, economic development, or political system' (García Canclini 1995: 111). We could say the same thing about the global appeal of the Disney creations, for example, and to a greater or lesser degree of much popular culture emanating from the United States, Britain, and to a certain extent Japan and China as well. Japanese *karaoke* and *anime* have struck a universal cord, for instance, as have *kung-fu* and other Asian martial arts.

The global economic and cultural marketplace motivates transnational communications activity like never before, generating unprecedented quantities of material and symbolic cultural resources. The Internet mushroomed to unbelievable popular proportions towards the end of the last century in part because the cost of processing information by computer decreased so radically (from US $75 million per operation in 1960 to less than one hundredth of a cent in 1990; Castells 1996: 45). But at a time when discussions about globalization and culture understandably tend to revolve around information technology and the Internet, it is very important to keep in mind that the phenomenon which manifests even greater significance in the global context with respect to the circulation of symbolic forms is the unprecedented expansion of all kinds of popular culture forms *not* transmitted by the Internet. The number of television stations in the world has quadrupled in just the past fifteen years, for instance, with most of the new channels looking for already produced, popular programming that falls into the categories of universal appeal mentioned above. Low-power radio stations are appearing in abundance now. Personal communications devices accompany the mass media expansion. In fact, commercial telecommunication systems, the international film industry, and radio, as well as other global cultural phenomena including tourism, theme parks, popular music, and professional sports cumulatively reach and influence a far greater proportion of the world's population than personal computers and websites do.

Given that the social consequences of cultural globalization extend beyond political borders and social classes, the overall effect of the technological explosion is the creation of a much greater range of cultural options. The astounding material and symbolic productivity stimulated by the international economic and cultural market is fundamental to the emergence of the superculture as a dominant cultural modality.

Widespread popular culture resources today are less tied to particular nations. The cultural situation in Mexico is an especially intriguing case, not least because it shares a long, tension-filled border with the United States. Nowhere else in the world do countries with such contrasting developmental profiles exist side by side, and no two cities in the world reveal this contrast more than San Diego and Tijuana. Current controversies about illegal immigration and drug smuggling only intensify the smoldering bad feelings. Moreover, American popular culture has long been regarded by many Mexican intellectuals as clear and detested evidence of cultural imperialism. The 'invasion' of American movies, television programs, pop music, and all the rest is considered by some Mexican critics to be especially insidious because, in addition to enthusiasm shown for their own cultural materials, Mexican people also eagerly consume and enjoy the symbolically charged cultural products from the United States.

That's why Néstor García Canclini's view of these issues is so interesting and important. Rather than follow the typical line of critical thinking, wherein the global market is condemned outright and American popular culture is roundly criticized, banned, or censored, García Canclini takes a more realistic and nuanced approach. He says that Mexican people have tired of their terribly inefficient state bureaucracies, the paralyzing political partisanship, corrupt labor unions, and elitist public media. They now look to commercial mass media 'to get what the civil institutions don't give them: services, justice, reparations, or simple attention' (García Canclini 1995: 13). He describes the Mexican populace's attitude towards 'citizenship' in globalization and the Communication Age: 'Where I belong, what rights I have, how I can learn things, and who represents my interests . . . these kinds of questions can be answered more in the private consumption of goods and on the mass media than in the abstract rules of democracy or in collective participation in the public spaces' (García Canclini 1995: 13). In García Canclini's view, this development suggests that 'we should ask ourselves if through consumption we are not making something that sustains, nurtures, and to a certain point constructs a new way to be citizens' (García Canclini 1995: 27).

Néstor García Canclini's argument does not proceed uncritically and it does not simply accede symbolic power to Mexico's wealthy and powerful neighbor to the North (García Canclini 1995; 1999). To the contrary, he has proposed a radical revision of Mexican (and Latin American) public cultural policy to downplay the high culture aspects, and connect more with the 'common culture' through development of national popular culture, a policy recommendation that has also been made in England (Willis 1990) and other countries. In many ways, the privatization of public media in Mexico and elsewhere has actually accomplished what García Canclini has encouraged the public agencies to do. We see the same tendencies in the Internet world. Most governments have been unable to supply their citizens with high technology and Internet access, so business has taken over that opportunity and turned it into a commercial venture. For instance, Brazil's banks, corporations, and Internet service providers now provide free (but heavily commercialized) access to the Internet. Yahoo and Hotmail from the USA offer free email and Internet access services (also loaded up with commercials, of course) to an international clientele.

The conclusion that the global market seems to be today's best source of symbolic inspiration understandably makes sensitive observers uncomfortable. But what are the superior alternatives? Even the French sociologist Pierre Bourdieu, who has been casting around desperately lately for some alternative to what he considers to be the destructive effects of globalization and the commercialization of media and information, can only unconvincingly retreat to the tired idea that state institutions, political parties, and labor unions will somehow rescue and resurrect the 'public interest' from the 'tyranny' of the market (Bourdieu 1998). Unfortunately, the ability of any nation-state or other entity to do so is seriously limited not only by the conceptual impracticality of such an idea but also by the technical impossibility of managing global technology. Every new form of communications technology accelerates and intensifies the transnational influence, and makes cultural supervision by any regulative body increasingly less viable.

Furthermore, while it is tempting to point at McDonald's, Blockbuster, Sony, rock and rap, Nokia, shopping malls, Coca-Cola, designer jeans, Disney, Honda, the National Basketball Association, and other highly visible globalized cultural themes frequently considered to be negative, homogenizing, Westernizing forces, many other types of symbolic representation circulate widely too. What started out as a distinctly American cultural phenomenon, the Internet, has given tremendous visibility, convenience, and power to various cultural and language groups almost everywhere. While the Internet should not be understood simply as a magical, technological generator of cultural democracy, the usual critical arguments made against communications technology as nothing more than tools of imperialism don't shed much light either. Instead of simply reproducing conditions of domination and repression, the market has created a rich source of material and symbolic resources which ultimately challenge the hegemony of state institutions. Where all this is headed, though, is anyone's guess.

Civilizations

'A big hug from Chile to all the Mexican people!'
(Chilean broadcast journalist reporting the presidential election victory in Chile of Ricardo Lagos to the Mexican national radio system, January 2000)

To a great extent our mediated and unmediated experiences reflect immersion in the civilizations to which we belong. This fact may seem quite unremarkable, perhaps even self-evident, but the very idea that differing civilizations demarcate global cultural organization with serious political consequences has generated much controversy in academic circles.

Although he was by no means the first to talk about culture in terms of broad civilizational groupings and alignments, Samuel P. Huntington stirred a tremendous reaction, certainly not all of it favorable, when his book *The Clash of Civilizations* was published in 1996. Part of the critical response to the book stems from many intellectuals' unwillingness to accept what they consider its main premises to be: that civilizations are essential human groupings, and that human conflict based on these essential differences is inevitable. Huntington argues, for instance, that:

> Civilizations are the ultimate human tribes, and the clash of civilizations is tribal conflict on a global scale . . . Cold peace, cold war, trade war, quasi war, uneasy peace, troubled relations, intense rivalry, competitive coexistence, arms races: these phrases are . . . descriptions of relations between entities from different civilizations. Trust and friendship will be rare.
>
> (Huntington 1996: 207)

A Harvard professor and former American government adviser on national security issues, Huntington interprets global cultural trends in ways that reflect his understanding and promotion of American national interests. However, we are not concerned here with the political implications and pessimistic cultural predictions Huntington makes. I am interested not in defending or interrogating the politics or subtleties of *The Clash of Civilizations* but in using the main theme of the book for establishing civilization as a primary cultural resource for supercultural formation. Even Huntington's most strident critics must grant that his dissertation on civilizations is extraordinarily comprehensive.

Where Huntington's analysis helps us most, I believe, is in the way he describes cultural developments on a global scale, and in the reasonableness of his claim that civilizations compose 'the broadest cultural entities' (Huntington 1996: 128). Huntington argues that the tendency for world populations to divide up according to civilizational differences has been particularly evident since the Cold War ended. Now, he says, 'the most important distinctions among peoples are not ideological, political, or economic. They are cultural' (Huntington 1996: 21).

Civilizations are made up of countries which group together according to common ancestry, religion, history, values, and customs. The civilizations derive from one of three historical criteria. Some civilizations take form according to a common world view based in religion (Islamic, Buddhist, Hindu, Orthodox, Sinic). Two more civilizations were created by colonial expansionism (Western civilization and Latin America), and two others developed primarily because of geographic circumstances (Japan and Africa).

People have extensive access to various features of their respective civilizations and draw liberally and creatively from those civilizational resources to fashion their supercultures. Civilizational ideas and materials represent distinct and coherent ways of thinking and feeling, and are expressed in verbal and non-verbal ways that are already familiar. People often feel more safe and comfortable sampling and using ideas and materials from their own civilizations than they do from other civilizations.

Strong economic and cultural ties between nations of any civilization encourage exposure to and involvement with the cultural features of that civilization, a trend which is given tremendous momentum by the dynamic processes of economic and cultural globalization. The nations which invest the most money in the United States, for instance, are Britain, Germany, France, Canada, the Netherlands, and Australia, while the United States invests most in Britain, the Netherlands, Canada, France, and Australia. In Huntington's world map, all these countries belong to the Western civilization. Such cultural alliances show up in virtually all aspects of everyday life. When people from the Nordic countries watch North American television, for instance, they can realistically imagine themselves in a North American cultural context because they are all part of the same civilization; in fact, centuries ago Nordic immigrants to the United States helped build what is now the United States of America and Canada.

Recent trends in intracivilizational economic activity in Latin America exhibit the same tendencies we see in nations that compose Western civilization. Development of the Mercosur Union (Brazil, Argentina, Chile, Paraguay, Uruguay) and the Andean Pact (Venezuela, Colombia, Ecuador, Peru, Bolivia), for instance, demonstrates how culturally harmonious nations can forge political alliances to solve social and economic problems. The international flow of money and other resources is based in cultural trust and comfort facilitated by common values, traditions, and languages. Most experts in these countries no longer expect to find solutions to Latin American problems from experts in Washington or New York.

Patterns of international exchange of cultural materials demonstrate how well civilizations are able to function as viable economic markets – a particularly strong test of the validity of civilizational theory. Staying with Latin America as our example, the flow of two staples of Latin popular culture – television dramas (*telenovelas*) and popular music – clearly shows how smooth and profitable the intracivilizational connections can be (Straubhaar 1991; Sinclair 1999). Television dramas and popular music bring out the expressive and emotional similarities of people who live in nations of the Latin American civilization. The global explosion of Latin American popular music that took off in the late 1990s through the success of singers such as Ricky Martin, Luis Miguel, Marc Anthony, Enrique Iglesias, and Jennifer Lopez was preceded by decades of intracivilizational exchange of musical talent throughout the Hispanic world. Two other popular television genres – the talk show and the variety show – have also become extraordinary civilizational resources in Latin America. For instance, the talk show *Cristina*, which originates in the new entertainment capital of Latin America, Miami, Florida, is aired in all Spanish-language countries of the world and attracts a huge weekly audience. Variety programs such as *Big Saturday* (*Sábado Gigante*), featuring Don Francisco of Chile, but recorded in Miami, likewise reaches an enormous audience in Spanish-language countries.

In the People's Republic of China people interpret and use foreign cultural materials quite differently depending on civilizational alignments (Lull 1991). While Chinese television viewers enjoy and learn from programs imported from North America, South America, and Europe, they are far more enthralled by Japanese productions. Japan is not part of the same civilization as China according to Huntington's scheme, but it shares cultural affinities with the Sinic civilization to which China belongs. Recognizing the ideological potential of the cultural overlap, the Chinese government has even imported certain Japanese television programs, hoping to inspire Chinese to work hard and succeed like Japan, particularly given that the two countries both 'started over' at about the same time – the mid- to late 1940s. Chinese viewers interpret Japanese programs in ways that differ from their involvements with cultural materials that are imported from other civilizations. Both the Chinese government's plan and the reactions of Chinese viewers to Japanese programs stem from a perceived civilizational resonance. Moreover, Chinese consumers more often recognize and greatly prefer Japanese commercial products over American goods. In virtually all respects, Chinese simply regard Japanese culture as closer to their own traditions, values, and ways of living than Western culture.

Civilizational discord

Cross-cultural interaction is commonplace in the globalized world. The contact can encourage co-operation, but it can also lead to conflict in even the most ordinary cultural contexts and social practises. For instance, both civilizational harmony and discord can be found in agricultural and social patterns of multicultural community garden plots in the Nordic countries. Barbro Klein (1990) observes that in Sweden, for instance, individual garden plots made by Swedes, Finns, Middle Easterners, and Chinese in these shared public spaces differ by botanical content and organization, and that 'ethnic neighborhood clusters' and 'outright segregation' exist on the multiethnic grounds. Any outward signs of sharing or joint purpose as 'gardeners' can be found 'only inside the ethnic groups . . . or ethnic coalitions such as the North European one' (Klein 1990: 20). The ethnic groups not only grow different things in different ways, they demarcate their space in the garden by putting up boundary fences, the likes of which do not exist between adjacent gardeners of the same civilization.

Analyzing cultural orientations and behavior strictly according to civilizational differences, however, obscures the fact that tremendous discord exists inside the various civilizations, and inside all the individual nations that make up any civilization. In the Swedish culture of Western civilization, for example, 'collectivist values such as equality, solidarity, and cooperation are officially sanctioned, whereas individualistic concepts such as freedom, independence, and personal success have a more oppositional flavor', according to ethnologist Billy Ehn (1990: 49). The ever-increasing influx of this 'oppositional' culture, especially that exported by the United States, brings with it a 'dog-eat-dog mentality, cheating, and ruthlessness . . . any sense of responsibility for public values and community are more or less non-existent' (Ehn 1990: 54). Such cultural differences can easily provoke discomfort in exchanges of all types between countries of the same civilization.

Koichi Iwabuchi's research on Asian regional cultural flows and cross-cultural consumption further underscores how this intercivilizational cultural resonance operates in complex, contradictory ways (Iwabuchi 1999). Iwabuchi shows how Japanese cultural materials travel and arrive in other Far East Asian nations, where the attractive civilizational commonalities are relativized by profound historical ruptures between and among the countries involved. In particular, Japan's odious imperialist history combines with enduring civilizational resonances to produce an historically constituted uneven relation with other Asian nations (Iwabuchi 1999).

And what about countries composed of a heterogeneous mixture of people who come from many different civilizations, a rapidly growing global trend? The United States, a nation of immigrants and multiple cultures from the beginning, may be the prototypical case. The racial, ethnic, and cultural differences of men and women who compose the United States' populace have been variously described as the country's greatest strength and as its greatest weakness. Such matters often take the form of debates about 'multiculturalism' in the United States. Those who oppose celebrating cultural difference and diversity typically argue that such cultural dividing and decentering will lead to the eventual destruction of the (dominant) 'American culture' and undermine its political and economic stability and power. This is especially true of race and ethnicity in the United States in the post-O.J. Simpson era. As he received the key to the city of Compton, California, a mainly African-American community near Los Angeles in 1998, Ji Jaga, an ex-Black-Panther (formerly known as Geronimo Pratt), told the gathering of African peoples from many nations at the World African Unity Festival: 'The bottom line is we are African. African unity is the key to bringing our solutions to fruition . . . we need to meditate on what our ancestors are telling us.'

The Islamic civilization and the Sinic civilization of Far East Asia will become extremely powerful forces in the twenty-first century, according to Samuel Huntington. The spread of Muslim faith and demography throughout the world, and the extraordinary economic growth of many Asian nations already signal world-level cultural alterations. While Western observers frequently credit the economic advances in Asia to positive Western influence, Huntington argues that the 'East Asians attribute their dramatic economic development not to the import of Western culture, but rather to their adherence to their own culture. They are succeeding, they argue, because they are different from the West' (Huntington 1996: 93). He continues:

> At the broadest level the Confucian ethos pervading many Asian societies stresses the values of authority, hierarchy, the subordination of individual rights and interests, the importance of consensus, the avoidance of confrontation, 'saving face,' and, in general the supremacy of the state over society and of society over the individual. In addition, Asians tend to think of the evolution of their societies in terms of centuries and millennia and to give priority to maximizing long-term gains. These attitudes contrast with the primacy in American beliefs of liberty, equality, democracy, and individualism, and the American propensity to distrust government, oppose authority, promote checks and balances, encourage competition, sanctify human rights, and to forget the past, ignore the future, and focus on maximizing immediate gains. The sources of conflict are in fundamental differences in society and culture.
>
> (Huntington 1996: 225)

Sinic and Islamic civilizations differ greatly from Western civilization, but also from each other 'fundamentally in terms of religion, culture, social structure, traditions, politics, and basic assumptions at the root of their way of life' (Huntington 1996: 185). Those foundational differences, according to Huntington, will prevent them from forming any anti-Western coalition.

Deterritorialization

Civilizational cultures endure when their members are deterritorialized too – when they live outside their places of geographic and cultural origin. Such cultural persistence can take the form of connections between diasporas and the homeland. 'Overseas Chinese', for instance, can consummate business deals in China much more effectively than Westerners can. Diasporic popular culture and media encourage cultural unity and comfort. At the extremely popular Club Miami in San Jose, California, for instance, a Mexican house band plays famous Puerto Rican and Colombian pop standards to unite and please the Peruvians, Venezuelans, Brazilians, Dominicans, and Salvadorans (as well as the Mexicans, Puerto Ricans, and Colombians) in attendance. Marisa Monte and Ricky Martin make Latinos everywhere proud – not of a place necessarily, but of a cultural style that emerges sensually from the Latin American civilization.

Deterritorialization, of course, is often very unpleasant. Cross-civilizational immigration is particularly difficult. Immigrating groups from the same civilization have a much better chance of 'fitting in' with the dominant cultural assumptions and legal system of the host civilization. Parents and teachers in many Asian nations, for instance, routinely spank, even bruise, the bodies of children when they lie, steal, skip school, or become involved with 'bad influences'. When Asian families immigrate to Western civilization nations, however, they often face tremendous difficulties adjusting to the new cultural and civilizational realities – particularly the concept of individual rights – which even grants children the right to hold their own parents legally responsible for abuse. In California, parenting classes are now being taught by acculturated Vietnamese-Americans to new immigrants from Vietnam so they can better understand life in the unfamiliar civilization.

Like all the cultural resources discussed in this chapter, civilizations function not only as material entities (real people in real physical places) but as discursive ideological and cultural spheres which people draw upon to establish and maintain their cultural identities, activities, and relationships. Mass and micro media contribute much to help keep the civilizations alive, despite the disruptions of geographical relocation.

Nation

The differences among us should be respected, but the shared values are more important.

(Bill Clinton in a public speech, 1997)

We live under one flag and it must fly supremely.

(African-American political leader Jesse Jackson arguing for government intervention to save 'affirmative action')

(Radical rightist) Bill Bennett, (leftist) Leon Panetta, and (lesbian
activist, daughter of Sonny) Chastity Bono on tomorrow's show . . .
hey, only in America!
(Larry King billboarding his CNN talk show)

Does Anything Bind us Together Beyond Cheeseburgers?
(Headline in *Portland Oregonian* newspaper)

A person's cultural identity traditionally has been shaped to a large extent by
his or her nationality, defined here to mean membership or citizenship in a
politically recognized nation-state. Nations are political organisms that organize
and reinforce cultural consciousness for a community of individuals in powerful and distinctive ways. People often refer to and explain themselves in terms
of an overarching national framework that is believed to apply fundamentally
to everyone who lives in a particular historical-geographical-political location,
especially if that place is relatively homogenous ethnically and racially.
Throughout the history of modernity, for a community of persons to declare
or win national independence has been a way to formalize, legitimize, and
defend common cultural values and practises.

Partisan interests dramatically shape the symbolic cultural imagery that
nations depend on for their political viability. As the legal scholar Monroe
Price points out, 'what is grandly called national identity may be no more than
the collection of myths, promises, and renderings of history that will keep one
political party rather than the other in power' (Price 1995: 64). Assumptions of
dominant cultural identity lie within the political-ideological framework of
any nation as well.

Like all hegemonic constructions, nations are more or less fragile entities.
They will be defended most strongly by those who stand to lose the most from
their disintegration. When the *Falun Gong* spiritual movement became so
attractive to urban Chinese around the turn of the century, for instance,
Chinese government authorities swiftly jailed the leaders of their ideological
competitor. That spiritual challenge to China's nationhood and to communist
ideological hegemony was, and still is, embedded in a matrix of other contradictory ideological discourses fueled by post-Tiananmen economic and
cultural developments. These developments included a dramatic increase in
private business and consumerism beginning in the 1980s, accompanied a
decade later by the dramatic entry of chaos-producing information technology
and the Internet. Like other totalitarian nation-states, China's political leaders
have had to walk a fine line that recognizes and utilizes the Internet as a
necessary tool for national economic development while trying to minimize
the potential ideological and cultural damage threatened by Internet communication. The challenge to hegemony presented by the Internet only
extends a long-term struggle between authorities and communications technology in China during the latter decades of the twentieth century (Lull 1991;

2000). We see the same kinds of nationalistic struggles today in communist Vietnam and North Korea.

On the other side of the world where the Internet was invented and attracts a greater proportion of users than anywhere else, and where individual rights are fundamental to national ideology, the latest challenge to nation comes from another direction. Less worried about the communist menace and a nuclear holocaust, debates in the United States today focus much more on internal questions of loyalty and commitment to the nation implicit in discussions of race, culture, and language. America's national identity, some claim, is under attack in the 'multiculturalism' movement, which brings our discussion of nation back to the issue of world civilizations and the question of nation as a viable *cultural* entity. As Samuel P. Huntington argues, 'the multiculturalists . . . wish to create a country of many civilizations, which is to say a country not belonging to any civilization and lacking a cultural core. History shows that no country so constituted can long endure as a coherent society' (Huntington 1996: 306).

The multiculturalism debate in the United States is closely linked to the roles of immigration policy and language in the construction of collective cultural unity. As the linguist David Crystal points out, 'some analysts consider the English language to have been an important factor in maintaining mutual intelligibility and American unity in the face of the immigration explosion which more than tripled the US population after 1900' (Crystal 1997: 118). The 'English only' and 'English as the Official Language' movements in the United States attempt to insure the long-term viability of the nation and national identity in the face of increasing cultural diversification.

Challenges to nation can be found all over the world. Often these challenges reflect the same cultural stresses that characterize recent debates and disturbances in the United States. The One Nation political party launched in Australia in 1997, with its anti-Asian-immigration platform and perceived anti-Aboriginal stance, is one example. European countries from Sweden and Finland in the north to Greece and Spain in the south invoke nationalist rhetoric as the 'immigrant problem' grows. Political debates surrounding the dismantling of the Nordic region's welfare societies, which have been in place since the early twentieth century and serve as a foundation of Nordic cultural identity and politics, are debated in terms of nation and national identity. Canadian and Québecois nationalism are deeply influenced by culture and language. The Chilean presidential election in 2000 – made particularly complex and emotional because of the Augusto Pinochet extradition struggle going on at the same time – was framed rhetorically in terms of the possibility for bringing the political right and left together to form some kind of post-Pinochet consensual national identity.

Nation as a cultural resource

In most cases, the nation is a formalized, relatively stable, homogenizing *social space* that citizens encounter every moment of their everyday lives, but it is also an 'imagined community' (Anderson 1983) that is sufficiently polysemic to allow personal interpretation and commitment to a *cultural space* that 'we share in common' (Chaney 1994: 126). This represents the crucial blending of ideology and the state with culture and community in the building and maintenance of the nation. Nations as political states, therefore, are constructed 'to be equivalent in all important aspects to a culture: a culture that has an identity through being distinctively different and thereby creates an identity for its members' (Chaney 1994: 126). This fact is key to our analysis. The nation 'works' as a fundamental cultural resource because it gives people a shared sense of difference that is endlessly reinforced, even outside conscious awareness, through the routines and rituals of everyday life, and through symbolic displays of the values and traditions, especially as they are expressed in a dominant language – a language, by the way, that should be spoken without a foreign accent.

But nations are much more than historically situated, geopolitical structures or communities of individuals who share the past and speak the same language. Nations are also complex and distinctive cultural narratives – mythical stories that people tell themselves that inscribe, reinscribe, and reinforce an idealized system of values. The nation has a personality and is experienced emotionally. Its fundamental elements – the legal system, religion(s), dominant language, system of commerce, and social customs – are all backed up by unifying material and symbolic forms including constitutions, flags, national anthems, school curricula, military forces, mass media, national museums, and advertising. Nations have always depended on symbolic forms for their political and cultural viability. The nation therefore is just as much a cultural construction as a political one, if not more so. Nation is a discursive product that is perpetually marketed back to its own people and to other nations. Nation thus continues to function as a defining, unifying, reinforcing, reassuring sociopolitical and cultural resource of extraordinary importance.

The symbolic character of nation – increasingly represented and promoted by various media in the Communication Age – stimulates levels of emotional involvement that contribute to the viability of any individual country as a legitimate political state. Indeed, the mass media have long played important roles in the process of nation-building: 'By ritualizing and sometimes creating great national events, such as those informal talks between President and people, the coronation of the Queen, the inauguration of the President, the first moonwalk, or the funeral of John F. Kennedy, government has played, and continues to play, a vital part in establishing the new mythologies of the state in modern times' (Price 1995: 11).

While such media representations are clearly motivated by political interests and indeed generally serve those interests, the rhetorical axes of nation and nationalism in the twenty-first century have moved away from an emphasis on political representations and interpretations to cultural displays and meanings. This does not mean that the political importance of nation is diminished, however. Cultural nationalism is key. The constant construction of an 'imagined dominant culture' that somehow represents 'who we are' is what keeps nations alive and functioning. That's why cultural divisiveness in any nation-state is in a way irrelevant to the discursive potential of 'nation'. In fact, as we have seen in several nations in the past decade especially, cultural divisiveness may lead even to violent conflict, but it also clarifies and strengthens the rhetorical status of those nations as discursive cultural constructs.

Nationalism as a *cultural field* exists worlds apart from the rationalistic, bourgeois public sphere of nineteenth-century Europe that Jürgen Habermas (1989) and his followers have had in mind. The Habermasian 'public sphere' implies trust and confidence in the public space and a sense of citizenship that simply does not exist in many parts of the world the same way it does in Germany and most of Europe. For the public sphere to function democratically, everyone must have a reasonable opportunity to participate in and influence political activities and decisions. For people in many parts of the world, cultural democracy is more important than political democracy and is easier to achieve. Mass media and popular culture play a pivotal role here too. In his analysis of Brazilian culture, for instance, the American anthropologist Conrad Kottak claims that 'soccer, television, and Carnaval . . . each create a democracy missing most areas of Brazilian life' (Kottak 1990: 43) because mass media and popular culture provide an equality of access to feelings and unite people in ways the political forces cannot achieve. Even the ouster of former president Fernando Collor de Mello in Brazil in 1992 was just as much a cultural action as a political one, and was made possible by the cultural media.

Nations come together, at least temporarily, through mediated, symbolic displays of common purpose. National sporting teams participating in the Olympics every four years are one example; World Cup football is another. Popular music is a vital domain of symbolic national unity. In Brazil, for instance, trans-generational, trans-regional, trans-racial, trans-class fans sing, dance, and emote along with Caetano Veloso, Roberto Carlos, Maria Bethania, Jorge Ben, Olodum, or Daniela Mercury and feel very Brazilian in the process. Mexicans of all ages and backgrounds create the same kind of cultural access and solidarity through the Olympics, the national football team, religious rituals, and popular music – the brilliant compositions of Juan Gabriel, the romances of Luis Miguel, and the mariachi-soaked *rancheras* of Vicente Fernandez all provoke profound feelings of 'Mexicanness' that are simply unachievable through political means.

For Latin American national cultures, the television novels (*telenovelas*) have the same ability to unite across age groups, regions, ethnic divisions, sexual orientations, and social classes. Pan-national television literacy enhances a sense of cultural equality by permitting fundamentally unrestricted access to the electronic medium, not only as an entertainment apparatus which connects so well with individual and collective feelings but as a conveyor of particular codes and conventions – a televisual aesthetic which supports and delivers the culturally rich melodramas to audiences. The *telenovela* draws from the collective cultural memory for its subject matter. Through the narrative of the *telenovela*, the romance and nostalgia of the imagined past are recontextualized into the romance and uncertainty of the imagined present. In the process images that make up the collective memory, long-term and short-term, become cultural resources which are interpreted and used in complex ways, all the while functioning to help construct a sense of national identity. In Mexico, for instance, viewers from Baja California to the Yucatan Peninsula, from the elite highrises of the Federal District to the tiny adobe homes in the villages of Chiapas, all participate in national cultural rituals via the *telenovela*.

The examples presented above indicate how communications media perpetuate political-economic-cultural systems by displaying cultural themes and discourses that touch and join people emotionally. In this way, the very concept of 'nation' serves as a crucial discursive stratagem for constructing meaning and identity.

Media are never ideologically or culturally seamless or coherent, however, and in capitalist countries at least they certainly do not always function to maintain national unity. Today's media are driven far more by the demands of the market than by the diatribes of government bureaucrats. And media don't respect political borders. The collapse of the Soviet Union, the Iranian revolution, and the disturbances in China are prime examples of the media's capacity to destabilize nations. Media content – especially scandals – can generate particularly potent challenges to the dominant culture in even the most stable and powerful nations (Lull & Hinerman 1997).

Symbolic forms of any kind do not serve but one purpose and they are never used up. It is exactly their abstract, infinite, symbolic qualities that make nations, civilizations, and universal values useful as discursive resources for collective political and cultural purposes, as well as for personal use as essential elements of customized supercultures. Having discussed four of the cultural spheres in the previous pages, we now turn our attention again to how the superculture functions as a contemporary cultural modality.

Superculture as cultural performance

Documenting the 'merger of globalized, customized mass media and computer-mediated communication', and noting how electronic communication now extends into 'the whole domain of life, from home to work, from schools to hospitals, from entertainment to travel', Manuel Castells worries about how 'our societies are increasingly structured around a bipolar opposition between the Net and the Self' (Castells 1996: 364, 3). His concerns are well founded. Statistics provided by Castells and many others clearly show that all cultural activity, old and new, is demarcated in important ways by basic social distinctions related to gender, race, class, age, and so on. The 'digital divide' is just the most recent way of talking about these social differences. In light of this, communications technology, the rampant circulation of symbolic forms, and supercultural construction should not be seen as any solution to social inequality, especially considering the brutal differences evident at the global level.

But while Castells's assertion that the world is now structured around an alienating and excluding opposition between Net and Self makes sense in macro terms, it fails to take into account how human communication works beneficially across social divisions in micro practices. The intensive crossing and meshing of symbolic and material cultural resources that characterizes the superculture is fundamental to even the most rudimentary varieties of cultural construction. Current tendencies towards cultural abundance, intensification, diversity, and hybridization affect everyone on Earth, and not just in negative ways. The 'indigenous' Maoris of New Zealand, for instance, have found a strong avenue for expressing cultural and political identity by appropriating North American rap music and hip-hop culture, whose African roots, sounds, attitudes, and images resonate well with the Maoris – dark-skinned, marginalized, tropical – by integrating the imported forms into local movements to reclaim land, language, and cultural history (Lull 2000: 246–9). Vietnamese who fled to Sweden as political refugees blend Vietnamese music videos made in Paris and California and social dances from Brazil and Argentina with the proximate cultural contours and welfare advantages of Scandinavia to invent productive supercultural matrices in unfamiliar territory. Poor Mexican farmers living in the shade of the volcanoes near Colima regularly gather together after going to Catholic mass on Sundays to cheer their favorite soccer teams on satellite television, comparing the Mexican sides with the Italians and the English who are playing on another channel, and later attend local *ranchero* music concerts amplified by a Japanese sound system. Meanwhile, their wives and girlfriends group together next door to laugh and cry their way through Mexican *telenovelas* and reruns of *Friends*, while preparing *enchiladas verdes* and drinking Coca-Cola.

The transformative assortment of ideas, styles, and activities that people choreograph to compose their cultural worlds reflects how meaningful and enjoyable (or less miserable) lives can be built in an era when cultural resources are more plentiful for nearly everyone, and when symbolic communication has assumed center stage in human experience. Constructing a superculture is like performing a spirited, unscripted, perpetual dance that oscillates between routine maneuvers reflecting the familiar deep structures of inherited 'internal cultural patterns' (Sowell 1994), and the trickier solo steps of cultural risk and innovation, back to the familiar once again, forever synthesizing and creating, never resting.

The power of the hybrid

The superculture is based on the premise that the *hybrid* – human, material, and discursive features of the cultural 'in between' (Bhabha 1996) – is the essence of contemporary cultural activity. Cultural hybrids are constructed through routine communication exchange, transforming existing cultural materials and signs into more elaborate material and discursive themes and representations, then melding those forms with other forms. Hybrids are not simply the cultural *products* of everyday interactions; they are the *sources* and *media* through which such phenomenological interactions take place. Hybrids spring from the indeterminate discursive ecologies of the cultural spheres, then connect with and mediate between and among the available cultural fields, reinforcing, contradicting, expanding, and undermining previous understandings while they simultaneously create new cultural frameworks and experiences.

The syncretic creativity characteristic of the popular culture industries (think of pop music forms such as country-western, *rock en español*, jazz fusion, or rock-rap, for instance), is now being routinely exercised by everyday cultural programmers, a trend that is made possible by widespread availability of the latest communication technologies and the abundance of symbolic forms stimulated by the globalized cultural economy. Culture has always been formed through such movements and mergings, but today all this activity takes place much faster and on a far broader scale. Contemporary cultural hybrids are then further mediated by the production of deterritorialized cultural styles created in new physical locations, and by the reintroduction of new cultural syntheses back into the 'original' locations – for example, Taiwanese culture entering the People's Republic of China, or Mexican-American culture returning to Mexico.

Supercultural identities

'Culture counts, and cultural identity is what is most meaningful to most people'.

(Huntington 1996: 20)

People all over the world even subconsciously assume cultural identities in order to understand their worlds, and try valiantly to create an overall sense of well being in the present and hope for the future. That has never been easy to do, as the spate of self-help pop psychology books, fundamentalist movements, and spiritualist crusades worldwide demonstrates. In some ways, today's cultural conditions appear to only exacerbate the confusion, isolation, and existential despair. As David Chaney has argued, the 'modern mass culture of urban-industrial societies' has become in many respects 'a culture of anonymity' (Chaney 1994: 96). Psychologist Kenneth Gergen believes that technology greatly disrupts cultural stability, and fears that the erosion of traditional cultures and the onslaught of unfamiliar cultural messages will create the 'burden of an increasing array of oughts, self-doubts, and irrationalities' because individual persons will be 'saturated' and overwhelmed by such information. He senses that a 'multiphrenic condition' is emerging 'in which one swims in ever-shifting, concatenating, and contentious currents of being' (Gergen 1991: 80). Moreover, the global mixture of communications technologies and cultural forms, acting together with the (often circular) flows of immigrants, guest workers, tourists, and international students, among others, adds to the cultural uncertainty and to the ontological instability that the rootlessness and apparent cold life of the global metropolises seem to produce.

One of our key theorists, Manuel Castells, who in this sense shares the view of Samuel Huntington, has suggested that these conditions often lead to cultural retreats: 'In such a world of uncontrolled, confusing change, people tend to group around primary identities: religious, ethnic, territorial, national' (Castells 1996: 3). Cultural identities in any era link the emotional-behavioral orientations of individual persons to the organized values and activities of the groups to which those persons perceive they belong – their human reference points, persons with whom they share experiences and routinely communicate. In cultural terms, the outcome of this social interaction should be feelings of security and belongingness for the persons involved.

Can contemporary multimediated streams of cultural information and personalized cultural hybrids such as those represented by the superculture generate the comforts of cultural identity? Here I would argue that in many respects, the answer is 'yes'. Castells, Huntington, Gergen, and others have not sufficiently taken the current era on its own terms. Key to bringing the cultural blur of postmodernity and globalization into focus is the inherent flexibility and polysemy of symbolic forms and the unbounded potential of the human imagination – the creative ability of people to synthesize the familiar with the exotic, and the material with the symbolic, in ways that make them feel secure, happy, and intrigued with life. The multicultural profile of the superculture reflects and extends the logic of communicative 'complex connectivity' (Tomlinson 1999), and the 'multiplicity of the self' (Maffesoli 1996: 10), into the realm of the cultural imagination. The multifunctionality of communications technology combining with the open-ended nature of contemporary cultural resources creates opportunities for construction of far more varied and dense matrices of 'niche' identities and lifestyle groupings that resemble forms of a dynamic, media-influenced, modern-day *habitus* (Bourdieu 1984).

While technology co-acts with social structure to help separate people in some unfortunate ways (e.g. the 'digital divide'), persons who are spatially distant can also join together via electronic networks of various kinds to develop, reinforce, and cultivate cultural contacts and communities. Mass media, information technologies, and the Internet dramatically enrich such processes of 'self-formation' because they encourage people to 'actively negotiate and participate in creating the kinds of mediated experiences they want' (Slevin 2000: 176). Although communications technology privileges rationality and cognition in many respects, the symbolic content that technology carries and the 'mediated co-presence' it facilitates (Thompson 1995) interact intimately with human emotions and the human body. Creating cultural experiences, relationships, and communities through mediated interaction, including the Internet, has become commonplace, even 'natural'. Technologically mediated information is brought close to the emotions and the body by stimulating the imagination. Communications media don't just 'get between' humans; rather they connect people to each other in ways that often overcome the (cultural) barriers imposed by physical distance. Moreover, the crystal-clear technical quality of digital audio and video transmission actually enhances emotionality by 'purifying' the desired 'information' to a level that greatly exceeds the acoustical expectations of unmediated, interpersonal exchanges of sentiment.

While it is true that much of cultural life continues to revolve around the 'local', and is strongly influenced by 'physical embodiment' which situates real flesh-and-blood human beings together in actual physical places (Tomlinson 1999: 9), spatial distinctions such as those drawn between the 'global' and the 'local', where the local is said to be experienced more profoundly, greatly oversimplify the way contemporary symbolic and cultural 'realities' are perceived and experienced. Our deepest emotions and our physical bodies are no longer just 'here'. A defining characteristic of culture in the Communication Age is that real human bodies and emotions interact with and are energized by the evocative, sensual qualities of multiple, ubiquitous, and ephemeral cultural spheres in ways that help individuals increase control over their life experiences.

A cosmopolitan utopia?

In his chapter in this book and in much of his other recent writing, Ulf Hannerz has used the term 'ecumene' to describe the scope and nature of globalized cultural activity. His choice of 'ecumene' to describe 'the interconnectedness of the world' (Hannerz 1996: 7) signals a distinct humanistic philosophy that promotes the (especially Swedish) idea of a 'global citizen'. In American English, at least, ecumene has less than subtle religious connotations. We hear about the 'ecumenical council of churches', for instance. The sole definition of 'ecumenism' given by the *American Heritage Dictionary* is 'a movement seeking to achieve worldwide unity among religions through greater cooperation and improved understanding'. The global ecumene – which Hannerz and others before him utilize to mean only 'worldwide' – clearly has spiritual, or at least moral implications, whether intended by the cultural theorists or not.

The ecumene refers to the site where twenty-first-century 'cosmopolitanism', another favorite expression of Hannerz, John Tomlinson, and others, takes place. Particularly in the rhetorical context of the 'ecumene', the idea of cosmopolitanism also enters scientific discussions with considerable metaphysical baggage. The cosmopolitan person should have a 'global sense of moral development', according to Tomlinson, which can be realized through positive actions such as exercising universal human rights in specific cases, or in the co-operative solving of common environmental problems (Tomlinson 1999: 204, 69). Concluding his insightful and hopeful analysis of contemporary globalization and culture, Tomlinson (1999) argues that there is room for universal themes and humanistically motivated behavior in the construction of cosmopolitan cultural politics at the local level. Complex global connectivity, he says, makes such progress possible.

However, as Tomlinson himself cautions, 'there is no guarantee that the lifting of general cultural horizons, the honing of semiotic skills, and the development of hermeneutic sensibilities [such as that which comprises superculture construction] will be followed by any necessary sense of responsibility for the global totality' (Tomlinson 1999: 202; insert mine). There are few social guarantees of any kind in the Communication Age. While culture retains a vital communal significance, and while contemporary communities can indeed inspire positive social acts and help people develop shared understandings and identities, the cultural networks and communities being formed today in many respects are based mainly on convenience and pleasure. They reflect and promote individual wants and needs rather than a unified collective identity or sense of well-being, such as more traditional manifestations of culture that are anchored in territory and ethnicity are expected to do.

Indeed, as many commentators from academia and the popular media have concluded, individualism and hedonism, not social responsibility and sacrifice, seem to be the order of the day. If cosmopolitanism is at work, it appears to be less an ecumenical cosmopolitanism associated with morality and global responsibility, and more an 'aesthetic cosmopolitanism' (Lash and Urry 1994: 253), representing the desire of people to explore new cultural vistas for personal reasons.

This does not mean, however, that the consumerism and aesthetic cosmopolitanism of personal globalization should necessarily be confused or conflated with blind self-interest. Other caveats also apply. It must be clearly understood, for instance, that not all the cultural choices people make have positive consequences. The superculture is not just a global shopping cart brimming with exotic cultural goodies; it can also represent a myriad of compromises influenced by the often harsh realities of socioeconomic location. Moreover, the general transition of culture and cultural identity away from the relatively collective and proximate toward the more individualized and mediated does not suggest by any means that other cultural imaginings do not exist or matter. For instance, people who struggle together for freedom, independence, or sheer recognition as collectivities often experience culture in powerful, immediate, and proximate ways – at least in certain respects and at certain times – that override all other cultural sensibilities and orientations, including the most complex, mediated, and personalized supercultures. In cases such as this, supercultural sensitivities simultaneously co-exist and interact with more pressing, often contested, local, regional, or national cultural aspirations. The new tribalisms from around the world represented spirited examples of these tendencies away from the eclecticism that inheres in superculture formation.

The superculture, thus, can best be regarded as one important general trend operating on a global scale – a cultural nuance reflecting new directions in cultural globalization, not some uncritical, exhaustive replacement for traditional collective understandings and identities. After all, cultural activity is not a zero-sum game under any conditions, but an ever more expansive and dynamic interplay of impulses and influences.

We are left now to ponder issues that have troubled other observers as well: can the material goods and symbolic resources of a market-driven, hyper-interconnected, globalized culture and economy truly meet people's needs, or does the mass marketing of lifestyle options only 'offer the illusion of equal participation' in the creation of what should be more integrated and unified societies and cultures? (Chaney 1994: 19). Are the kinds of cultures that are created by means of today's complex communication processes producing a 'veneer of shared experience that informs and amuses, but does not necessarily serve or unite people' (Dertouzos 1998), or is development of a cosmopolitan global ecumene of moral responsibility, a democratic 'mediated public sphere' (Thompson 1995), or a shared, civilizational 'public space' (García Canclini 1995) really possible or even desirable? Under any present-day scenario – from the most daunting doomsday nightmare to the most Pollyannaish utopian fantasy – symbolic, communicational, and cultural complexity inevitably contribute to the increased fragmentation, acceleration, and personalization of life experience, exactly what the superculture addresses and represents. Through it all, one fact is clear: creativity and hybridity have always been at the heart of cultural construction and embody some of the best human tendencies. In my view, those tendencies should be reflexively respected and embraced, not unreasonably feared, now that the range of cultural improvisation has reached global proportions.

Note

1   The concentration of many major media and culture industries in the hands of few corporate owners remains an issue that in some respects contradicts the shift of power to individual user/interpreters, but does not undermine the significance of the general transition of certain kinds of power from institutions to individuals.

References

Anderson, B. (1983). *Imagined Communities. Reflections on the Origin and Spread of Nationalism*. London: Verso.

Annan, K. (1998). What can I do to make things better? *Parade Magazine*, 20 December.

Augé, M. (1995). *Non-places: Introduction to the Anthropology of Supermodernity*. London: Verso.

Bhabha, H. (1996). 'Culture's in-between'. In S. Hall and P. du Gay (eds), *Cultural Identity*. London: Sage Publications.

Bourdieu, P. (1984). *Distinction*. Cambridge, MA: Harvard University Press.

——— (1998). *Acts of Resistance*. New York: The New Press.

Castells, M. (1996). *The Rise of the Network Society*. Oxford: Blackwell.

Chaney, D. (1994). *The Cultural Turn: Scene-setting Essays on Contemporary Cultural History*. London: Routledge.

Crystal, D. (1997). *English as a Global Language*. Cambridge: Cambridge University Press.

Dertouzos, M. (1998). *What Will Be: How the New World of Information Will Change Our Lives*. New York: Harper.

Ehn, B. (1990). 'The rhetoric of individualism and collectivism in multi-ethnic Sweden'. In B. Ehn *et al.* (eds), *The Organization of Diversity in Sweden*. Stockholm: Stockholm University.

García Canclini, N. (1995). *Consumidores y Ciudadanos*. Mexico City: Grijalbo.

——— (1999). *La globalizacíon imaginada*. Barcelona: Paidos.

Gergen, K. (1991). *The Saturated Self*. New York: Bantam Books.

Giddens, A. (1991). *Modernity and Self Identity*. Cambridge: Polity Press.

Habermas, J. (1989). *The Structural Transformation of the Public Sphere*. Cambridge: Polity Press.

Hannerz, U. (1992). *Cultural Complexity: Studies in the Social Organisation of Meaning*. New York: Columbia University Press.

——— (1996). *Transnational Connections*. London: Routledge.

Hofstede, G. (1984). *Culture's Consequences*. Beverly Hills, CA: Sage Publications.

Huntington, S. P. (1996). *The Clash of Civilizations and the Remaking of World Order*. New York: Simon and Schuster.

Iwabuchi, K. (1999). *Returning to Asia: Japan in the Cultural Dynamics of Globalization, Localization, and Asianization*. Doctoral dissertation. University of Western Sydney, Australia.

Johnson, S. (1997). *Interface Culture: How New Technology Transforms the Way We Create and Communicate*. San Francisco: HarperEdge.

Klein, B. (1990). 'Plotting boundaries and planting roots: Gardening in a multi-ethnic Swedish town'. In B. Ehn *et al.* (eds), *The Organization of Diversity in Sweden*. Stockholm: Stockholm University.

Kottak, C. (1990). *Prime-time Society: An Anthropological Analysis of Television and Culture*. Belmont, CA: Wadsworth.

Lash, S. and Urry, J. (1994). *Economies of Signs and Space*. London: Sage.

Lull, J. (1991). *China Turned On: Television, Reform, and Resistance*. London: Routledge.

——— (2000). *Media, Communication, Culture: A Global Approach* (revised ed.). Cambridge: Polity Press; New York: Columbia University Press.

Lull, J. and Hinerman, S. (1997). *Media Scandals: Morality and Desire in the Popular Culture Marketplace*. Cambridge: Polity Press; New York: Columbia University Press.

Maffesoli, M. (1996). *The Time of the Tribes*. London: Sage Publications.

Martín-Barbero, J. (1997). 'Globalizacíon comunicacional y descentramiento cultural'. *Dia-logos de la Comunicacíon*, 50: 28–42.

Office of the United Nations High Commissioner for Human Rights (2000). *Universal Declaration of Human Rights.* www.unhchr.ch/udhr/lang/eng.htm

Price, M. (1995). *Television, the Public Sphere, and National Identity.* Oxford: Oxford University Press.

Real, M. (1989). *Super Media: A Cultural Studies Approach.* Newbury Park, CA: Sage Publications.

Sinclair, J. (1999). *Latin American Televison: A Global View.* Oxford: Oxford University Press.

Slevin, J. (2000). *The Internet and Society.* Cambridge: Polity Press.

Sowell, T. (1994). *Race and Culture: A World View.* New York: Basic Books.

Straubhaar, J. (1991). 'Beyond media imperialism. Asymmetrical interdependence and cultural proximity'. *Critical Studies in Mass Communication,* 8: 39–59.

Thompson, J. (1995). *The Media and Modernity: A Social Theory of the Media.* Cambridge: Polity Press.

Tomlinson, J. (1999). *Globalization and Culture.* Cambridge: Polity Press.

Willis, P. (1990). *Common Culture.* Boulder, CO: Westview Press.

Section Three

CONTEMPORARY
CULTURAL FORMS

8

CULTURAL THEORY IN POPULAR CULTURE AND MEDIA SPECTACLES

Michael Real

Popular culture, that omnipresent manifestation of widespread representational practices in contemporary life, has been problematic for cultural theory. The distance between general cultural theory and popular culture theory creates an opportunity here to debate issues in the development of cultural theory. An intellectual history of such communication study – of which this analysis is a small part – notes first the distance between the two and then questions why rapprochement has been difficult.

From the one side, in popular culture studies, attempts to theorize popular culture have frequently trailed off into narrow expressions of a singular concept from literary or social theory. Baseball is examined as a quasi-literary narrative, or intertextuality is traced in hip-hop music. From the other side, general theories of culture may not highlight important dimensions of 'the popular'. A minor art clique is given the same weighting as (or greater weighting than) the massive popular involvement in media sports. In many respects, general cultural theory applies to popular culture only with important new distinctions and extensions: 'commercial' forces in popular culture, for example, are more obvious than in face-to-face folk cultural interaction. In this examination, I attempt to draw out some of the lessons learned about culture from those theories especially associated with popular culture.

Defining culture and 'destabilizing privileged assumptions'

Popular culture theory has fought an uphill struggle against many forces lined up against it as the phenomena of popular and mass culture have evolved over the past century and a half. In contrast to the assumption that true research and theory serve to 'build theory' in a cumulative way, popular culture theory has often first been forced to dethrone opposing assumptions in order to clear the way for its own insights. In the useful phrase of Ulf Hannerz in Chapter 3, popular culture theory has been challenged to 'destabilize privileged assumptions' in order to carve out and justify its own position.

One basic dimension of the struggle of popular culture theory has been definitional. This definitional conflict has continued throughout more than a century of evolution of cultural theory. Both cultural theory in general and popular culture theory in particular have attempted to create rational understandings of non-rational dimensions of social life. To do this, nineteenth-century anthropology 'discovered' the life of 'savages' and attempted to find rational and aesthetic coherence in that life. Generations of groundbreaking ethnographies of preliterate societies found pragmatic and symbolic power in primitive rituals, myths, kinship patterns, tribal behavior, and everyday practices. This was 'culture' in the anthropological sense. Anthropology by the late nineteenth century had thus come to define culture as the systematic way of constructing reality that a people acquires as a consequence of living in a group.[1]

At the same time, however, 'culture' in the literate West was defined and studied in the aesthetic sense championed by Matthew Arnold as 'the best that has been known and said in the world'. The West was by many uncritically assumed to be rational, other cultures irrational. Ethnographies were conducted in non-technological societies in the service of the British Empire and other European colonial powers, but the same kinds of studies of everyday culture were much less common or respected when conducted within the imperial countries and cultures themselves.

The definitional (and imperial) conflict forced popular culture theory to distinguish at least four levels of culture, clarifying them with definitions that were not solidified before the middle of the twentieth century. First, 'elite' or high or serious culture was that produced by known artists within a consciously esthetic context judged according to an accepted set of rules, norms, and classics.[2] This marks the British literary meaning of culture. Second, 'folk' culture or art, in contrast, is that expressed in face-to-face interactions within traditional or tribal cultures and created through anonymous contributions from within the group where close interaction between performer and community is the norm. This reflects the anthropological emphasis. Third, 'mass' culture emerged from sociological and critical theory by mid-century as those large-scale expressions of culture that were created for a mass market and were known for their standardization of product, commercial promotion, and mass behavior. Mass culture theory was developed through a sociology of the masses, beginning with Max Weber, and by the critical theory of the Frankfurt School in the works of Adorno, Horkheimer, Benjamin, Marcuse, and others.

The fourth level of culture, 'popular' culture, was at times defined as narrowly identical with mass culture over and against elite and folk culture. Or, popular culture has alternately been identified as a middle ground, romantically situated between the localisms of folk culture and the grossness of mass culture, a kind of moderately ambitious and widespread aesthetic expression that maintains legitimacy and integrity. But more generally and more recently it has taken on a comprehensive meaning for any cultural expressions or products that are found broadly among a population, whether the popularly shared culture has elite, folk, or mass elements at work. In the Americas, 'the popular' became an inclusive term in the work of Latin American critics and North American academics, particularly those associated with the organizations and publications centered in the Center for the Study of Popular Culture at Bowling Green State University. The popular became, as well, especially associated with mediated forms of communication, those cultural expressions relayed through technology both in interactive forms shared through the Internet or the telephone, and in the mass media.

The definitional development of an accepted category for 'popular culture' provides an effective tool for destabilizing other privileged assumptions. The elitist rejection of popular culture as unworthy expressions of the unwashed masses has been unmasked as class bias. Value judgments built into the vocabulary of elitist theory for upper-class culture have had to make way for more eclectic and egalitarian recognition of the legitimacy and even the functionality of working-class culture. The struggles of Richard Hoggart and Raymond Williams in the 1950s to legitimize studies of music hall culture or pop fiction represented the first generation of 'Oxbridge' scholars whose class background and sympathies broke from the elitism of Eliot, Arnold, and the classicists. In parallel developments in the United States, mass communication research was validating the cultural power of sports, popular music, prime-time television, Hollywood movies, and other non-elitist expressions within advanced industrial society. Bernard Berelson (1949) found that 'What "Missing the Newspaper" Means' included primarily non-rational, non-informational factors. The 1947 New York newspaper strike not only left readers without political and public information but also left them with nothing to do at breakfast or on a commuter train; it left a huge *ritual* hole in their day. From this and similar influential pioneering studies – Herta Herzog on soap operas, Kurt and Gladys Lang on the MacArthur Day parade in Chicago, for instance, the literate, technological, industrialized West was indeed found to be non-rational in its dominant cultural expressions.

Stuart Hall and the Birmingham School took this definitional destabilizing further. For example, feminist scholarship examining the popular culture of teen magazines and romance fiction underscored the paternal biases in previous definitions of significant culture. 'Popular culture' meant not only working-class expression and life but also all those traditionally marginalized cultural practices most popular with, or even found only among, women. Angela McRobbie's (1978) stencilled Occasional Paper from the Birmingham Centre for Contemporary Cultural Studies, '*Jackie*: an ideology of adolescent femininity', was one of the pioneering studies that took seriously the expressions of youth culture and feminine experience.

McRobbie's thorough study of a teen magazine aimed at a female market can be seen to bring together the lenses provided by the multiple approaches to defining culture: the traditional ethnographer's interest in unsophisticated, seemingly non-rational culture, the elitist's sense that cultural products crystallize and express the group sensibility, the anti-elitist's interest in working-class people, the mass culture theorist's attention to mass marketing and commodification, the feminist's interest in expression idiosyncratic to paternal culture, and the popular culture theorist's interest in the unvarnished 'what is'. Ethnographers, elitists, mass culture critics, popular theorists, feminists, and post-modernists all look through the lenses provided by popular culture definitions and theory and only collectively begin to come to terms with the complexity of contemporary culture as actually lived and expressed. It takes all this and more to create thorough examinations of phenomena as superficially simple but culturally complex as Disneyland, the Olympics, the World Cup, the Super Bowl, or blockbuster movies.

Historical convergence: colonial anthropology and media technology

As the nineteenth century unfolded, two movements developed that were completely unrelated to each other yet destined to meet with significant consequences for cultural theory and popular culture. In the course of the twentieth century, these separate movements came together, at first awkwardly and in conflict but more recently with harmonious mutual benefits. The movements were, on the one hand, the development of colonialist anthropology with its previously mentioned attempt to define 'culture' among what were then considered the 'primitive peoples' of the world and, on the other hand, the development of new media of communication technology which enabled humans to communicate over distances with speed and increasing sensory completeness.

In our own time the coming together of these two movements has resulted in what James Clifford (1988) calls 'the predicament of culture', a sense of culture in which communication technologies, interacting with vastly increased travel and commerce, contribute to an everyday life that is in every part of the globe lived as a multilayered, syncretic complex of cultural impulses and components drawn from a diverse, fragmented, heterogeny of representational beliefs, behaviors, and meanings. With cultural lives that are almost everywhere heterogeneous and postmodern, in the convergence of anthropology and technology we see at work the importance of the historical shaping of concepts (culture) and definitions (elite, mass, popular, commodification, gender, etc.), as well as the theoretical understandings they facilitate or impede.

It is in this historical-cultural context that the importance of 'popular culture' becomes more clear. Once dismissed as insignificant trivia, the popular culture of music, film, radio, television, pulp fiction, advertising, telephone, Internet, and the rest, has become a cultural force on the global stage that is at once pervasive, intrusive, dominating, contradictory, and irresistible. The evolved aesthetic of 'the popular' – news stories in sound bites, music with predictable lyrical and melodic structures, pre-programmed emotions of movies and entertainment television, conventions and formulas known by all – this popular aesthetic plays an inescapable and profound role in everyone's life today, from the elite sophisticate who may erroneously think herself above it to the philistine presumed too dense to express himself through it. The popular culture competes with and incorporates every other cultural source – high culture and classical arts, traditional culture and folk arts, face-to-face experience, everything from masterful creativity to unconscious, inherited practices. The result is a form of everyday life today that is culturally impure, that is, a life that is neither traditional culture nor modern culture, that may uncritically combine the elite, the folk, and the mass, and that is postcolonial and postmodern in its essence.

The way humans mark the major moments in life always exposes cultural roots and today reflects this postmodern syncretism. Birth, coming-of-age, marriage and death are turning points in life and invariably receive ritual treatment in standardized ceremonies that vary from culture to culture. Consider, for example, how funeral practices illustrate this dynamic. Funerals in Western culture were historically built on classic liturgy in High Church traditions of Catholics, Lutherans, or Episcopalians. In Low Church traditions, funerals incorporated elements of folk culture with increased emotionalism in hymns and outbursts of response and lamenting. With the incorporation of recorded music, guitars, and pop songs in such services, the popular culture made its presence newly felt. But today a single funeral can incorporate every dimension of syncretic, postmodern culture, as we all saw in late 1997.

Diana's funeral and popular culture theory

Taking all the above into account, what do we make of a funeral like that for Lady Diana Spencer, 'Princess Di', following her death in a high-speed accident in Paris on 31 August 1997? What concepts of culture does it underscore? An estimated 1.2 billion people all over the globe watched the funeral of Diana, making it one of the most widely shared events in human history. Public concern over the death of Diana was ritually worked through in this massive transnational media experience. In this 'media event'[3] we have one of the purest and best-known expressions of popular culture, most strikingly as seen in the popular ritual functions of television and the rest of the media apparatus.

The televised ceremony was elitist in its origins within traditions of British royalty but was distinctly 'popular' in style. Variations from the classical funeral liturgy gave it a pop quality and reflected Diana's well-known struggles against orthodox traditions of royal life, Windsor property, marital submission, and the tasteful avoidance of controversy. The most famous variation from Anglican liturgy was the allowance of Elton John's performance of his Diana-adapted

'Candle in the Wind', originally a tribute to Marilyn Monroe. Just as Diana had won popular favor by opposing the stuffier of Windsor traditions, this intrusion of the pop amongst the sacred won favor with a vast world audience that quickly made John's song a global bestseller.

Popular and elite mixed elsewhere in the ceremony as well. The world cyber-pulpit presented by Diana's funeral was seized by the Church of England but more so by Diana's brother Charles, the ninth Earl of Spencer. His moving tribute to Diana was spiced with righteous criticism of the royal family, Satanic paparazzi, and the media exploitation of celebrities. Adding to the postmodern pastiche, those attending the funeral reflected the many spheres of media celebrity. There were royalty from many countries, politicians (Tony Blair and Margaret Thatcher), foreign dignitaries (Hillary Rodham Clinton and Henry Kissinger), fashion designers (Valentino and the Versaces), and entertainers (Luciano Pavarotti, Tom Cruise, Richard Attenborough, Tom Hanks, Nicole Kidman, Sting, Steven Spielberg, *et alii*).

An understanding of the intriguing power and role of such a 'media celebrity' is another example of the definitional advance of popular culture theorizing.[4]

The sheer *scale* of popular cultural practice, technological systems, and the global media spectacle is of theoretical significance. Huge numbers of people are connected through the televised funeral, and that fact alone makes the event distinct from the small-scale face-to-face culture of colonial anthropology. Under the title 'TV once again unites the world in grief', Tom Shales (1997) notes, 'The simple point of the whole amazing international ordeal may be that the entire world felt it needed a good cry, and the ceremony and its coverage was certainly designed to inspire one'. The concept of 'ritual power' in popular culture theory helps explain the funeral experience of viewers. Caryn James (1997) found that television began its final Diana watch immediately after her death by 'serving a communal function and uniting the country in grief and acceptance . . . Like a wake, watching television allows viewers to overcome their disbelief and grasp the reality of death'. But this soon gave way to 'wall-to-wall trivia about her life' in a 'voyeuristic overload'. Finally, when the funeral procession began a week later, James notes, 'television returned to its significant communal function' with elements 'typical of wakes and funerals in real life'.

This is classical mythic ritual at work, as first theorized by colonial anthropologists and later complexified through mass media. In the ritual act, the participant feels and expresses a unity with the ritual story and meaning, with others in the ritual, with the origins and purposes of human life and death. In Diana's funeral, television ritual showed its power to connect the participant to richer meanings and larger forces. Its liturgical relay took the global audience through the profane to reach out towards the sacred. The ritual participant was transported. For the collective, the Diana funeral ritual marked a suspension of normal activities and structure and a transformation towards a better community. The trans-human model and the repetition of an exemplary scenario unified us ritually and re-awakened our sense of drama and the uniqueness of individual events. The televised funeral ritual celebrated unifying, emotional, symbolic objectifications of collective experience. It established order and defined roles as it restructured time and space. It offered a security blanket against the terror or boredom of mere profane existence. It celebrated central tendencies and values in our global culture. These are the larger theoretical concepts that classical anthropological theory and popular culture theory have contributed.[5]

The importance of 'the popular' and media celebrity

'The popular' today has the prominence the Church had in medieval society. In the broadest sense, all areas of life today relate to and are subsumed by a kind of media 'noosphere', to borrow a word from Teilhard de Chardin, that global mental and spiritual environment expressed in the bytes of media circulating everywhere and captured in human minds. Diana's death and funeral illustrate the ways in which popular media play the traditional social role of the Church in today's secular, pluralistic society.

The canonized saint can be of the humblest origins and the slightest worldly accomplishments but is offered up for emulation as a role model for symbolic purposes: 'Be like Saint Teresa.' Today the media celebrity plays this role. 'Be like Mike' (Michael Jordan), that is, be delivered from your worldly miseries by losing yourself in his celebrity. Diana became a celebrity par excellence. Even when she separated herself from her largest claim on worldly power as the wife of England's future king, she remained in the public eye and continued to be celebrated. She is a classic example of historian Daniel Boorstin's observation that a modern celebrity is famous simply for being famous, that is, that 'worldly achievement' is not necessary to celebrity.

The scale of Diana's celebrity cannot be denied. During her life and death, she was featured on magazine covers in unprecedented numbers. Jacqueline Sharkey (1997: 20) notes, 'Economic and technological developments made Diana's image such a marketing force that broadcast network news operations devoted more time in one week to her fatal accident than to any news event since the 1991 coup attempt against Soviet leader Mikhail Gorbachev'. Her death was the number one news story of 1997 according to the Associated Press. Diana's significance has been the subject of at least fifteen conferences. Opinion polls in the UK rank her as high as second among the twentieth century's most important figures.

Such celebrity as Diana's, in many respects, achieves what canonization was intended for, role modeling and relief writ large, but does so on a scale unimaginable to Church instruments of beatification and canonization. The number of people affected, however slightly, by the Diana phenomenon is a challenge to the theoretical imagination. Diana in life and death symbolized so many things to so many people – beauty, compassion, glamour, responsibility, parenting, independence, uncertainty, commitment. To one media professional, the coverage of her death 'represented an important public catharsis about all sorts of different issues – about women and their place in society, about how the famous and their fans interact' (Sharkey 1997: 21).

The globalization of media sport culture

The scale of some popular spectacles does not mean there is one uniform, multinational form of culture taking over the world today, quite the contrary. Within the popular are multiple contradictions and differences that make any specific manifestation of culture today distinctive in its peculiar combinations of the elite and the mass, the new and the old, the global and the local, the borrowed and the invented. Popular culture theory takes very seriously how technology, popular ritual, the spectacle, commerce, hegemony, and other dynamics of the popular create representation and meaning in everyday life.

At the turn of the millennium, current technologies of the Internet, digitization, interactivity, and broadband instantaneous multimedia manage to accelerate the technological trends begun with the telegraph, telephone, sound recording, electricity, film, wireless, and other technologies of the nineteenth century. Cultural theories of collage, displacement, historical contingency, intertextuality, transnationalization, postcolonialism, and everyday life complexify and correct the work of nineteenth-century colonial anthropology. Clifford Geertz's (1973) essay on the cockfight in Bali, perhaps the most widely cited piece of cultural theory in the past half century, added a more humble, postmodern reading of 'other' cultures, deleting the imperialism of colonial-era ethnographers while opening up the 'textual' interpretation of culture.

At the millennium, theorizing about the 'media sport nexus' reflected the consensus in popular culture theory in a global context. David Rowe's *Sport, Culture and the Media* (1999) joined the anthologies *MediaSport* (Wenner 1998) and *SportCult* (Martin and Miller 1999) in bringing together cultural theory and case studies of specific instances of media-transmitted sports activities. These works held in common that global factors are central to current popular culture; witness the parallel developments in mediated sports in different countries as media moguls buy up sporting events and teams. Disney buys baseball and hockey teams (the Anaheim Angels and Mighty Ducks) at the same time that it buys a television network (ABC), and similar media/sport combinations emerge in Australia, the UK, Europe, Asia, and Latin America.

But, in addition to that parallel-development form of globalization, a more multinational form of globalization was also taking place as a single individual or corporation would buy up and merge media and sports institutions simultaneously in different countries. Illustrating this, Rupert Murdoch appears repeatedly in each of the three media/sport/cult books. His empire is the living embodiment of the most blatant 'globalization' of popular culture. Murdoch controls or is part-owner of television rights around the globe. In America, through his Fox Network, Murdoch owns NFL football and NHL hockey. Via British-based Foxtel, British-based BSkyB, German-based Vox, Australian-based Channel Seven, and Hong-Kong-based Star TV, Murdock controls dominant television rights in one form or another to all major spectator sports: soccer, rugby, cricket, boxing, Australian football, auto racing, tennis, golf, badminton, motorcycling, table tennis, American football, and baseball (Rowe & McKay 1999).

In fundamental ways, only a unified theory of culture, heavily indebted to popular culture theory, makes the three media/sport/cult books possible and coherent. One book, *Sportcult*, is organized around 'building nations' through studies of *kung fu* cinema in Tanzania and cricket in South Africa and Sri Lanka, 'building bodies' through aerobics, bodybuilding, and wrestling, 'buying and selling nations and bodies' through ownership struggles, internationalized golf, and trash-talking basketball, and 'signifying sport' in upward-mobility documentary, women sports journalists, and battles over sports trademarks. A second book, *MediaSport*, examines institutions, texts, and audiences of the sports/media complex. The themes include games, commodification, marketplace, race and gender, audiences, cyberspace, nationalism, and globalization. This last theme is developed most extensively in David Whitson's 'Circuits of promotion: Media, marketing and the globalization of sport'. Whitson finds 'a new kind of corporate integration in the media and entertainment industries'. At one level this means transnational investment and marketing on a global basis. At another level it means vertical integration between ownership of distribution media and ownership of popular entertainment properties. This represents a global 'shift towards integrated corporate ownership of both content *and* distribution' (59). Similarly, Rowe's examination of *Sport, Culture and the Media* revolves around his chapter on global political economy, 'Money, myth and the big match: The political economy of the sports media'. The media sport text has become a valuable commodity, especially as economies have shifted away from material goods and direct services and towards control of information and images. Rowe represents a concern of recent important work in popular culture: 'There is a marked globalizing trend in media sport which makes it increasingly hard to insulate any aspect of sport and media in any particular country from external, disruptive forces' (1999: 75).

Imagine nineteenth-century colonial anthropologists hearing their theories of non-rational tribal belief and behavior applied to global experiences touching more than a billion people at once. They would be bewildered. The applications of popular culture theory today explode the face-to-face scale of social analysis known to colonial anthropologists. Because of this, theories of classical myth and ritual must be complemented with theories of the media text and political economy and more. Popular culture cases today take us well beyond the limits of classical definitions and applications.

Unscrewing the inscrutable: over-rationalizing culture in the name of theory

Life is not a problem to be solved but a mystery to be lived.

(Gabriel Marcel, *The Mystery of Being*: 1984)

A final contribution of popular culture theory to cultural debates is pop cult's insistence on not losing contact with the lived experience of culture, with the actual practices and products which theory is meant to explain and possibly direct. General cultural theory can position itself at such a high level of abstraction that the reader despairs of actually comprehending the theory in specific personal experience. Popular culture theory, even at the expense of appearing atheoretical or anti-intellectual, has long insisted on celebrating and criticizing 'the immediate experience', in the wonderful phrasing of Robert Warshow concerning moviegoing. The immediacy of popular culture protects it against theorizing at too high a level of abstraction, while at the other end its bewildering variety and importance demands some degree of serious explaining.

Popular culture theory's closeness to reality also protects against any unfortunate confusion between the rational explanation of the pop cult phenomenon and the actual experience of it. It is not that rational explanations are untrue or are not valuable; they are essential to a self-determining society. But the true attraction and value of popular culture, and all culture, is the existential experience of it, its phenomenological place. Love of a sports team or rapture over a celebrity's funeral is neither selected nor enjoyed because of or through its rationality. Rather its emotionality, its pleasure, its rich evocation and multiple associations, serve to draw and hold the human subjects who engage in it. The popular culturalist has little trouble sensing the wisdom behind taking life as a mystery to be lived rather than as a problem to be solved.

The historical sweep of the development and contribution of popular culture theory, notably in its accomplishments flowing to and from general cultural theory, lays out before us a rich set of definitions, concepts, interrogations, and explanations. They place us in an advantaged position despite the many complications, obscurities, and inconsistencies still occupying space in the theoretical mix. In the effort to hyper-rationalize culture through theory, we create false hope and a false goal if our theoretical rationality attempts to convert all cultural experience into elite culture or folk culture or some other rationally approved alternative. The true goal of popular culture theory is to come to terms with the popular *as it is* and not as translated into something else. This can be a helpful check on all cultural theory. After all, we do ourselves a disservice on many levels if we lose sight of the fact that culture is above all, in fact, our experience of fun, challenge, history, conflict, love, meaning, joy, friendship, death, and all that makes life worthwhile.

Notes

1 Ernst Cassirer has critiqued the early developments of anthropological theories of myth and ritual to argue for their 'symbolic' power. Myth is one of his six basic symbolic systems alongside language, science, religion, art, and history; such theoretic power for myth as a symbol system provides a basis for accenting the importance of popular culture and its theoretical constructions. See Cassirer (1944, 1946, 1965).
2 The definition of elite is especially drawn from Russell Nye (1970), that of folk from Oscar Handlin (1961) and Joseph Arpad (1975), and the definitions of mass and popular are drawn from Harold Wilensky (1974), Raymond Williams (1974), and Herbert Gans (1974).
3 See Dayan and Katz (1992) for the characteristics and consequences of live international media events, of which Diana's funeral was a classical example.
4 For theories of celebrity and stardom, see Richard Dyer (1979 and 1986) and the readings in Drucker and Cathcart (1994).
5 Such mythic functions are explained here drawing from the works of Mircea Eliade, Bronislaw Malinowksi, Ernst Cassirer, Victor Turner, and, in their more recent mediated forms, by James Carey and Dayan and Katz.

References

Arpad, J. (1975). 'Between folklore and literature: Popular culture as anomaly'. *Journal of Popular Culture*, 9: 404.

Berelson, B. (1949). 'What "missing the newspaper" means'. In P. Lazarsfeld and F. Stanton (eds), *Communication Research 1948–1949*. New York: Harper and Bros.

Cassirer, E. (1944). *Essay on Man*. New Haven: Yale University Press.

—— (1946). *The Myth of the State*. New Haven: Yale University Press.

—— (1965). *The Philosophy of Symbolic Forms*. New Haven: Yale University Press.

Clifford, J. (1988). *The Predicament of Culture: Twentieth-century Ethnography, Literature, and Art*. Cambridge, MA: Harvard University Press.

Dayan, D. and Katz, E. (1992). *Media Events: The Live Broadcasting of History*. Cambridge, MA: Harvard University Press.

Drucker, S. J. and Cathcart, R. S. (1994). *American Heroes in a Media Age*. Cresskill, NJ: Hampton Press.

Dyer, R. (1979). *Stars*. London: BFI.

Dyer, R. (1986). *Heavenly Bodies: Stars and Society*. London: BFI.

Gans, H. (1974). *Popular Culture and High Culture: An Analysis and Evaluation of Taste*. New York: Basic Books.

Handlin, O. (1961). 'Mass and popular culture'. In N. Jacob (ed.), *Culture for the Millions*. New York: Van Nostrand.

Geertz, C. (1973). *The Interpretation of Cultures*. New York: Basic Books.

James, C. (1997). 'A medium at its best, when not at its worst'. *New York Times*, 7 September: 10.

McRobbie, A. (1978). *Jackie*: An Ideology of Adolescent Femininity. Stencilled Occasional Paper. Birmingham, England: The Centre for Contemporary Cultural Studies.

Marcel, G. (1984). *The Mystery of Being*. New York: University Press of America.

Martin, R. and Miller, T. (eds) (1999). *SportCult*. Minneapolis: University of Minnesota Press.

Nye, R. (1970). *The Unembarrassed Muse: The Popular Arts in America*. New York: Dial Press.

Rowe, D. (1999). *Sport, Culture and the Media: The Unruly Trinity*. Buckingham: Open University Press.

Shales, T. (1997). 'TV once again unites the world in grief'. *The Washington Post*, 7 September. Reprinted in Ray Eldon Hiebert (ed.), *Impact of Mass Media: Current Issues*, 4th edition (1999). New York: Longman.

Sharkey, J. (1997). 'The Diana aftermath'. *American Journalism Review*, November: 18–25.

Wenner, L. A. (1998). *MediaSport*. London: Routledge.

Whitson, D. (1998). Circuits of promotion: Media, marketing, and the globalization of sport'. In L. A. Wenner (ed.), *MediaSport*. London: Routledge.

Wilensky, H. (1974). 'Mass society and mass culture: Interdependence or independence?' In G. Tuchman (ed.), *The TV Establishment: Programming for Power and Profit*. Englewood Cliffs, NJ: Prentice-Hall.

Williams, R. (1974). 'On high and popular culture'. *The New Republic*, 23 November: 15.

9

VISUAL CULTURE

Paul Messaris

One need not be a technological determinist to recognize that the globalizing, mass-mediated, commercially driven visual culture that so much of the world lives in today – a culture embodied in movies, television, advertising, and other pictorial media – is in part the product of technological developments in those media. Whereas one can conceive of complex verbal cultures based only on rudimentary means for the dissemination of the written word, contemporary visual culture would be inconceivable without the technologies that make it possible to produce automatic images of the visual world, to manipulate, copy, and store those images, to make them seem to move, and to transmit them instantaneously across vast spaces. This overview of visual culture will focus on four visual technologies, and on the implications of each. In order of the chronology of their invention, these four technologies are: print-making, photography, cinematography, and television. In connection with these technologies, this discussion will examine the relationship between visual culture and cognition; the nature of photographic truth and falsehood; the impact of visual fiction and fantasy on viewers' evaluations of their own lives; and visual culture's increasingly international character.

Print-making and cognition

The roots of contemporary visual culture lie in the centuries-old technology of print-making. As William Ivins has pointed out, the development of printing, which seems to have originated in China, made it possible for the first time to create 'exactly repeatable pictorial statements' (Ivins 1953). In this sense, printed copies of images were the first pictorial mass media. Ivins's seminal analysis of the social consequences of early print-making places major emphasis on the scientific and cognitive implications of this mass medium. Following his lead, an examination of cognitive consequences may be an appropriate starting point for considering the nature and ramifications of visual culture.

Writing primarily about the development of woodblock printing, engraving, and etching in fifteenth and sixteenth century Europe, Ivins argued that the new-found ability to produce exact replicas of pictorial information provided a tremendous boost to all intellectual endeavors that deal with spatial structures, ranging from architecture and engineering to such disparate fields as geography, anatomy, and botany. Much of Ivins's account deals with specific applications of print-making in such tasks as the construction of blueprints or the illustration of textbooks in herbal pharmacology. However, going beyond such particulars, Ivins also believed that the spread of pictorial mass media was responsible for a more general shift in human cognitive capabilities, away from the verbal abstractions of the ancient world and towards types of reasoning that were more directly attuned to the forms of material reality.

Ivins's conjectures about the broader cognitive concomitants of a cultural shift towards visual media are as pertinent to the present state of visual communication as they were to the historical period that his book was about. Among contemporary cultural critics, it has become commonplace to argue that the increasing societal shift towards visual media is responsible for a large-scale impoverishment of people's cognitive capacities. As the editors of a volume on American cultural decline have pointed out, the term 'dumbing down' appears to have been first used in reaction to the intellectual level of Hollywood movies (Washburn and Thornton 1996: 12). In contrast to such indictments of movies or other visual media, Ivins's work points to the possibility that, far from dumbing viewers down, visual culture may actually entail important cognitive benefits.

Ivins's optimistic view of the cognitive dimensions of visual culture is shared by more recent authors such as Edgerton (1991), who argues that Renaissance artists' discovery of linear perspective made a significant contribution to architecture and engineering, and Tufte (1983, 1990, 1997), whose books on informational graphics contain abundant testimony to the intellectual sophistication that goes into the creation of such taken-for-granted visuals as maps or temperature charts. Still, all of these writers deal with visual media that are directly linked to scientific or technological activities. As far as the broad public's reactions to visual communication are concerned, it may be more appropriate to focus on entertainment media such as movies or television.

The familiar argument that television is responsible for a decline in young people's intellectual abilities has been examined in research reported by Neuman (1995). The findings indicated that there does indeed appear to be a negative correlation between amount of television viewing and some aspects of children's school performance. However, even if this correlation is due to an underlying causal link, we need to be cautious in drawing any broader conclusions from these results. Because measures of school performance tend overwhelmingly to be verbal, the data reported by Neuman could indeed be a sign that television depresses verbal skills by displacing some amount of leisure-time reading. However, unless one believes that verbal skills are the only, or the predominant, component of cognitive ability, these data cannot be taken as a more general indictment of the cognitive effects of visual media. Instead, they can be seen as a reminder to look beyond words in assessing the relationship between cognition and visual culture.

For more than a decade, the most prominent conceptual framework for investigations of the non-verbal aspects of cognitive ability has been Howard Gardner's theory of multiple intelligences (Gardner 1983, 1993). Gardner's basic argument is that intelligence is not a single, largely verbal entity but, rather, comprises a variety of intellectual abilities, which are not necessarily correlated with each other. Among the eight or so basic intelligences that Gardner discusses, there is one in particular, namely, spatial intelligence, that is directly relevant to any consideration of viewers' cognitive engagement with visual media. Spatial intelligence is the ability to form accurate mental representations of the relationships among objects or parts of objects in two- or three-dimensional space. Spatial intelligence also encompasses the ability to perform mental transformations of those relationships. In other words, this is a type of mental skill that is absolutely crucial in such professions as carpentry or airplane navigation, but it also plays a more routine, and often unconscious, role in many facets of everyday life, whenever we have to interact with physical structures or orient ourselves in our environment.

It seems reasonable to suppose that spatial intelligence may be enhanced by one's dealings with visual media. Gardner appears to take this relationship for granted, but the assumption is also supported by systematic research, most notably perhaps in an Israeli study by Tidhar (1984), where fifth-grade children who were taught movie-making attained a significant increase in spatial intelligence over the course of a semester (see also earlier related research by Salomon 1979). A crucial point about Tidhar's study is that it had to do with a medium that is commonly used for entertainment, whereas the arguments of Ivins and his successors were concerned mainly with scientific or informational uses of visual media. In this respect, Tidhar's study takes us beyond the realm of professional users of images and points toward the broader, society-wide concomitants of visual culture. In other words, the study suggests that the positive impact of visual media on cognitive skills may go beyond those sectors of the population in which visual media are used as direct aids to cognition.

An especially intriguing aspect of Tidhar's findings was the fact that children who were taught movie-editing experienced a greater improvement in spatial intelligence than children who were taught camerawork. This finding suggests that it is the characteristic syntax of movies – their way of carving up reality into discrete units and reassembling those units according to medium-specific conventions – that may be most conducive to the sharpening of mental skills. Any movie (or television program, or video) forces us to see reality in a new and distinctive way. Instead of being immersed in a continuous visual surround, we are confronted with a succession of sharply delimited visual fragments, which we ourselves must mentally reassemble into a coherent world, one which fits together not just spatially but also in terms of narrative logic. It is not surprising that this continual mental challenge should serve to extend our cognitive abilities.

Furthermore, although previous discussion of these issues has focused largely on spatial intelligence, it seems more than likely that other aspects of cognitive functioning also receive a beneficial boost from the experience of visual syntax. Much editing – or, more broadly, montage – is based on the principle of analogy (for example, in the realm of advertising, the ubiquitous juxtapositions of products with images that metaphorically mirror the products' attributes), and analogical constructions are prevalent in conventions of visual composition and camerawork as well (Messaris 1996). It may well be, then, that analogical thinking is another area of cognitive functioning in which visual media play an activating role. More generally, the arguments that we have just reviewed converge on the notion that the evolving visual culture of the mass media is not only a system of social representation but also a distinctive blueprint for cognition.

Truth and falsehood in photography

If the technologies of print-making had remained the only methods for producing pictorial mass media, some facets of contemporary visual culture would not look very different from the way they do today. Comic books would be largely unaffected, and so would a certain fraction of such media as magazine ads, billboards, or greeting cards, among others. However, the bulk of the imagery in today's visual media is based on the major successor to print-making, namely, photography. The nineteenth-century invention of photography brought into being for the first time a series of mass media (including cinema, television, and video) that could lay claim to reproducing certain features of human perceptual experience directly, that is, without the intervention of the artist's hand. In the well-known semiotic terminology of C. S. Peirce (1991), photographs are 'indexical' representations, meaning that they are actually the physical products of the things they represent. Traditional photography is the result of the action of light rays on photosensitive chemicals, while television, video, and digital images arise from the effects of light on electrical circuits. Hence the notion that photographic images are 'objective' records of reality.

Much of the character of contemporary visual culture is colored indelibly by this 'indexicality' of photographic images. The importance of indexicality is most obvious in cases in which our interaction with a certain medium is explicitly premised on the medium's putative capacity to deliver the visual truth. News imagery and some forms of advertising are perhaps the two most prominent examples of this phenomenon, and it is not surprising that much scholarly and critical writing about these media has dealt explicitly with the potential deceptions that lurk behind the façade of photographic truth.

As far as television news imagery is concerned, the foundational study on this

topic was Lang and Lang's (1952) investigation of viewer responses to an incident from the Korean War period, a public ceremony held in Chicago in
honor of General Douglas MacArthur following President Harry Truman's
decision to remove him from the command of US forces in the war. Employing
research assistants who were trained in the observation and coding of human
behavior, the Langs compared the televised version of the event with what
was actually happening at the event itself. The results indicated that television's
selective presentation of some incidents and not others created an exaggerated
sense of the public's degree of enthusiasm for General MacArthur.

The overall point of the Langs' study – namely, how much difference the
simple process of selection can make to the final impression conveyed by any
photographic medium – goes to the heart of the issues raised by the seeming
veridicality of visual representations. A more recent demonstration of the same
point occurred during the Persian Gulf War, when television images of amaz-
ingly precise 'smart bombs' appear to have led many, if not most, viewers to see
the war as a 'remote, bloodless, pushbutton battle in which only military targets
were assumed destroyed' (Walker 1992: 84). As it happens, however, subsequent
reports revealed that, 'of all bombs dropped on Iraq, only seven percent were
so-called smart bombs, and of these at most 70 percent were thought to have
hit their intended targets' (Lee and Solomon 1990: xx). Moreover, in stark
contrast to the image of a war without human victims, it appears that there
were substantial numbers of Iraqi civilian casualties, especially in the city of
Basra (Walker 1992: 87–8; see also Sifry and Cerf 1991: 336n). In other words,
the selective images of precisely guided smart-bomb strikes may have given
viewers a misleading impression of one of the most serious consequences of the
war.

Selective representation, in the sense in which we have just encountered it in
these examples, is an inherent and unavoidable feature of all photographic
image-making. In that respect, potentially misleading selectivity is arguably a
ubiquitous possibility in any facet of visual culture in which photographic
evidence serves as the guarantor (whether stated or implicit) of objectivity or
truth. And yet, when contemporary visually oriented scholars raise concerns
about abuse of photography's indexical character, they are much more likely to
focus on relatively more complex forms of potential deception, namely,
unacknowledged staging and digital manipulation of images. Unacknowledged
staging is exemplified by such cases as the news report in which a truck was
rigged with explosives to demonstrate its supposed tendency to detonate in
accidents; or the television commercial in which a car's body was reinforced
with steel I-beams to demonstrate its supposed ability to withstand the attacks
of a 'monster truck' (Messaris 1997: 271–2).

To an even greater extent than is the case with unacknowledged staging,
digital imaging has become a major focus of concerns about the problematic
truth value of photographic images. In fact, as Stephen Prince (1993) has noted,
the emergence of digital techniques for the alteration of images calls into

question the very indexicality of photography. If an image or part of an image that looks like a photograph can now be created by non-photographic means, the notion that a photograph is a direct record of visual reality is no longer a defining principle of the medium as a whole. Critics of potentially deceptive digital imaging are usually concerned about its consequences for the viewer who has not detected the presence of digital manipulation and may, indeed, be more generally unaware of the ubiquity of digitally manipulated imagery. However, a different, somewhat contrasting school of criticism focuses on how photography's loss of indexicality affects those viewers who are, in fact, aware and may even be practitioners of digital imaging in their own right. Such viewers, it is argued, will eventually lose all faith in the photographic medium, and photography will no longer be accorded its privileged place among media with a stake in appearing faithful to fact (Ritchin 1990).

This possibility is demonstrated very vividly in a story told by the distinguished landscape and nature photographer Galen Rowell (Dalai Lama and Rowell 1990). While taking photographs of the palace of the Dalai Lama in Tibet, Rowell noticed a gorgeous rainbow in the sky. He also realized that from a different vantage point – a great distance away – the rainbow would appear to terminate on the palace itself. Anxious to get this more dramatic view before the rainbow disappeared, Rowell set off in a great hurry over difficult terrain. He arrived at the spot exhausted, but the rainbow was still there, and his efforts were rewarded with a spectacular photograph. However, when he showed the photograph to audiences in the United States, he found that, instead of admiring his compositional skills and the sheer physical effort required to produce this picture, viewers who were unaware of the circumstances surrounding its creation were inclined to assume that the photograph was simply the product of digital manipulation, a routine case of superimposing one image on top of another.

The assumption that increasing awareness of potentially misleading photographic practices may result in a growing public distrust of the medium is supported by the outcome of a study by Slattery and Tiedge (1992), who found that labeling portions of a newscast as 'staged recreations' led to a more general erosion of faith even in those segments that were not so labeled. As people become more familiar with digital imaging practices and as abuses of photography's documentary qualities receive increasing attention from media watchdogs, it may well turn out that photographic images will lose some of their traditional aura of being true-to-life. Still, such predictions should be tempered by a recognition that the public's faith in photographic truth may never have been as blind as some media critics have assumed. The manipulation of photographic reality has a history that is essentially as long as that of photography itself, and there is good evidence that, even in the earliest years of the medium, its potentially misleading nature had not escaped public notice. There is also good reason to believe that ordinary viewers are perfectly capable of challenging photographic evidence when it doesn't fit their own preconceptions – as when German prisoners-of-war in the Second World War dismissed filmed documentation of Nazi concentration camps (Fincher 1995). Consequently, rather than assuming that people are taken in by photography because they don't know better, it may be more accurate to say that people buy into photographic truth when it accords with what they want to believe.

Movie fantasies and personal realities

Although the photographic process is the basis of most pictorial mass media, it was not until the advent of moving pictures that visual images began to occupy the central role that they currently play in so many people's leisure time. One of the distinctive qualities of life in the twentieth century has been the increasing amount of time that people spend in the imaginary visual worlds of movies and fictional television programs. In both qualitative and quantitative terms, this experience is sharply removed from that which characterized the movies' two most obvious predecessors, namely, the theater and written fiction. The theater may be closer to reality in certain respects, and fictional reading may be as consuming an activity – at least for some segments of the population – but it is only movies and television that combine the true-to-life appearance of photographic media with the ubiquity that most media have acquired thanks to late-nineteenth- and twentieth-century techniques of mass production.

What does it mean to be immersed, day in and day out, in the parallel visual universe provided by television, video, and film? A crucial feature of this experience is the compelling imitative realism of the motion-picture image. This realism goes beyond the true-to-life quality of all photographs. Rather, as many film theorists have noted, it is a realism that stems just as much from the way in which movies manipulate space and time as from the photographic basis of the movie image (Ray 1985). In film theory, this topic is usually discussed under the heading of 'illusionism', namely, movies' ability to create a fictional world which sucks the viewer in and suppresses his/her awareness of the essential artificiality of what he/she is watching. The most frequently cited ingredient of movie illusionism is 'invisible editing', a set of principles for creating image sequences that seem to flow naturally, deflecting the viewer's attention away from the fact that, each time there is an edit, there is also a radical, 'impossible' shift in a movie's point-of-view.

In the Hollywood style of film-making that dominated the world's theaters and television screens for much of the twentieth century, this illusionism has been combined with another important attribute, the idealization of the people, places, and events represented on the screen. To sit through most Hollywood movies is to enter a world that can seem engagingly lifelike and yet also better, more desirable than everyday life in many ways. Typically, people in movies are more glamorous than people in real life, the physical environment of movies is more opulent than people's real-life surroundings, and movie happenings are more exciting, more rewarding, more satisfying in their resolutions than the everyday experiences of real people. What are the consequences of being immersed mentally in such a world for a large and regular portion of one's existence, as so many people are in a culture of full-time television and neighborhood video stores? And how do those consequences mesh with people's responses to commercial advertising, a form of visual communication that is even more tightly wedded to idealization than most Hollywood movies are?

A suggestive answer to these questions is provided by a brief item of gossip that appeared in a supermarket tabloid some years ago. This story concerned an aging (now deceased) Hollywood actor who had had the reputation of being a 'ladies' man'. Somehow, a reporter asked him if he ever watched pornographic movies. No, the former film star replied, he did not enjoy seeing people do in the span of an hour and a half what he himself was no longer able to do in a whole week. This comment is mirrored by the responses of subjects in systematic research on the effects of pornography. As Zillman and Bryant (1989) have found, a regular diet of pornographic movies tends to lower men's level of satisfaction with their own sexual relationships. At first blush, these findings and the movie star's personal story may seem somewhat far removed from the world of non-pornographic cinema and advertising. However, on closer inspection it turns out that what the movie star was describing appears to be a common response of viewers exposed to any form of fantasy, be it sexual, romantic, or whatever.

In the realm of non-pornographic sexuality and romance, a study by Goldfarb (1987) has documented viewers' responses that were strikingly similar to those of Zillman and Bryant's pornography-viewing subjects and the aging movie star. Goldfarb was interested in how people respond to media representations of romance, and she explored this topic through individual interviews with some forty young men and women. At the end of the interviews, she explicitly asked each of her interviewees whether they ever felt inadequate or disappointed about their own lives in comparison to images of romance in movies or television. A majority of the people in her sample – men as well as women, and college graduates as well as those who had not gone beyond high school – said that they did. For example, here is the reply of a female college grad:

> Oh definitely! Even the sex scenes I feel really . . . small that I'm not like that. Or the women who have really good careers, I'll feel really inadequate and say 'how come I'm not as good as they are?' I get so wrapped up in the movie, I feel I'm the only one there. I get so involved that I compare myself to their relationships, their careers, what they look like. I sit there and look at that hairdo, those shoes, this dress, the way she acted, and I just compare myself and I feel lousy.
>
> (Goldfarb 1987: 86)

In fact, it seems that even professional observers of the media are not immune from feelings of this sort. The famous film critic Molly Haskell once wrote a whole essay about her repeated disappointment at the discrepancy between the loves in her real life and the love-life she had experienced vicariously in movies. The essay's title was, 'Movies ruined me for real romance'.

Furthermore, as the quotation from Goldfarb's respondent suggests, it is not just images of romance and sex that give rise to such feelings of personal inadequacy. The quotation's hint at career dissatisfaction is a theme that emerges in other accounts of viewers' comparisons between their own professional or economic circumstances and the images they witness in the visual media. For example, in a psychotherapeutic exploration of people's responses to advertising, Carol Moog cites the case of a young lawyer who felt frustrated because she hadn't lived up to her potential as a member of 'the Pepsi generation – that is, beautiful, sexy, happy young people . . . a generation that didn't slog through law school, work twelve-hour days, or break up with fiances' (Moog 1990: 15). Moog suggests that advertising is actually in the business of making people feel bad in such ways, on the assumption that personal frustration can motivate compensatory purchases. In the case of movies and fictional television images, on the other hand, similar feelings seem to arise despite the fact that the producers of these images are presumably in the business of making people feel good.

Feelings of dissatisfaction in response to visual fantasy seem especially significant when they occur in children, whose evolving world views are probably more fluid and malleable than those of adults. Some indication of how children feel about idealized media images comes from a study by the present author (Messaris 1987). Based on interviews with mothers, the study was an investigation of what children and parents say to one another while watching television. Without any special prompting on the part of the interviewers, a substantial number of mothers mentioned that their children had occasionally expressed feelings of inadequacy or resentment in response to television programs or commercials. More specifically, it was images of material well-being and glamorous lifestyles that appeared to trigger these expressions of dissatisfaction, and what the children were objecting to was the discrepancy between these highly alluring images and the more constrained circumstances of their own lives. As one mother put it, 'Both my own and children in school seem to feel that that [i.e., television] is – at that age, at the sixth, seventh, and eighth grade level – they seem to feel that that's reality and what they're living in is somehow a mistake' (see Messaris 1987: 100). Not surprisingly, these kinds of comments were more common among the less well-off families in the study. According to our interviews, mothers often respond to such comments by telling their children that television images paint a false picture of reality. However, as we have seen, adults themselves are not immune from feeling that reality is at fault for not being able to match the attractions of the television image.

From a broader sociocultural perspective, these ramifications of our involvement with visual fantasy may perhaps be seen as elements of the overall workings of a consumption-driven economy and culture, geared to the satisfaction of individuals' material desires. The notion that there can be no upper limit in one's pursuit of such desires is part and parcel of the operation of such an economy and culture, and this notion is bound to create a sense of personal failure in individuals who subscribe to it, since, where there are no upper limits, there can be no point at which success has been attained. In that sense, the visual culture of movie and television fantasy may be interpreted as an expression of deep-seated social imperatives.

Television and global media

With the advent of movies, 'Western' visual culture became increasingly international in its reach, and this process has been accelerated by the instantaneous global dissemination of television images. If there is any validity to the 1960s notion of an emerging 'global village', the shaping of that village's common culture will be largely tied to the mass-produced visual images of movies, ads, and news. The notion of a global village is sometimes put forth (as it was by Marshall McLuhan) as a self-evident fact of contemporary life or, alternatively, as a rhetorical construct, something to strive for or wish for, rather than a description of existing reality. However, there is some intriguing empirical research that can be interpreted as actually demonstrating the workings of a global-village effect on specific societies and individuals.

Perhaps the most important set of findings on this topic comes from a study by Forbes and Lonner (1980), conducted in Alaska in the late 1970s. At that time, with the advent of large-scale satellite transmission, television had begun to appear in areas of the state that had hitherto not been able to receive it. Through systematic interviews, the researchers set out to investigate the effects of the medium on the lives of young people who were being exposed to it for the first time. In particular, these interviews focused on how children belonging to the various Native Alaskan ethnic groups responded to television images of two other ethnic groups, African-Americans and European-Americans. These responses, obtained through before-after questionnaire ratings, indicated no change in the perception of European-Americans, but a significant positive change in the children's attitudes toward African-Americans. Given the fact that the Native Alaskan children were previously familiar with European-Americans (who constitute the majority of the state's population) but had little or no prior familiarity with African-Americans, these findings suggest that increased contact with another group through a visual medium may indeed create the sense of community and commonality that the term 'global village' connotes. This interpretation is supported by the fact that the children's post-television ratings of African-Americans included an increase in perceived similarity to themselves, while European-Americans were already rated high on that attribute.

On the assumption that the process envisioned above can also be brought about by deliberate design, several researchers have used visual media – mostly movies and video, rather than single images – in attempts to bring about a greater sense of fellowship among members of different social groups. It is possible to give a short summary of the results of such efforts without doing too much violence to the individual studies. In brief, what happens is this: when these experiments are performed with children and adolescents, they almost always 'work', in the sense of having the desired outcome; however, when the subjects of the experiments are adults, the results are much more variable and ambiguous (Messaris 1997: 118–25). These findings are not surprising, of course. They confirm one's intuitive sense that adult attitudes are much more resistant to change than those of younger people. So, while there does seem to be empirical support for assuming that the international flow of images could create the cultural preconditions for a 'global village', the likelihood that such changes in consciousness might ever occur on a large scale should be weighed against the fact that attitude changes arising in childhood may not always endure beyond that stage in life.

Moreover, any discussion of global visual culture must take into account the fact that, at present, much of that culture originates in one society, the United States. Although the film industries of Asia have recently been making some notable inroads into that position of dominance, global visual culture may still be described, without too much exaggeration, as being saturated with the products and influence of Hollywood, Madison Avenue (as a metaphor, not a geographical fact), and CNN. The standard, and obvious, concern about this state of affairs is that it leads to an erosion of local values and beliefs and an adoption of cultural perspectives that may be maladaptive to one's local circumstances. A study that could be interpreted from this perspective was performed some years ago by Dumas (1988). At a time when people living in China had more limited access to US media than they do today, Dumas studied recently arrived Chinese graduate students' responses to the images in US print advertising. One of the major patterns in her findings was that the Chinese viewers would express approval of various US cultural practices that differed sharply from traditional Chinese values: for example, lack of formal displays of respect by children to parents; lack of restraint in the public display of sexual attachments; lack of restraint in the expression of other strong emotions, etc.

Leaving aside the possibility that the Chinese students were merely expressing polite approval of the culture of their host country, it is easy to see Dumas's findings as a demonstration of the steamroller effect of the individualistic culture of US media, and that is probably how a traditional cultural critic would see things. In other words, the emphasis in such criticism has tended to be on the seductions of US media values and their putatively baneful consequences. What is often overlooked in such criticism is the other side of the coin, that is, the reasons that a particular person may have for rejecting the values of her/his ancestral culture. In the case of Dumas's study, many of her interviewees made it clear that they were not merely responding to the positive appeal of the US ads' version of reality but were also motivated by a measured, reflective self-distancing from some of the problematic elements of the world view they had grown up with in China. To see people who undergo such transitions as merely passive victims of 'Westernization' is to deny them the capacity for reasoned choice.

Conclusion

One safe prediction that one can make about the four aspects of visual culture discussed above is that at least three of them are bound to undergo major transformations in the years ahead. The cognitive impacts of visual culture are likely to accelerate as people's informational uses of media continue to shift from verbal to visual sources – in other words, as the realm of information goes through the same changes that have taken place in that of fictional entertainment. This process may be retarded somewhat by the present state of the Web, which is still not very good at delivering high-quality images at high speed, but this road block is surely not going to be up much longer. The status of photography as evidence may also be affected by technological developments, as increasing numbers of people gain access to user-friendly software for rudimentary image manipulation. If there is any truth to the common belief that knowing about the workings of the media makes one more resistant to their influence, then faith in the indexical character of photographic images may indeed erode as predicted. Finally, as high-quality media production continues to become less expensive, it seems more than likely that the trend toward a global, multi-directional flow of media images will continue (Lull 2000). But what those images will consist of, and which culture they will reflect, is far from clear. The fantasies designed in Hollywood over the past century have been remarkably persistent, and they show no sign of changing in any fundamental way. It should not be surprising if those fantasies become a primary ingredient in visual images that have nominally originated outside the Hollywood system. Indeed, some facets of visual culture seem likely to prove very durable.

References

Dalai Lama and Rowell, G. (1990). *My Tibet.* Berkeley: University of California Press.

Dumas, A. A. (1988). *Cross-cultural Analysis of People's Interpretation of Advertising Visual Clichés.* M.A. thesis, Annenberg School for Communication, University of Pennsylvania.

Edgerton, S. Y., Jr (1991). *The Heritage of Giotto's Geometry: Art and Science on the Eve of the Scientific Revolution.* Ithaca, NY: Cornell University Press.

Fincher, J. (1995). 'By convention, the enemy never did without'. *Smithsonian*, 26: 26–143.

Forbes, N. E. and Lonner, W. J. (1980). *Sociocultural and Cognitive Effects of Commercial*

Television on Previously Television-naive Rural Alaskan Children. Bellingham, WA: Western Washington University.

Gardner, H. (1983). *Frames of Mind: The Theory of Multiple Intelligences.* New York: Basic Books.

—— (1993). *Multiple Intelligences: The Theory in Practice.* New York: Basic Books.

Goldfarb, E. (1987). *Romance and Media: The Role of Romantic Portrayals in Perceptions of Real-life Romantic Experiences.* M.A. thesis, Annenberg School for Communication, University of Pennsylvania.

Haskell, M. (1976). 'Movies ruined me for real romance'. *The Village Voice,* 5 April: 65–6.

Ivins, W. M., Jr (1953). *Prints and Visual Communication.* Cambridge, MA: MIT Press.

Lang, K. and Lang, G. E. (1953). 'The unique perspective of television and its effect: A pilot study'. In W. Schramm and D. F. Roberts (eds), *The Process and Effects of Mass Communication.* Urbana, IL: University of Illinois Press: 169–88.

Lee, M. A. and Solomon, N. (1990). *Unreliable Sources: A Guide to Detecting Bias in News Media.* Secaucus, NJ: Carol Publishing Group.

Lull, J. (2000). *Media, Communication, Culture: A Global Approach* (revised ed.). Cambridge: Polity Press; New York: Columbia University Press.

Messaris, P. (1987). 'Mothers' comments to their children about the relationship between television and reality'. In T. R. Lindlof (ed.), *Natural Audiences: Qualitative Research of Media Uses and Effects.* Norwood, NJ: Ablex: 95–108.

—— (1996). 'Video ergo cogito: Visual education and analogical thinking'. *Young: Nordic Journal of Youth Research,* 4: 46–59.

—— (1997). *Visual Persuasion: The Role of Images in Advertising.* Thousand Oaks, CA: Sage Publications.

Moog, C. (1990). *Are They Selling Her Lips? Advertising and Identity.* New York: Morrow.

Neuman, S. B. (1995). *Literacy in the Television Age: The Myth of the TV Effect* (second ed.). Norwood, NJ: Ablex.

Peirce, C. S. (1991). *Peirce on Signs: Writings on Semiotics by Charles Sanders Peirce.* Chapel Hill: University of North Carolina Press.

Prince, S. (1993). 'The discourse of pictures: Iconicity and film study'. *Film Quarterly,* 47: 16–28.

Ray, R. B. (1985). *A Certain Tendency of the Hollywood Cinema, 1930–1980.* Princeton, NJ: Princeton University Press.

Ritchin, F. (1990). *In Our Own Image: The Coming Revolution in Photography.* New York: Aperture.

Salomon, G. (1979). *Interaction of Media, Cognition, and Learning: An Exploration of How Symbolic Forms Cultivate Mental Skills and Affect Knowledge Acquisition.* San Francisco: Jossey-Bass.

Sifry, M. L. and Cerf, C. (eds) (1991). *The Gulf War Reader: History, Documents, Opinions.* New York: Times Books.

Slattery, K. and Tiedge, J. T. (1992). 'The effects of labeling staged video on the credibility of TV news stories'. *Journal of Broadcasting and Electronic Media,* 36: 279–86.

Tidhar, C. E. (1984). 'Children communicating in cinematic codes: Effects on cognitive skills'. *Journal of Educational Psychology,* 76: 957–65.

Tufte, E. R. (1983). *The Visual Display of Quantitative Information.* Cheshire, CT: Graphics Press.

—— (1990). *Envisioning Information.* Cheshire, CT: Graphics Press.

191

—— (1997). *Visual Explanations: Images and Quantities, Evidence and Narratives*. Cheshire, CT: Graphics Press.

Walker, P. (1992). 'The myth of surgical bombing in the Gulf War'. In R. Clarke (ed.), *War Crimes*. Washington, DC: Maisonneuve Press: 83–9.

Washburn, K. and Thornton, J. (eds) (1996). *Dumbing Down: Essays on the Strip-mining of American Culture*. New York: Norton.

Zillman, D. and Bryant, J. (eds) (1989). *Pornography: Research Advances and Policy Considerations*. Mahwah, NJ: Lawrence Erlbaum Associates.

10

STAR CULTURE

Stephen Hinerman

Being a Western, middle-class traveler in the modern global environment can be quite disconcerting. Traveling has always been the experience of difference – going from the familiar to the novel. But today such a traveler – especially someone from the United States – may well be struck by how similar a foreign community is to one's own home. While cultural features including language, food, and religion often change as we cross borders, much that awaits the Western traveler in almost any new land is already well-known. The films one leaves back home play in movie theaters across the globe. The music video channel in the hotel room will likely feature songs the traveler knows well. Sporting events from back home appear on the screen at the local bar. Visual images of pop culture stars from the traveler's homeland are often plastered all over street-corner kiosks and urban walls.

Familiar things awaiting the traveler do not stop there. Imagine two people – one a traveler, the other a local – making lists of their most admired heroes. We would not be surprised if both lists feature many of the same names – movie stars, music celebrities, sports heroes, and television personalities. Perhaps the lists would include Madonna, Ricky Martin, Tom Hanks, or Jean-Claude Van Damme, for example.

Should the overlap of these lists trouble us? Where are the people who have traditionally been seen as heroes – individuals who have changed the world – the political figures, public servants, civil rights leaders, and generals? Are we all the same in our likes and dislikes the world over? For some critics of popular culture, it seems so. They lament that the entire world has been duped into worshipping global media entertainment celebrities more than real heroes. These critics argue that the corporate power of the culture and media industries has become so pervasive that only a commodified stock of superficial stars is widely recognizable these days. According to the doomsayers, the 'cult of celebrity' has taken over the world to the detriment of positive values and clear-headed thinking.

This issue has been part of twentieth-century debates over culture, media, and globalization. From the sincere and sophisticated critical concerns of

Frankfurt School theorists early last century to the rants and raves of some neo-conservative guardians of culture at the onset of the new millennium, the rise of the cult of celebrity has been blamed for destroying core values and for eradicating individual and local differences.

Is this an accurate representation of the role of stardom in modern and postmodern culture? Certainly Frankfurt School theorists Max Horkheimer and Theodor Adorno thought so. Writing during the Second World War, they attempted on one level to explain the rise of Adolf Hitler, whom they considered to be a celebrity-like figure foisted upon a vulnerable public by the power of propaganda and the then new electronic media. They later became concerned about the power of entertainment and stardom in general. In a landmark study, 'The culture industry: enlightenment as mass deception', Horkheimer and Adorno argue that modern entertainment and media corporations use stardom and celebrity to pacify the masses. Essentially, they believe that the culture industries use stars as vehicles mainly to create false hopes of upward social mobility and meaningful social change among audience members:

> Those [stars] discovered by the talent scouts and then publicized on a vast scale by the studio are ideal types of the new dependent average. Of course, the starlet is meant to symbolize the typist in such a way that the splendid evening dress seems meant for the actress as distinct from the real girl. The girls in the audience not only feel that they could be on the screen, but realize that great gulf separating them from it . . . Whenever the culture industry still issues an invitation naively to identify, it is immediately withdrawn. No one can escape from himself anymore.
>
> (Horkheimer and Adorno 1972: 145)

For Horkheimer and Adorno, film and other media initially use stars to entice identification among audience members. But, they argue, audience members simultaneously realize that the chances of living the life they see on screen are staggeringly slim. This makes stardom 'part of a system of false promise in the system of capital, which offers the reward of stardom to a random few in order to perpetuate the myth of potential universal success. The masses are by their very nature psychologically immature and thus are drawn to these [stars] . . . in the same way children identify with and implicitly trust their parents' (Marshall 1997: 9). The result is that the audience indirectly learns 'obedience to the social hierarchy' (Horkheimer and Adorno 1972: 131). People learn not to challenge power but to accept it, and to remain passive in the face of corporate authority.

To be fair, Horkheimer and Adorno did not lump all popular culture stars into the same class. They took great pains to distance more 'artistic' global celebrities like Charlie Chaplin and Greta Garbo from others of the 1940s. Yet, their view of stardom and its potential danger provided them a logical explanation for the object of their original analysis: the rise of Hitler and fascism in their native Germany. The masses are ripe for passivity and obedience, according to this line of thought, provided that the media are manipulated effectively, as Hitler certainly was able to do.

This pessimistic view of popular culture, media, and stardom has dominated critical academic theory since the end of the Second World War. Although not all contemporary critical theorists argue that stars create a sense of social malaise or political obedience, many do. Indeed, some critics press the Frankfurt School arguments even farther, arguing that stardom poses real dangers to the social order as celebrity images increasingly dominate the globe. They argue that whereas past societies could anchor their positive, substantive values to genuine political heroes, today we live in a world of celebrity worship where style routinely stands in for substance. The consequences of such superficiality and sensationalism include the failure of proper moral judgments, and generally reveal a global breakdown in authority and virtue.

This argument is taken up, for instance, in Daniel Boorstin's important study, *The Image*, where he claims that the actions of modern celebrities comprise 'human pseudo-events'. From this perspective, today's celebrities are famous simply for being famous, not for the substantial or heroic acts attributed to figures of the past (Boorstin 1961: 57). James Monaco makes a similar argument, distinguishing between the 'heroes' of an earlier time and the 'celebrities' of today:

> Before we had celebrities we had heroes . . . [W]hat these hero types all share, of course, are admirable qualities – qualities that somehow set them apart from the rest of us. They have *done* things, acted in the world: written, thought, understood, led. Celebrities, on the other hand, needn't have done – needn't do – anything special. Their function isn't to act – just to be.
>
> (Monaco 1978: 5–6)

Contemporary critical theorist Stuart Ewen agrees with the idea that character has become divorced from the images stars project in modern life. Ewen says we therefore need a 'reconciliation of image and meaning' for society to function healthily again (1989: 271). Even some critics sympathetic to the emergence of modern celebrity admit that the link between stars and everyday people is 'not necessarily a deep one . . . the experience of it is not necessarily weighty' (Gamson 1994: 6). This argument resonates throughout the writings of Jean Baudrillard too. The French sociologist implies that stars, as dimensions of fashion, are *simulacra* – empty signs that circulate free of values and without connection to any stable reality (Baudrillard 1988: 6). While Baudrillard seems to take some joy in describing this 'playful' meaninglessness, his foundational view of all media – and, by implication, stardom – is not much different from that of the Frankfurt School theorists. Stars are empty figures – fool's gold – which dazzles, but offers little of value to its audience.

Such negative reasoning, of course, is not the only way to explain the significance of the rise of celebrity in global culture. Yes, it *is* true that stardom permeates the globalized economy. Famous people *are* recognized across borders. Their images *are* common coins in a cultural economy driven by media, the culture industries, and information technology. But this does not mean that the relationship of stars to fans is without deep meaning, that stars 'dupe' their publics, or that media-intensive cultures of celebrity are less meaningful than earlier, 'genuine hero'-oriented cultures.

Previous critical accounts of stardom and celebrity lack complex discussions of how modern audiences work with star images culturally. As P. David Marshall observes in one of the few studies to treat celebrity as a positive cultural resource, for many theorists the 'meaning of celebrity is largely an elitist strategy' in that it appears to materialize hierarchically from the 'top' (the star and the media corporation) down, ignoring the audience (Marshall 1997: 27). While stars do help media corporations sell their products worldwide, they also help people form positive identities in postmodernity. They grant audiences pleasure. To argue therefore that modern stardom is less vital or less worthy than earlier forms of hero-worship demeans contemporary identities unfairly and ignores the vital roles that media play in postmodernity. A less didactic approach to the study of stardom and celebrity in modernity is needed. I will argue in this chapter that stardom as one imaginary glue of globalization is not a 'problem' but a blessing in the chaotic conditions of modern life.

The parameters of global media stardom

To be well understood, any theory of global media stardom must account for two phenomena. First, it must consider how images are produced by media corporations and consumed by media audiences. Second, it must locate the rise of celebrity in the nexus of time and space that characterizes modernity. If global media stardom can be understood in terms of these two parameters, perhaps it can be rescued from critiques which assign it a dangerous role in modern history.

Returning, then, to the first of the two phenomena – the production and consumption of media images – it is clear that the means of production in media industries in modernity and late modernity have undergone vast transformations. Global corporations flourish, constantly recombining in mergers and buy-outs, which in turn reduces the number of smaller, localized media producers. These multinational, mega-entertainment companies make videos, CDs, movies, television shows, webcasts, and countless other cultural forms, often using the same properties and personalities across the various media. They sponsor rock concerts, theme parks, ice capades, and sporting events. Stars are important components in all these activities, helping to sell 'product' while engendering feelings of familiarity, reliability, and trust within the consuming public.

Concerning time and space, stars often cross borders with startling speed. Movies play in many parts of the world the same week. An actor can become an 'overnight success' in many different parts of the globe at the same time. The World Cup and Super Bowl create instant sports celebrities. Identical videos are seen minutes apart in Europe, Asia, and North and South America. Time – as a unitary, regulating, sequencing of events – collapses. Star images circulate through geographic space where the only border checkpoints are local cable systems and satellite providers. Space stretches to the point where the concept of 'country' becomes almost quaint. Even 'local' telecommunications networks scramble to describe themselves as 'global'. Observing time and space as they manifest themselves in the creation of modern entertainment and the production of stardom, we sense a true new world order where time and space not only change, but merge in new, accelerated ways. McGrew elaborates upon this process:

> [we can] conceive of globalization as having two interrelated dimensions: scope ('stretching') and intensity (or 'deepening'). On the one hand, the concept of globalization defines a universal process or set of processes which generate a multiplicity of linkages and interconnections between states and societies which make up the modern world system: the concept therefore has a spatial connotation. Social, political and economic activities are becoming 'stretched' across the globe, such that events, decisions, and activities in one part of the world can come to have immediate significance for individuals and communities in quite distant parts of the global system. On the other hand, globalization also implies an intensification in the levels of interaction, interconnectedness, or interdependence between the states and societies which constitute the modern world community. Accordingly, alongside this 'stretching' goes a 'deepening' . . . Thus globalization involves a growing interpenetration of the global human condition with the particularities of place and individuality.
>
> (McGrew 1992: 68–9)

Fame is by no means unique to the contemporary world; heroes have always been with us. What has changed is the manner by which symbolic forms are produced, and the contexts in which they are consumed. These changes are intimately tied up with modernity and postmodernity and compose a crucial component of cultural life today. Only by examining the historical development of fame, modern notions of time and space, and the changing modes of production and consumption in the mediated world, can we begin to explain the impact of stardom on modern life. The need for such a theoretical overview was recognized years ago by Richard Dyer:

Although stars form the basis of probably the larger part of everyday discussion of films, and although the majority of film books produced are fan material of one kind or another, very little in the way of sustained work has been done in the area. No work, that is, elaborates some kind of theory of the phenomenon and uses this theory to inform empirical investigation of it.

(Dyer 1979: 1)

While some theorists, including Dyer himself (1986), have attempted just such an elaboration in the meantime, none has sufficiently explained how identity, time, and space play crucial roles in the ways celebrity works in modern culture. That is the specific goal of this chapter. I will now provide a short introduction that outlines concepts that are basic to a modernist approach to time and space. Then I will illustrate how fame has changed in modernity in response to changes in perceptions of time and space. Finally, I will examine in some depth how stardom works together with modern communications technology in cultural production and consumption, and how these aspects of celebrity adapt to alterations in time and space brought on by modernity.

Fame and renown in history

Recognizability and renown appear universally throughout history. Many of the words that refer to stardom – *fama, ambitio, celebritas* – can be traced to the Roman world. The ideas they describe go back even farther (Braudy 1986: 57). From the beginning of time, some individuals have hoped to see their reputations live beyond their death. Historically, more renown has been granted when such reputations transverse space and reach wide audiences. Investigations of fame, like Braudy's *The Frenzy of Renown* (1986), comprehensively illustrate how fame has always been caught up in the subtleties and nuances of time and space. Braudy argues convincingly that stardom is anything but a recent phenomenon.

For Braudy, fame represents an attempt by individuals to 'last longer than any specific action' (1986: 15). This impulse, he believes, is fundamental to human nature, as people have always been interested in leaving legacies that don't just reproduce, but transcend, their deeds. As Braudy observes, 'In great part the history of fame is the history of the changing ways by which individuals have sought to bring themselves to the attention of others and, not incidentally, have thereby gained power over them' (1986: 3).

Braudy believes that famous persons (the 'renowned') often model themselves on previously famous individuals. Although media technologies have changed the way fame is spread, and while the development of communication technology has increased the number of widely recognized and admired people, the genesis of fame is quite uniform, whether the famous person is Alexander the Great or Greta Garbo (Braudy 1986: 4). Apparently, a 'will to power' drives

198

those who seek renown. Once fame is granted, the famous know they will be rewarded with political, material, or cultural influence.

While this 'will to power' may be constant throughout history, the means by which fame is spread and the conditions under which it is received by audiences have changed drastically. These processes have altered the nature of the quest for fame. Braudy suggests that substantive changes have taken place in the motivation for fame and the time span within which renown is granted:

> Although the urge to fame originally was the aspiration for a life after death in the words and thoughts of the community, it has evolved over the centuries into the desire for fame in one's own lifetime, fame not as the crown of earthly achievement but as psychic medicine for a pervasive sense of loss and personal failure . . . For the ancient Romans, your genius was in the stars. Now, with little thought for either posterity or transcendence, genius is entirely within.
>
> (Braudy 1986: 605)

Braudy argues that the very psyche of modern culture has been altered by changes in modern communication technology and the culture industries. He writes: 'Through the media of sound, sight, and print individuals can aspire to a dream of ubiquity in which fame seems unbounded by time and space: constantly present, constantly recognizable, and therefore constantly existing' (1986: 553). Yet, for Braudy, the consequences of these changes are purely negative, particularly for the famous person, who is the true subject of his investigation. The modern famous person becomes alienated from his or her own nature in a web of communication technology, and metamorphosizes into a mere image that circulates without links to the 'authentic moral self'. Braudy mourns this loss of 'authenticity', which he believes characterized earlier heroes and gave moral force to their actions. Braudy suggests that today's stars are 'performers' instead, and 'the performer's lesson [is] that to be caught in the attention of others is in great part to mean what they want you to mean', often 'intimately accessible, unthreatening, enclosed – turned by [media] into an ironic version of [one's] self' (Braudy 1986: 583).

This condemning view of modern renown fails to accept the fact that time and space have *always* been implicated in fame, and that it is audiences – not the famous themselves – who are the final arbiters of who will or will not win fame. Because celebrity status depends so much on currents of time, space, and audience involvement, any changes in the ways time and space are experienced by the public will also change the specific nature of fame. For instance, if one looks up to a famous person in a culture where time is elongated and spatial borders cannot easily be transcended, that will be a very different experience from idolatry in an instantaneous, 'global society'. The impact of the relationship between star and consumer will differ in intensity, in reach, and in the manner it shapes the self-image of the audience member or 'fan'. To place a value judgment on such changes without fully understanding those changes in a larger context easily leads to flawed judgments.

Ultimately, modern fame assumes importance not for what it says about the feelings or reputations of famous people but for what it does for audiences. Some scholars, particularly those who work from the 'top down' in their critiques of modern stardom, forget that it is the audience that determines celebrity. These critics sometimes become more seduced by the aura of stars than the masses they fret about so much.

The impact of time and space on audiences' relationships with famous people has always been vital to understanding how renown is granted. We can find examples as far back in time as classical Greece. When Aristotle in the *Rhetoric* describes the qualities of people who have *ethos*, and are able to engender emulation in others, he is telling us about fame:

> They are the ones who possess . . . courage, wisdom, public office; for men in office can render service to many, and so can generals, orators, and all who have the like power and influence. Emulation is excited, too, by those who have many imitators; or whose acquaintance or friendship many desire; or whom many admire, or whom we ourselves admire. And it is excited by those whom poets or panegyrists celebrate in praises and encomiums.
>
> (Aristotle 1960: 130)

Aristotle places the onus of fame not on individual persons but on the collective audience. It is the community which bestows fame. The only way to understand fame, therefore, is to understand those who emulate the famous and how they do so.

In Aristotle's time, fame was rooted firmly in time-bound expectations of the audience at the very moment the famous sought to transcend those temporal boundaries. Fame was a set of historical valuations, an accumulation of actions and subsequent public manifestations of praise which granted a kind of immortality. Reputation in the ancient world, therefore, resulted from an accretion of historical, lineal acts, viewed from a distance over time, and finally valued and fixed by public speeches of praise or blame emanating from the marketplace or the battlefield. Public honoring of renown was an important aspect of classical culture, given how the famous exemplified, personified, and modeled ideal behavior and values. Ulf Hannerz notes that this phenomenon still occurs in many non-media cultures: 'small-scale, non-media societies make sure that much meaning is effortlessly kept alive at least in microtime, through redundancy. Knowledge and beliefs are inscribed into the environment, and personified by individuals' (1992: 147). These renowned individuals mark the 'ideal life' of the community.

Aristotle also implied that classical fame depended not only on accumulated time but on geographically discrete space. The 'technologies' for spreading fame (via poets and orators) assured that renown was, ultimately, local. Pericles may have had wide-ranging success in battle, but his glory was not simultaneously celebrated in Africa or Babylon. If word spread, it circulated slowly and was confined to particular places and spaces. Moreover, the meaning of Pericles' work would have been interpreted through the filter of local concerns as well. To use another example, while Alexander the Great's fame spread slowly throughout the Mediterranean world, it was inevitably bound by geographical space and restricted to those social classes that had access to particular information in specific forms – persons who were privileged to have heard songs, poems, or speeches, or were privy to military reports or gossip.

Fame in the premodern, pre-mediated world, therefore, was clearly rooted in fixed notions of time and space which directly influenced the audiences' experience. But time and space have undergone radical transformations in the last hundred years. Individuals now experience the world, and their selves in it, in many different ways. Notions of what fame and renown mean to individuals have changed as well.

Time, space, and fame in modernity and postmodernity

Anthony Giddens, David Harvey, and John B. Thompson among others have contributed much to current understandings of time and space which have implications for the changing nature of fame. They all agree that globalization and postmodernity have altered basic perceptions of the self and the experience of time and space. Giddens's now-familiar point is that globalization creates 'time-space distanciation' (1990: 14). Contemporary communication technologies and economies 'disembed' long-established relationship patterns from their local contexts and create new global patterns where 'place' takes on a new meaning. Human relationships no longer depend upon physical geography. This does not mean that individuals no longer talk to people who are physically near them, or that local issues no longer matter. But as numerous theorists have stated, social interaction today no longer depends solely on geographical proximity. As the increasing growth of on-line relationships demonstrates, for instance, feelings of intimacy can grow between persons who are physically absent. For Giddens, then, 'globalization concerns the intersection of presence and absence, the interlacing of social events and social relations "at a distance" with local contextualities' (1991: 21).

Harvey claims that modern economic changes and technological developments have 'compressed' time and space (1989: 240). Time is speeded up; space is collapsed. People now experience simultaneous events in quick bursts, without much regard for geographical constraints. For Harvey, these changes have come from periodic reformations of capitalism. When capitalism has undergone any one of its periodic crises, it has generally resulted in a speeding up of both economic and social processes. This speeding up has had major consequences in cultural life. Harvey argues, 'we have been experiencing [since the 1960s] an intense phase of time-space compression that has had a disorienting and disruptive impact upon political-economic practices, the balance of class power, as well as upon cultural and social life' (1989: 284)

The stretching of time and collapsing of space affects much more than the global economy. It has also greatly altered understandings of fame. While the scope of fame in premodernity was limited to a considerable degree by 'real' time and space, now the potential reach and depth of fame and celebrity have expanded. At the same time, however, fame functions centrally as an engine that drives economic realities linked to modern communications technologies. Given that these technologies entail elaborate symbol systems, famous, repetitive images become the perfect means to suture audience loyalty to communication media and to the economic system behind them. In an age where time is stretched and space is collapsed, highly valued common images provide individuals with shared communication experiences across geographical boundaries. In the process, global stars are born.

Thompson notes that a specific form of social relationship which he calls 'non-reciprocal intimacy' has developed in late modernity. For our purposes here, this suggests that fans can feel close to famous individuals, yet that closeness is not tied to any physical locale. The familiarity exists despite the fact that the fan has never met the star; indeed, the star may never have set foot in the fan's home country. Still, the fan feels he or she knows the celebrity and experiences an emotional intimacy made up of shared knowledge, understandings, taste, and style. The relationship 'grows' despite the fact that only a one-way flow of communication over vast geographic distance has taken place. As Thompson notes:

> Since mediated quasi-interaction is stretched across space and time, it makes possible a form of intimacy with others who do not share one's own spatial-temporal locale; in other words, it makes possible what has been aptly described as 'intimacy at a distance'. Second, since mediated quasi-interaction is non-dialogical, the form of intimacy established through it is non-reciprocal in character.
>
> (1995: 219)

This change has profound implications for fan psychology. Modernity has loosened our sense of self. No longer do central institutions like Church or government grant ready-made identities to citizens, making clear one's place in the universe, or one's function in hierarchical society. Marx's key insight that the accumulation of capital loosens the bonds of society has proved to be accurate in the symbolic realm as well. The dislocation which results from the collapsing of space and the speeding up of time makes it difficult for individuals to assimilate information coherently (Thompson 1995: 209). What is left is a crisis of identity formation for the modern individual.

Stars and trust

With modern identity formation being so problematic, institutions that normally provide and rely upon stable identities are threatened too. As Giddens observes, the changing nature of time and space has implications for basic social concepts like trust, where premodern kinship, local community, and religion are replaced by abstract systems and future-oriented thought (1990: 102). Searching for any sort of stable identity, people increasingly seek intimacy from a distance and fashion their identities from mediated forms of communication. Giddens does not mention stardom, and actually has very little to say about media and the culture industries overall. But we can extend his argument to assert that, if trust is no longer provided by the Church or state, it can be bestowed by allegiance to mediated images that are recognizable, predictable, and consistent.

As an example of this phenomenon, many of us today feel a sense of loss when we enter our local bank. New tellers seem to arrive daily, and the desks that used to accommodate loan officers are empty. Those officers now are only accessible by phone, on-line, or in some mythical central office far away. Such changes may very well make us feel that the bank can no longer be trusted. This experience can be repeated at any number of institutions – the Health Maintenance Organization (HMO), where our 'family doctor' changes daily, or the customer service phone operator, whose name changes with each call. In a world of constant flux, uncertainty, and impersonality, the common, stable, recognizable faces we encounter most often are those of pop culture celebrities, and media narratives are some of the rare stories we hold in common with others.

Stardom, as it is served up by modern telecommunications industries for global consumption, is thus a perfect trust-building, self-locating mechanism. Stardom has become a 'glue' that can connect individuals across time and space, create identities, and hold them together. Stars grant modern people a sense of self and a sense of (placeless) place. Rather than argue that star culture engenders only a 'hollow, superficial' human experience, therefore, it is far more interesting to consider how stardom provides significant emotional connections for otherwise relatively disconnected individuals.

The production of stardom

If fame and its heroes characterize premodern forms of renown, then stardom and celebrity reflect renown in late modernity and postmodernity. Stardom stitches together cognitive and cultural elements that have been loosened by modernity. The contemporary brands of stardom, however, emerged only when modern communications technology came into wide use. Production of star images by media corporations must therefore be seriously taken into account in any theory of stardom and modernity.

It is no coincidence that stardom emerged alongside the changing notions of time and space that were under way at the start of the twentieth century. Kern (1983) has shown how early conceptualizations of time and space were linked with specific technological developments characteristic of the period 1880–1910, especially invention of the cinema. He argues that 'the cinema portrayed a variety of temporal phenomena that played with the uniformity and irreversibility of time', while the 'close-up' and the 'quick cut' altered notions of space (Kern 1983: 29, 218). In addition, film distribution – with American movies later beginning to dominate European markets – started to alter perceptions of what constitutes 'national' entertainment, and what temporal increment is necessary to distribute information across borders and continents.

Examining the origins of modern celebrity illustrates these developments. The modern star and the cinema developed together. DeCordova (1990) places development of the film star between 1910 and 1914, and argues that, because of the nature and pervasiveness of film distribution, the film star was a very different kind of celebrity from the theater star which preceded it. The geographic reach of movie stars, of course, was much broader. Their recognizability was faster and more certain. Stars who could traverse space and be preserved limitlessly in time entered the stage. A new era of popular culture had begun. Stars were born; so were fans.

The reshaping of fame that resulted was catapulted by new technological media and capitalist business practices. Suddenly worldwide markets required product, and the more this product could be uniform in content, the less capital investment was needed for healthy economic returns. Modern stardom did not arise by accident. Financial success was not a coincidence, and the stardom it featured was not simply an extension of premodern forms of notoriety. Stardom resulted from film technology in the first two decades of the twentieth century, the mass production and distribution of audio recordings in the 1920s, and the beginning of worldwide media and pop culture markets created by the global capitalist system for the rest of the century. Such developments required stardom as much as stardom required them. Celebrity has always been organic to modernity.

The star system

The star system may have begun with the development of the movies, but it did not stop there. Development of multinational business practices coupled simultaneously with industry's desire to reach large audiences have been central to the function of modern communications technologies. Stardom and the star system have been crucial to these processes.

According to Donald, stardom involves both industrial and psychic processes. He suggests a connection exists between star as center of profit (the exchange value), and star as granter of pleasure (the use value):

The object in which we make (an) investment is always provided for us – some would say imposed on us – by the 'machine' of culture. This machine involves not just the bricks and mortar of Hollywood studios and chains of cinemas, but also certain cultural orientations and competencies (shared language, for example, and shared conceptions of time, personality, and aesthetic value) and the psychic processes whereby we enter culture and negotiate shifting, insecure positions within it ... The implications of this argument are that, in investigating the phenomenon of stardom, we are not dealing with a person or an image with particular characteristics (talent, beauty, glamour, charisma, etc.) but with a rather complex set of cultural processes.

(Donald 1985: 50)

Stardom has two general trajectories. First, stardom functions as part of the production process – it is vital to representation, narrative, and marketing. Once produced, stardom is then consumed by audiences, located in particular, but mobile, sites of time and space. The two dimensions – production and consumption – thus work together to generate specific meanings of stardom.

Conditions of popular culture production and its effects on stardom have been elaborated by Alberoni (1972), who argues that stardom requires an efficient bureaucracy, a large-scale capitalist society, and significant economic development. King (1987) adds to the list the necessity for a commodity-producing industry, and a strict temporal and cognitive distinction between work and leisure into which such productions can move. Gamson (1994: 42–3) points out that modern innovations in stardom beginning in the 1940s relied on production-oriented practices such as scientific target marketing, increased 'info-tainment' media outlets, and 'non-entertainment' sectors becoming increasingly interested in public relations. All these authors agree that stardom requires well-financed institutions and systems of professional practices to produce and circulate images for fans to consume.

To understand more fully how stardom is crucial to media production practices generally, we can look at how stardom emerged first in the film industry. According to DeCordova, competing theories try to explain *how* stardom developed in the cinema business, but little disagreement exists as to *why* (1990: 2–8). Movie stars were cultivated to draw consumers back, time and again, into film theaters. The standard account of this historical development is that stars were created by the small, independent film companies battling the motion picture monopoly, while at the same time these independents took ownership of star images (King 1986: 161). It gave the independents a chance to compete with the big studios because stars drew repeat audiences.

Yet this is hardly the only commercial benefit reaped by the 'production' of stars. Stardom also allowed the culture industries to minimize risk and enhance predictability, which is crucial to any capitalist venture. Film stars made it possible for entertainment companies to raise capital more easily (King 1987: 149).

205

Popular actresses and actors pre-sold pictures to a considerable degree, assuring built-in audiences and revenues for the film companies and their financial backers. Furthermore, stars as professional actors were generally dependable. They could be counted upon to show up for work, deliver first-rate performances, and work efficiently within a budget.

The type of star chosen for a particular role also helped to move production along smoothly. Stars often achieved fame via particular genre roles. Studios routinely placed stars back into movies of the same genre, thereby enhancing predictability and audience loyalty (Dyer 1982: 53). Stars also made it possible for the studios to promote films by developing an entirely new enterprise, 'publicity', around the star. Consumers could be enticed back into the theater because they were interested in the life of the stars outside their character roles. In fact, the very distinction between the public life of a star and the private life of the actor developed when stars were first used as the main means of merchandising films by their companies (DeCordova 1991: 26). King elaborates on the central importance of stardom to film production:

> Not only is it possible to point to the fact that the star is central to the raising of finance, as the least problematic advance guarantee of a certain level of audience interest. It is also relatively easy to detail the various ways in which stars stabilize the process of representation itself by focusing a disparate range of specialisms and narrational inputs around a relatively fixed nucleus of meaning, which is given in advance of any specific instance of narration or, for that matter, context of production. Likewise, the mobilization of publicity and advertising around the moment of consumption of film itself – not to mention the consumption of derived commodities such as fan magazines, fashions, and consumer goods – relies on the star as cybernetic monitor which returns all efforts to the same apparent core of meaning.
>
> (King 1987: 149)

Stardom is the perfect vehicle for cultural production in a mass-mediated, modern world. What better lure than consistent, recognizable, attractive, marketable commodities available for public display that can ensure relative predictability in a business that is historically unpredictable? Stars deliver desired production values while they nearly guarantee a profit. Stars function instantaneously across media technologies and genres to introduce, glamorize, focus, and stabilize new cultural commodities, as well as media and cultural production itself. Many definitions of stardom take this anchoring function into account. For instance, Ellis's definition of a star as 'a performer in a particular medium whose figure enters into subsidiary forms of circulation, and feeds back into future performances' reflects this idea (Ellis 1982: 91).

To look solely at the production side of stardom, however, misses a vital component of popular culture. We know from countless failed examples that it is impossible to simply create a star on demand. For every rising star we see, many never get off the ground despite expensive efforts to circulate and market their images, and some even fall off the launch pad in flames. In the final analysis, Aristotle was correct when he insisted that we should look beyond the source to determine the effect of renown. Fame, it must be said, depends upon the audience; it is in the consumption of pop culture imagery that stars are made.

Consuming stardom

Stars grant pleasures to their audiences. Through gestures, manners of speech, and body movements, actors, singers, and sports figures create performances that build on their reputation and previous symbolic work (Naremore 1988; Smith 1993). We watch an actor navigate a role with knowledge of his or her previous performances, and we delight in how the actor assumes a new identity. For instance, Robert DeNiro plays a man paralyzed by a stroke. Audiences will be impressed by the degree to which his performance differs from previous roles, while at the same time they appreciate his skill enacting a condition he clearly does not have in real life. In music, the performer's voice or instrument creates an identity as well, as it makes manifest the sound of personal feelings (Frith 1996: 211). When, for example, Celine Dion sings a series of deeply felt notes, her audience assumes the pain or joy signified to be hers, something she has experienced in the past and perhaps is re-experiencing now. In sports, we watch stars bodily enact a series of physical skills that define their public personality (Rowe 1994: 8). Kobe Bryant makes a move that is at once in the tradition of basketball, yet seems new, exciting, never imagined until now. Stars of all kinds fascinate because they consistently create and delight. They invent and challenge within formulaic confines.

Their personalities, the repertoire of techniques at their disposal, and their public and private histories all help make up the potential pleasures that stars can inspire. Engaging stars repeatedly, audiences begin to invest their heroes with qualities that brim with individuality. Especially when a star gets caught in a media scandal, fans 'personally' begin to evaluate in great detail a media figure they have never met (Lull and Hinerman 1997). The bigger the star, the more the celebrity is assumed to be known, and the more interest the story will inspire.

This idea that the public 'knows' a star gives rise to a central aspect of how stardom is consumed today. Audiences assume they know what a star 'is really like' away from the screen, concert hall, or sports arena. Modern media stars thus have two distinct personae: a public, external persona (made up of physical appearances and images), and a private, internal persona (made up of the star's 'real' feelings, thoughts, and private concerns). A major fascination for fans is the blurring and narrativizing of the space between the public and private domains of celebrities. Audiences know the singer is not always the song, the actor not always the character. Still, curiosity about the symbolic space between 'roles' remains and stimulates even more interest.

This powerful tension between the public and private selves of stars stems from the way media narratives work. As DeCordova observes about film stars:

> The body that appears in fiction films actually has an ambiguous and complex status: at any moment one can theoretically locate two bodies in the one: a body produced (that of the character) and a body pro-ducing (that of the actor). Attention to the former draws the spectator into the representation of character within the fiction. Attention to the latter, on the other hand, draws the spectator into a specific path of intertextuality that extends outside the text as formal system.
>
> (1990: 19, 20)

Ambiguity and tension around the public/private nexus create provocative questions of 'authenticity' which swirl around stardom. There are many ways to try to resolve the uncertainty: by reading fan magazines, watching info-tainment shows, conversing with friends and co-workers. Still, the soul behind the mask will always be enigmatic.

The paradigmatic tension between the public and private life of the star began to be exploited by film companies as soon as stardom arose (DeCordova 1991: 26). Celebrity gossip and fanzines appeared simultaneously with the creation of stars, all of which helped build a sense of the exciting internal life of the star, which then stimulated more public curiosity. Studios soon learned to appreciate the market value of this public/private duality; indeed, the dialectical spin between the star as star, and the star as human being, has become an essential element of stardom. Tributary media such as the tabloid press, enter-tainment television shows, and overnight paperback biographies are all cogs in the machinery of modern star production (Smith 1993: xvi).

Fan identity

Why do we need the pleasures we derive from star gazing? Do these pleasures simply give us a temporary thrill as we move from one star to the next? Research on fans (Lewis 1992) suggests otherwise; it indicates that the pleasures experienced by consuming stars take on stable meanings that are central to the identities of modern people. Let us return briefly, then, to the role of identity in modernity.

John B. Thompson observes that the non-reciprocal intimacy created by modernity puts great pressure on individual personalities. With the speeding up of time and the collapsing of space, individual identities today develop though a process Thompson calls 'quasi-mediated interaction'. According to Thompson:

the process of self-formation becomes more reflexive and open-ended, in the sense that individuals fall back increasingly on their own resources to construct a coherent identity for themselves. At the same time, the process of self-formation is increasingly nourished by mediated symbolic materials, greatly expanding the range of options available to individuals and loosening – without destroying – the connection between self-formation and shared locale.

(1995: 207)

In this world, Thompson continues, 'the self is a symbolic project that the individual actively constructs' (1995: 210). Mediated texts – including those concerning the lives of stars – provide a constant flow of material used by modern individuals to piece identities together and affix them in a relatively stable way.

Stars frequently embody idealized appearances or behaviors, while at other times they are effective because they represent 'typical' ways of being (Dyer 1979: 24). But stars can also be admired for being completely outrageous. Audiences thus look to stars to gauge the ideal, the typical, and the unconventional, and count on stars to illustrate the perfect, the mundane, and the extraordinary. Stars become personal guides to the imagined future who sensitize audiences to the limits of everyday life, while at the same time they transcend those very limits. Such images may appear to be contradictory, but they are not. As Frith notes, 'identity is always already an ideal, what we would like to be, not what we are' (1998: 274). Through their private and public sides, stars encourage us to think that the unreachable may actually be within reach.

Rather than bemoan the star-studded situation (as Horkheimer, Adorno, Ewen, and other cultural theorists do) by arguing that the distance between star and audience only creates dashed hopes and passive acceptance of a highly orchestrated, oppressive social order, some critics argue that stardom should be theorized instead as a stabilizing anchor for the kind of identity transformations described by Thompson (1995). I return here as well to the ideas of Anthony Giddens, who argues that trust in modernity must be enacted in a dynamic tension between faceless systems and persons with whom facework is possible. We achieve trust by 're-embedding' (that is, by sustaining faceless commitments via facework) through 'access points', spaces where individuals or groups can meet abstract systems (Giddens 1990: 88). Stardom is just such an access point. It is here we meet, non-reciprocally, the 'faces' who help us to form our social and personal identities. Giddens speaks of these faces as doctors, dentists, and travel agents (each representing a larger institution), but popular culture stars are every bit as powerful as any professional person. Through stars we learn to trust our own ideals, determine where we 'fit' in the global milieu, and formulate our social and cultural identities.

The future of celebrity

There is no escape from the culture of stardom. Famous images meet us on buses, in magazines, and on Web pages. Their voices ring out from CDs, radios, television sets, and personal computers. We cannot escape them by traveling to distant lands or hiding in our homes.

Despite the growing uniformity of star images worldwide and the money-driven services celebrities perform by selling product for global corporations, it is unwise simply to condemn stars, the culture industries that promote them, and the multitude of fans who love them. We most certainly are not creating a world that is devoid of difference, nor are audiences turning into passive consumers of some predigested media menu. In fact, the diversity of voices, types, and ethnicities of stars today, as well as the creative and critical ways that people evaluate the performances and lives of their favorite celebrities, make it clear that star culture may be pervasive, but is by no means bland or banal.

Changes in the nature of time and space brought on by the advent of modern and postmodern environments have made identity formation today particularly problematic and complex. In the global context, stars act as cultural resources that help audiences construct their identities and stable selves. To assume that these audiences will automatically 'misuse' such symbolic resources – turning themselves into unthinking zombies or desperate loners in the process – simply ignores the vitality, intelligence, and creativity that people bring to cultural enactment. It is time to appreciate the global star culture in which we live with an open mind, and to acknowledge the determining roles we all willingly play in its tireless creation.

References

Alberoni, F. (1972). 'The powerless "elite": theory and sociological research on the phenomenon of stars'. In D. McQuail (ed.), *Sociology of Mass Communications*. Harmondsworth: Penguin Books.

Aristotle (1962). *The Rhetoric of Aristotle*, trs. L. Cooper. New York: Appleton Century-Crofts, Inc.

Baudrillard, J. (1988). *Jean Baudrillard: Selected Works*, ed. M. Poster. Cambridge: Polity Press.

Boorstin, D. (1961). *The Image: A Guide to Pseudo-events in America*. New York: Harper and Row.

Braudy, L. (1986). *The Frenzy of Renown: Fame and Its History*. New York: Oxford University Press.

DeCordova, R. (1990). *Picture Personalities: The Emergence of the Star System in America*. Urbana: University of Illinois Press.

—— (1991). 'The emergence of the star system in America'. In C. Gledhill (ed.), *Stardom: Industry of Desire*. London: Routledge.

Donald, J. (1985). 'Stars'. In P. Cook (ed.), *The Cinema Book*. London: British Film Institute.

Dyer, R. (1979). *Stars*. London: BFI.

—— (1986). *Heavenly Bodies: Film Stars and Society*. New York: St Martin's Press.

Ellis, J. (1982). *Visible Fictions: Cinema, Television, Video*. London: Routledge & Kegan Paul.

Ewen, S. (1989). *All Consuming Images: The Politics of Style in Contemporary Culture*. New York: Basic Books.

Frith, S. (1998). *Performing Rites: On the Value of Popular Music*. Cambridge, MA: Harvard University Press.

Gamson, D. (1994). *Claims to Fame: Celebrity in Contemporary America*. Berkeley: University of Calfornia Press.

Giddens, A. (1990). *The Consequences of Modernity*. Cambridge: Polity Press.

—— (1991). *Modernity and Self Identity*. Cambridge: Polity Press.

Hannerz, U. (1992). *Cultural Complexity: Studies in the Social Organization of Meaning*. New York: Columbia University Press.

Harvey, D. (1989). *The Condition of Postmodernity*. Oxford: Basil Blackwell.

Horkheimer, M. and Adorno, T. (1972). 'The culture industry: enlightenment as mass deception'. In *Dialectic of Enlightenment*, trs. J. Cumming. New York: Continuum.

Kern, S. (1983). *The Culture of Time and Space: 1880–1915*. Cambridge, MA: Harvard University Press.

King, B. (1986). 'Stardom as an occupation'. In P. Kern (ed.), *The Hollywood Film Industry*. London: Routledge & Kegan Paul.

—— (1987). 'The star and the commodity: notes towards a performance theory of stardom'. *Cultural Studies*, 1/2: 145–61.

Lewis, L. (1992). *The Adoring Audience: Fan Culture and Popular Media*. New York: Routledge.

Lull, J. (2000). *Media, Communication, Culture: A Global Approach* (revised ed.). Cambridge: Polity Press; New York: Columbia University Press.

Lull, J. and Hinerman, S. (1997). *Media Scandals: Morality and Desire in the Popular Culture Marketplace*. Cambridge: Polity Press; New York: Columbia University Press.

McGrew, T. (1992). 'A global society'. In S. Hall, D. Held, and T. McGrew (eds), *Modernity and Its Futures*. Cambridge: Polity Press.

Marshall, P. D. (1997). *Celebrity and Power: Fame in Contemporary Culture*. Minneapolis: University of Minnesota Press.

Monaco, J. (1978). *Celebrity: The Media as Image Makers*. New York: Delta Publishing.

Naremore, J. (1988). 'The performance frame'. In J. Butler (ed.), *Star Texts: Image and Performance in Film and Television*. Detroit: Wayne State University Press.

Rowe, D. (1994). 'Accommodating bodies: celebrity, sexuality and "tragic Magic"'. *Journal of Sport and Social Issues*, 18/1: 6–26.

Smith, P. (1993). *Clint Eastwood: A Cultural Production*. Minneapolis: University of Minnesota Press.

Thompson, J. (1995). *The Media and Modernity: A Social Theory of the Media*. Cambridge: Polity Press.

11

COMPUTERS, THE INTERNET, AND VIRTUAL CULTURES

Steve Jones and Stephanie Kucker

In an essay titled 'Thinking the Internet: Cultural studies vs the Millennium', Jonathan Sterne (1999) notes that a central issue for cultural studies approaches to 'thinking the Internet' is quite literally how to think about it beyond traditional dichotomous perspectives. Instead of asking whether the Internet leads us to utopia, or whether it will destroy the fabric of society, how might we examine the Internet as another media technology situated in routine social practice and everyday life? Scholars must pay attention to the routines undergoing transformation because of networking, for it is in the realm of the mundane that we most clearly see the consequences of the Internet in culture and society. Sterne asks us to imagine a day in the life of one of his students, and to note the ways in which the Internet, or more appropriately perhaps *Internetworking*, is embedded in mundane routines and practices. Stopping in a computer lab between classes to check email, for instance, or sending a note to a professor while doing homework, are examples he cites of common practices altered by Internetworking.

To Sterne's request we add another. We should examine the routine practices of myriad occupations, relationships and events (including ones within academia) if we are best to determine the ubiquity of Internetworking and its cultural consequences. For instance, a scholarly conference examining the WorldwideWeb was held in 1998 at Drake University. Many of those assembled had known one another for years, from other scholarly conferences, from graduate school, or from publications. But prior to that conference only one or two were known to be interested in studying the Web. How did it come to be that all were in one place at one time discussing the Web, its metaphors, and meanings?

What became clear at the Drake conference was the participants' common interest in a technology that somehow managed to encompass previous intellectual interests (if not in some ways swallow them whole), but also managed to put a 'twist' on previously held theories and concepts. For instance, those who had been studying popular music and its audience quite literally had an entirely new medium with which to contend, a medium that challenged popular music's industrial processes, and therefore challenged theories concerning the relationships between performers, fans, and the music business. As has been noted in a volume on cyberpsychology:

> An overarching issue is the manner in which these technologies implicate the objects and subjects of scholarship, along with scholars themselves, in new webs of significance and meaning that impart new frameworks to our experiences and encounters. In addition to encapsulating us in any variety of Foucauldian panopticons, like some global Hawthorne effect, network technologies affect our thinking and behavior as much because of the attention we pay the technology (and ourselves embedded in it) as because of anything else.
>
> (Jones 2000)

Similarly, Internetworking has come to encompass culture in particularly interesting ways, especially so for those who have mined the territory of cultural studies. The Internet could, in some ways, be seen as a 'carrier' of culture, in so far as it serves both as a medium of transmission and as a medium whose users selectively attend to texts others have made available. But to have it seen as such means that we will likely overlook practice, space, and emotion in favor of text. Of course, the Internet is embedded within culture in important ways. The Internet, it may be said, creates a 'virtual culture' (Jones 1997a). As Strate noted, echoing many Internet theorists: 'Communication adjusted to meet the demands and biases of cyberspace is cybercommunication, and as communication and culture are intimately linked (to some they are consubstantial), culture itself is altered' (Strate *et al.* 1996: 271).

But a virtual culture cannot (at least, not yet) be entirely disassociated from 'real' life (Jones 1998). Wellman and Gulia (1999) noted that most Internet research 'Treats the Internet as an isolated social phenomenon without taking into account how interactions on the Net fit with other aspects of people's lives. The Net is only one of many ways in which the same people may interact. It is not a separate reality' (Wellman and Gulia 1999: 334).

Our conditions of existence, to borrow from James Carey's (1997) excellent essay on American cultural studies, are not all consumed by cyberspace, no matter how often or how much we may log on. How we, as scholars and Internet users, draw the boundaries between the online and offline will largely determine the phenomenological and ontological dimensions of our analyses.

Most research on the Internet and culture has taken a decidedly sociological, and to a slight degree psychological, turn. Our own work (Jones 1995, 1997a, 1998), for instance, has focused on questions like 'Who are we when we are online?' Such questions are prompted by elements of Internetworking technology's interface with our human selves, by the feelings of bodily projection on to a field, matrix or grid, and by the dispersion of selves externally (as we traverse cyberspace) and internally (as we adopt personas in interaction). However, these questions insufficiently address the cultural consequences of Internetworking.

Perspectives on Internetworking

To understand best the limited role culture has played in Internet studies, it is necessary to historicize and review the main threads of Internet research.

Much of the early research on Internetworking stems from studies of computer-mediated communication (CMC) targeted toward work-related uses within organizations, with studies of electronic mail messaging and groupware prevailing. Electronic mail (or 'electronic messaging systems') has most commonly been used as a model of electronic communication, and has reinforced text as a paradigm in Internet studies. In this representative role, email is approached with assumptions (which it has also reinforced) about the properties and uses of CMC technologies. One assumption has been that CMC is in essence a medium of transmission. That is, not only has early research on CMC employed what Carey (1989) terms a 'transmission model' for understanding communication, it has come to view CMC as fundamentally a means of transmission. Furthermore, it is taken for granted that the point of CMC is *interpersonal* messaging, whether multiple persons receive the message or not. Users of CMC are thus abstracted from the contexts within which they use CMC technologies.

A consequence of such abstraction is that research centralizing the importance of technological characteristics regards text-based CMC (i.e. listserv, Usenet, email) as lacking in social context cues – verbal and non-verbal information – that are presumed essential to interpersonal exchange (Kiesler, Siegel, and McGuire 1984; Sproull and Kiesler 1986). The argument that a lack of context cues limits socio-emotional information led early CMC scholars to brand these media as inherently impersonal and thereby best suited to unequivocal, work-related tasks (Kiesler, Siegel, and McGuire 1984). Of course, the very perception of CMC as task-centered would likely lead to no other conclusion. Moreover, the organizational settings used for the earliest CMC studies, the 'newness' of the technology in organizations and workgroups, and its insertion in pre-existing work processes would also tend to support such a conclusion.

Culnan and Markus (1987), using elements of social presence and media richness theory, explained the early findings of CMC researchers (that CMC lacks social context cues and is ill-suited to interpersonal interactions) by naming them 'cues filtered out' approaches to CMC. The 'cues filtered out' perspective assumes that the number of channels available for the transmission of impression-bearing data, and specifically non-verbal cues, marks the critical difference between CMC and face-to-face (F2F) communication. While F2F is regarded as a more encompassing form that provides an essential blend of verbal and non-verbal cues for social interaction, CMC is diagnosed as utilizing fewer channels, and thereby 'bereft of [the] impression bearing data' that makes for effective interpersonal communication (Walther 1993: 384).

The 'cues filtered out' perspectives dominated CMC scholarship in the 1980s. Under the assumption of CMC's social deficiency, studies of email systems revolved around the application of these technologies to work-related tasks within organizations, where interpersonal exchange was believed to be limited and unnecessary (Hiltz, Johnson, and Turoff 1986). Driven by administrative interest in enhancing productivity and improving operations, these studies were focused on how email could mediate internal corporate communications and what effect this mediation would have on work-related activities, such as decision-making (Garton and Wellman 1995; Wellman *et al.* 1996). Though culture does not appear as a central theme in these early studies, it is important to consider that these technologies were not widely diffused outside of organizational settings. Early adopters at this time consisted of government agencies or corporations (and, in some cases, educational institutions) that deployed CMC for particular purposes. Nevertheless, by the 1980s notions of 'corporate culture' were themselves widespread, and it is at least somewhat surprising not to find CMC scholars forming opinions regarding the influence of CMC on organizational culture. It is equally surprising given that, even in the early days of development of ARPANET, non-task-oriented communication took place. For instance, one can consider as a precursor to listservs and Usenet discussion groups the SF-LOVERS mailing list and the development of UUCP (the Unix-to-Unix Copy Program that enabled files to be passed easily across networked computers running Unix) in the 1980s (Salus 1995). These developments were not widely reported at the time, for Internetworking had many years to go before it would capture the public imagination. But these developments did not go unnoticed in the networking community, and they have been acknowledged recently among CMC scholars as important moments in the development of a network culture (Hauben and Hauben 1997). Still, what is surprising is that no studies of the ARPANET (and other Internet precursors) were undertaken at the time of their development (or quickly thereafter) by CMC researchers.

Instead, comparisons between CMC and F2F characterized the bulk of early CMC research, as did organizational context. Research on organizational email systems was characterized by comparative studies of CMC and F2F interactions with regards to how the inherent properties of communication media influence individual media choice (Wellman *et al.* 1996). Consequently, forms of uses and gratifications research gained a foothold as well, and foreground rationality as a means by which one could explain CMC use. Media richness scholars argue that, when faced with a given task, individuals will make a rational choice among available communication media based on consideration of how well each medium matches the task (Daft and Lengel 1990; Webster and Trevino 1995). Driven by the 'cues filtered out' orientation, much research on media choice concluded that individuals faced with interpersonal communication objectives made a conscious choice to use F2F over CMC owing to CMC's social deficiencies (Lea 1991).

Despite the dominance of cues-filtered-out, task-based research programs in the 1980s, some early research did reveal the emergence of 'social uses' of these technologies, and particularly email (Rice and Love 1987; Steinfeld 1985). Steinfeld's (1985) study of organizational email messaging systems found that the mail system was used for a wide variety of purposes, with two major dimensions – 'task' and 'socio-emotional'. While the former mostly involved the transfer and acquisition of information (not unexpected), the latter related to the maintenance of personal relationships, 'feeling a part' of the organization, and being 'in touch'. Similarly, a study by Rice and Love (1987) revealed that workers find social support, companionship, and a sense of belonging online.

In the early 1990s, scholarly dissatisfaction with perspectives that regard CMC technologies as impersonal and ill-suited to interpersonal interactions led to the emergence of new theoretical lenses through which to explore the social aspects of CMC. The 'social information processing perspective' used the comparison of CMC with F2F to illustrate that 'interpersonality' does indeed form via CMC, but at a slower rate than in F2F interactions (Walther and Burgoon 1992). When viewed from this perspective, the difference between CMC and F2F was not the 'amount of social information exchanged', as argued by early theorists, but rather 'the rate of social information exchange' (Walther 1996: 10). By centralizing the role of rate, the social information processing perspective pushed for more longitudinal research designs that could account for relational development over time. It was argued that early perspectives regarding CMC as impersonal by nature were misinformed by programs of research that targeted workgroups over limited-time engagements (Walther 1992).

A more recent outgrowth of this perspective, the 'hyperpersonal' view, suggests that there are instances when CMC may be 'more socially desirable than [individuals] tend to experience in parallel F2F interaction', and thereby may surpass F2F communication in the ability to establish interpersonal relationships (Walther 1996: 17). This assertion is based on the premise that, even though CMC may reduce non-verbal context cues (i.e. facial expressions, gestures, tone of voice, etc.), such a lack of cues may enhance interpersonal communication in a range of situational contexts, and particularly where status differentials are present.

Both the 'cues filtered out' and 'social information processing' research programs have been anchored within the organizational setting and fixed to a workgroup context. Moreover, they have foregrounded interpersonal communication and de-emphasized the role culture may play not only in organizational terms but also extra-organizationally. As such, while issues of social relationship formation are addressed, they are considered as a function of the group task, or as a side effect of work relations. Social aspects of CMC are not central to those research programs in which technology is seen as driving media choice, use, and relationships (Bordia 1997). However, as suggested by Schmitz and Fulk (1991), media use is influenced by more than rational choices made in consideration of message content and the situation or task at hand; the use of media is also influenced by social forces and symbolic cues. Context is important. The primary focus of CMC research has been on CMC as a transmission tool for communication and information exchange, and not on CMC as a tool for social connectivity (Jones 1995).

Internetworking and community

Robins noted that 'the mythology of cyberspace is preferred over its sociology' (1995: 153), to which we would add that its sociology is preferred over its phenomenology and philosophy. In recent years, the rapid expansion of CMC's favorite (and favored) progeny, the Internet, has opened up new doors with regards to the study of electronic communication as more than a technological phenomenon but also as a social one (Jones 1995, 1997a). Researchers have come to the study of the Internet and its associated applications (i.e. Usenet, MUDS, IRC, WWW, and electronic mail) with social implications at the center of their inquiry, expanding their questions, contexts of investigation, and approaches to studying these new media both theoretically and methodologically.

Those scholars concerned with social aspects of the Internet and CMC have centralized 'connection' in their research, arguing that human-connecting computer networks are by nature social networks (Jones 1995; Wellman et al. 1996). They also emphasize context, both that surrounding and that encompassed within these media. While the former refers more to the physical environment and user demographics existing outside the enveloped media, the latter attends to the notion of 'social space', which is created and re-created in the course of technologically mediated interactions. This last consideration of context has helped to move scholarship away from the dominant view of CMC as a 'tool' for communications transmission and information exchange towards one that views CMC as a place of 'production and reproduction' of social relations (Jones 1995).

However, one cannot consider these studies to be cultural approaches to Internetworking. Online community studies and studies of community networks (Garton and Wellman 1995; Jones 1995; Rheingold 1993) tend to explore a particular group of people who, driven by a common interest, develop a shared sense of community in the course of virtual interaction, typically on Usenet groups, listservs, or in multi-user dungeons (MUDS). The phenomenon of central interest is how individuals come together via CMC and develop a group identity (as well as a sense of personal identity) in the absence of F2F interaction. Studies in this area have witnessed the development of status cues, rules of order, and interpersonal bonds in text-based applications, which were previously regarded as socially deficient (Wellman 1997). While comparisons have been drawn between these online developments and 'real life' interactions, scholarly attempts to address the relationship between life online and life offline have fallen by the wayside (Jones, 1995; Kiesler 1997). Even in those online studies that do consider what happens when members of an online community meet 'in real life', the primary focus remains on how these 'virtual communities of interest' develop and remain online in 'cyber-space' (Blanchard and Horan 1998; Rheingold 1993). As Blanchard and Horan (1998) point out, there are also 'physically based virtual communities' which result when proximal communities add electronic resources.

Virnoche and Marx define community networks as a particular type of computer-mediated community when they note that 'Community networks are systems that electronically connect individuals who also share common geographic space' (1997: 85). The focus is on geographic connection as ongoing, as opposed to intermittent, and augmented with shared virtual space. Recent inquiries have started to ask: what happens when physically proximal communities go online? While this relationship has been considered in the early organizational literature, most of that research was focused on how the introduction of CMC can contribute to changes in workplace satisfaction, with the primary concern resting with CMC-enhanced outcomes. Recent inquiries exhibit more concern for the social implications of networked communities, and address how the addition of new communication technology can alter social interactions and social structure. While there is debate surrounding whether the effects of CMC technology will be positive or negative for a given community of users, there is the strong indication that the implementation of CMC technology does contribute to the process by which social relationships exist.

Community, connection, space, and culture

In his masterful examination of culture, narrative, and space, David Nye noted that 'the computer did not always have a screen full of text and images' (1997: 161). He discerned three phases in the development of cyberspace:

> The first lasting from the end of World War II until the end of the 1970s. Computers were integrated into large institutions, notably banks, airlines – white-collar organizations of all kinds. Second, at the end of the 1970s computers began to emerge into everyday life and consumption, as computer chips were installed in many products. The decentralization of the personal computer lasted until the early 1990s, when the rapid spread of the Internet marked the start of a third phase.
> (Nye 1997: 161)

Similarly, one can discern three phases in Internet studies – the early CMC research rooted in organizational studies emerged first, followed by research on the insertion of computers in everyday life. We are at the brink of a third phase, namely research on the decentralization of Internetworking and its diffusion across and through cultural processes and practices.

Culture has clearly played a role in much of the literature in Internet studies during the mid-1990s and onward. Culture was conceived and deployed in two limited ways. First, it was understood by some as largely non-Western, that is, as something in opposition to online culture as monolithic (usually invoked in terms of language, particularly English, or commercialism). Particular cultures thus could be considered under threat from the ubiquity of capitalist, Western culture online (Brook and Boal 1995), or they could be thought to be undergoing profound revitalization as they fight being subsumed by 'mainstream' online culture, finding new outlets for their spread (Nardi and O'Day 1999). Such discourses can be found also in the rhetoric surrounding rural communities going online (Smith and Kollock 1999). Second, it was understood as an artifact of online interaction, as 'virtual culture'. In this case one can find fascinating work, such as that by Donna Haraway, Sandy Stone, Anne Balsamo and others, on the racial, political and sexual dimensions of online experience and online culture. However, in these cases it is typically assumed that there is either a boundary between the online and the offline that, though transgressed, is necessary for the analysis of virtual culture. Alternately, one finds work based on the premise that online culture is the digital manifestation of offline culture. As Gackenbach, Guthrie, and Karpen put it, 'The Internet is the collection of information and interactions which flow over it; the users and their usage which generate the information, and their experiences of it' (1998: 323).

But culture is neither information nor interaction as they describe it. Neither is it usage, or experience, at least as regards online interaction alone. Clifford Geertz reminds us that the 'proper object' of cultural analysis is 'the informal logic of actual life', rather than the 'arrang(ement of) abstracted entities into unified patterns' (Geertz 1973: 17).

What is lacking from Gackenbach et al. and others' conceptions of online culture is a connection between space and culture, a connection formed, as Alexander, Ishikawa, and Silverstein note, by the promenade, a place where people 'gather together to rub shoulders and confirm their community' (1977: 169). At present one senses that, online, rubbing shoulders, as a metaphor, consists of a continuum between lurking and going elsewhere. But that is precisely why the non-textual online phenomena are of such great importance. What goes unsaid by the myriad Internet users, what is not revealed between the lines, is of critical importance, because there is nothing but lines. The in-between spaces are, for all practical purposes, impossible to mine from online interaction alone, just as, offline, it is impossible during a card game to determine the intentions of a poker-faced player. Sherry Turkle summed it up

219

well when describing her first encounter with a MUD. 'I was reminded of kissing games', she wrote, 'in which it was awful to be chosen and awful not to be chosen' (1999: 206). In short, even in offline social situations lurking can be the most desired choice, though proximity in real life borne of a lack of mediation won't allow it. Simply put, real life does not allow so many multiple and immediate options with which to mediate social situations as does CMC.

The Internet, on the other hand, is entirely mediation, and the most commonly chosen social role is that of the lurker. Whether lurking and voyeurism are linked (which we believe they are) and how they may be linked is a discussion beyond the scope of this chapter. Suffice to say that there are clearly important issues to be considered in relation to lurking, voyeurism, surveillance, the gaze, image, and metaphor (Foucault 1980). What is central to the argument presented here is that culture is overlooked by those who study the Internet because 'overlooking' is, if you will, the main activity of being online, being in cyberspace. As we more and more textualize cyberspace we more and more destabilize the relationships between space and culture. As Nye puts it, 'What appears on the computer screen seems a curious combination of space and story' (Nye 1997: 186). The story, however, is not that of a machine 'impinging', as he puts it, on space, but is rather that of a narrative incursion into an existing culture. In an important sense, if cyberspace is an 'information superhighway', it is not built into and through space (be it cyber or otherwise). It is a road built into and through a cultural landscape that before its construction knew not of traffic.

Traffic is, in fact, antithetical to community. As Alexander, Ishikawa, and Silverstein point out, 'the heavier the traffic in an area, the less people think of it as home territory. Not only do residents view the streets with heavy traffic as less personal, but they feel the same about the houses along the street' (1977: 82–3). We can glean an important distinction between the conception of a highway, meant to carry traffic, and a road or path, meant to foster habitation, from Milan Kundera's novel *Immortality*:

> Road: a strip of ground over which one walks. A highway differs from a road not only because it is merely a line that connects one point with another. A highway has no meaning in itself; its meaning derives entirely from the two points that it connects. A road is a tribute to space. Every stretch of road has meaning in itself and invites us to stop. A highway is the triumphant devaluation of space.
>
> Before roads and paths disappeared from the landscape, they had disappeared from the human soul. [We] no longer saw life as a road, but as a highway: a line that led from one point to another, from the rank of captain to the rank of general, from the role of wife to the role of widow. Time became a mere obstacle to life, an obstacle that had to be overcome by ever greater speed.
>
> (Kundera 1990: 223)

The speed with which we move from place to place online itself renders any traditional notions of community obsolete (Jones 1997b). Online community is usually considered as spatial or cyberspatial, but temporality is rarely a matter of analysis. For that reason, a useful concept may be that of 'habitation', the commitment not only to being in the same place as others but to staying there for some length of time. We experience where we visit and where we live very differently both spatially and temporally.

However, habitation is a key element in current industrial discourses about the Internet. Terms like 'community', 'portal', 'stickiness', all point to the same issue, namely that it is increasingly difficult, in a medium built (and continuously imagined) for movement, to develop the relatively stable communities desired by marketers and advertisers (and, may we add, by most people). Or, to put it another way, it is increasingly a concern to content providers that they cannot puzzle out how to deliver audiences to advertisers. Community online seems an accident, even in its earliest incarnations. Salus tells the story of Brian Redman, a pioneering developer of UUCP, who 'began "sending electronic mail on a regular basis", leading to a community' (1995: 133).

This is not a new phenomenon. In Marshall Berman's insightfull book *All that Is Solid Melts into Air*, a description of Georges Haussmann's nineteenth-century Paris should hold particular interest for Internet scholars:

> When Haussmann's work on the boulevards began, no one understood why he wanted them so wide: from a hundred feet to a hundred yards across. It was only when the job was done that people began to see that these roads, immensely wide, straight as arrows, running on for miles, would be ideal speedways for heavy traffic . . .
>
> The archetypal modern man, as we see him here, is a man alone contending against an agglomeration of mass and energy that is heavy, fast and lethal. The burgeoning street and boulevard traffic knows no spatial or temporal bounds, spills over into every urban space, imposes its tempo on everybody's time, transforms the whole modern environment into a 'moving chaos'. The chaos here lies not in the movers themselves – the individual walkers or drivers, each of whom may be pursuing the most efficient route for himself – but in their interaction, in the totality of their common movements in a common space.
>
> (Berman 1982: 158–9)

One can easily mine this passage of Berman's solely for the multiple parallels to Internetworking. But the important point Berman makes later is that twentieth-century architects did all they could to leave the metropolis behind, to create 'supercontrolled environments' (1982: 246) and, ultimately, malls and gated communities. Only by controlling access – traffic – does it become possible to control trafficking, be it in conversation or commodities, as those in the Internet business who have been in the process of creating 'portals' know well.

The economic project of localizing communities in terms of real estate is strikingly similar to the project of localizing (and commercializing) communities in virtual space. But to take a cultural approach to the study of virtual space means, as Carey points out, to accept the notion that Americans, particularly, 'are a people who are always creating new communities and then trying to figure out a way to get out of town' (Carey 1997: 23). With the Internet, at first a particularly American technology, we have invented at once the community and the way out of town.

Conclusion

If we are to begin to understand culture in cyberspace, we therefore need to adapt to our analyses, as Grossberg suggests, by 'rethink[ing] articulations of culture and power' (1997: 354). Adopting a strategy set forth by Deleuze and Guattari, Grossberg exhorts 'that cultural studies explore the concrete ways in which different machines – or, in Foucault's terms, apparatuses – produce the specific spaces, configurations, and circulations of power' (1997: 355–6). An articulation that must be made is between the real and the virtual. As Robins pointed out:

> It is time to relocate virtual culture in the real world (the real world that virtual culturalists, seduced by their own metaphors, pronounce dead or dying). Through the development of new technologies, we are, indeed, more and more open to experiences of de-realization and de-localization. But we continue to have physical and localized existences. We must consider our state of suspension between these conditions. We must de-mythologize virtual culture if we are to assess the serious implications it has for our personal and collective lives.
>
> (Robins 1995: 153)

To do so will require our thinking to move beyond the hyperbole of 'connection' between people, beyond analyses of social networks, groups, and communities, that demonstrate that the Internet 'connects'. Online we are not solely and simply expressing cultural identities we maintain offline; we may be expressing ones entirely unfamiliar to us in other realms and repressing others. But the important issue is that culture and community, though in many ways seemingly inseparable from communication, are nevertheless *not communication*. To study the ways the Internet allows connection and then do little else is not only an acritical approach to the study of life online but it ultimately reifies technology and subsumes human, interpretive activity to the tyranny of the Internet itself.

We would do well instead to examine the Internet's own connections to other realms of human endeavor. At the outset of this chapter we noted the appropriateness of Jonathan Sterne's remarks concerning Internetworking and everyday life, and they are pertinent as a conclusion, too. If cultural studies can 'denaturalize and radically contextualize the Internet itself' (Sterne 1999: 277), scholars must think less about the connections users make online and more about what it is that connects the expression of particular interpretations and what compels repression of others. We must delve into the how and why of the connections made, the formation and reformation of the structure of the Net both as apparatus and as spatializing force, not in the sense of 'creating space' (such as cyberspace) but rather in the sense that it creates affective spaces. Only by problematizing the relationship between the triumvirate of space, connection, and culture will we make it possible to do so. To borrow from Geertz, how might we 'reduce the puzzlement to which unfamiliar acts emerging out of unknown backgrounds naturally give rise' (1973: 16)? The goal should not be to merely 'connect' the real and the virtual; it should be to embed one within the other. The choice one must make when doing cultural studies of the Internet, there-fore, is deciding which one, the real or the virtual, is to be embedded in the other.

References

Alexander, C., Ishikawa, S. and Silverstein, M. (1977). *A Pattern Language*. New York: Oxford University Press.

Berman, M. (1982). *All that Is Solid Melts into Air*. New York: Simon and Schuster.

Blanchard, A. and Horan, T. (1998) 'Virtual communities and social capital'. *Social Science Computer Review* 16: 293–307.

Bordia, P. (1997). 'Face-to-face versus computer-mediated communication. A synthesis of the experimental literature'. *The Journal of Business Communication*, 34: 99–120.

Brook, J. and Boal, I. A. (1995). *Resisting the Virtual Life*. San Francisco: City Lights.

Carey, J. (1989). *Communication as Culture*. Boston, MA: Unwin Hyman.

—— (1997). 'Reflections on the project of (American) cultural studies'. In M. Ferguson and P. Golding (eds), *Cultural Studies in Question*. London: Sage Publications.

Culnan, M. J. and Markus, M. L. (1987). 'Information technologies'. In F. M. Jablin, L. L. Putnam, K. H. Roberts, and L. W. Poole (eds), *Handbook of Organizational Communication: An Interdisciplinary Perspective*. Newbury Park, CA: Sage.

Daft, R. L., Lengel, R. H., and Trevino, L. K. (1990). 'Message equivocality, media selection, and manager performance: Implications for information systems'. *MIS Quarterly*, 11: 355–68.

Foucault, M. (1980). *Power-Knowledge*. New York: Pantheon.

Gackenbach, J., Guthrie, G., and Karpen, J. (1998). 'The coevolution of technology and consciousness'. In J. Gackenbach (ed.), *Psychology and the Internet*. London: Academic Press.

Garton, L. and Wellman, B. (1995). 'Social impacts of electronic mail in organizations: A review of the research literature'. In B. R. Burleson (ed.), *Communication Yearbook*, 18: 434–53. Thousand Oaks, CA: Sage.

Geertz, C. (1973). *The Interpretation of Cultures*. New York: Basic Books.

Grossberg, L. (1997). *Bringing it All Back Home*. Durham, NC: Duke University Press.

Hauben, M. and Hauben, R. (1997). *Netizens: On the History and Impact of Usenet and the Internet*. Los Alamitos, CA: IEEE Computer Society Press.

Hiltz, S. R., Johnson, R., and Turoff, M. (1986). 'Experiments in group decision-making: Communication process and outcome in face-to-face versus computerized conferences'. *Human Communication Research*, 13, 225–52.

Jones, S. (1995). *Cybersociety*. Newbury Park, CA: Sage Publications.

—— (1997a). *Virtual Culture*. London: Sage Publications.

—— (1997b). 'The Internet, communication and electromotion'. In A. Roesler (ed.), *Mythos Internet*. Frankfurt: Suhrkamp Verlag.

—— (1998). *Cybersociety 2.0*. Newbury Park, CA: Sage Publications.

—— (2000). 'The cyber and the subjective'. In A. Gordo-Lopez and I. Parker (eds), *Cyberpsychology*. New York: Macmillan.

Kiesler, S. (1997). *Cultures of the Internet*. Mahwah, NJ: Lawrence Erlbaum.

Kiesler, S., Siegel, J., and McGuire, T. W. (1984). 'Social psychological aspects of computer-mediated communication'. *American Psychologist*, 39: 1123–34.

Kundera, M. (1990). *L'immortalité*. Paris: Gallimard.

Nardi, B. and O'Day, V. (1999). *Information Ecologies*. Cambridge, MA: MIT Press.

Nye, D. (1997). *Narratives and Spaces*. Exeter: University of Exeter Press.

Rheingold, H. (1993). *The Virtual Community: Homesteading on the Electronic Frontier*. New York: Harper.

Rice, R. E. and Love, G. (1987). 'Electronic emotion: Socioemotional content in a computer-mediated network'. *Communication Research*, 14: 85–108.

Rice, R. E., Grant, A. E., Schmitz, J., and Torobin, J. (1990). 'Individual and network influences on the adoption and perceived outcomes of electronic messaging'. *Social Networks*, 12: 27–55.

Robins, K. (1995). 'Cyberspace and the world we live in'. In M. Featherstone (ed.), *Cyberspace / Cyberbodies / Cyberpunk*. London: Sage Publications.

Salus, P. (1995). *Casting the Net*. Reading, MA: Addison-Wesley Publishing Co.

Schmitz, J. and Fulk, J. (1991). 'Organizational colleagues, media richness, and electronic mail'. *Communication Research* 18: 487–523.

Smith, M. and Kollock, P. (1999). *Communities in Cyberspace*. London: Routledge.

Sproull, L. and Faraj, S. (1997). 'Atheism, sex, and databases: The Net as a social technology'. In S. Kielser (ed.), *Cultures of the Internet*. Mahwah, NJ: Lawrence Erlbaum.

Sproull, L. and Kiesler, S. (1986). 'Reducing social context cues: Electronic mail in organizational communication'. *Management Science*, 32: 1492–512.

Steinfeld, C. W. (1985). 'Computer-mediated communication in an organizational setting: Explaining task-related and socioemotional uses'. In M. L. McLaughlin (ed.), *Communication Yearbook 9*. Newbury Park, CA: Sage.

Sterne, J. (1999). 'Thinking the Internet: Cultural studies vs. the Millennium'. In S. Jones (ed.), *Doing Internet Research*. Newbury Park, CA: Sage Publications.

Strate, L., Jacobson, R., and Gibson, S. B. (1996). 'Meaning: Cybercommunication and cyberculture'. In L. Strate, R. Jacobson, and S. B. Gibson (eds), *Communication and Cyberspace*. Cresskill, NJ: Hampton Press.

Turkle, S. (1999). 'Tinysex and gender trouble'. In Liberty (ed.), *Liberating Cyberspace*. London: Pluto Press.

Virnoche, M. E. and Marx, G. T. (1997). '"Only connect": E. M. Forster in an age of electronic communication: Computer-mediated communication and community networks'. *Sociological Inquiry*, 67: 85–100.

Walther, J. B. (1992). 'Interpersonal effects in computer-mediated interaction: A relational perspective'. *Communication Research*, 19: 52–90.

—— (1993). 'Impression development in computer-mediated interaction'. *Western Journal of Communication*, 57: 381–98.

—— (1996). 'Computer-mediated communication: Impersonal, interpersonal, and hyperpersonal interaction'. *Communication Research*, 23: 3–43.

Walther, J. B. and Burgoon, J. K. (1992). 'Relational communication in computer-mediated interaction'. *Human Communication Research*, 19: 50–88.

Webster, K. and Trevino, L. K. (1995). 'Rational and social theories as complementary explanations of communication media choices: Two policy-capturing studies'. *Academy of Management Journal*, 38: 1544–72.

Wellman, B. (1997). 'An electronic group is virtually a social network'. In S. Kiesler (ed.), *Cultures of the Internet*. Mahwah, NJ: Lawrence Erlbaum.

Wellman, B. and Gulia, M. (1999). 'Net-surfers don't ride alone'. In B. Wellman (ed.), *Networks in the Global Village*. Boulder, CO: Westview Press.

Wellman, B., Salaff, J., Dimitrova, D., Garton, L., Gulia, M., and Haythornthwaite, C. (1996). 'Computer networks as social networks: Collaborative work, telework, and virtual community'. *Annual Review of Sociology*, 22: 213–38.

INDEX